Crime and Punishment:
Interpreting the Data

Crime and Punishment: Interpreting the Data

A. KEITH BOTTOMLEY
University of Hull

KEN PEASE
University of Manchester

Open University Press
Milton Keynes · Philadelphia

Open University Press
Celtic Court
22 Ballmoor
Buckingham
MK18 1XW

and
1900 Frost Road, Suite 101
Bristol, PA 19007, USA

First Published 1993
Reprinted 1994

British Library Cataloguing in Publication Data

Bottomley, A. Keith
   Crime and punishment: interpreting the data
   1. Crime and criminals — Great Britain
   I. Title   II. Pease, Ken
   364'.941   HV6947

   ISBN 0–335–15390–9
   ISBN 0–335–15389–5 Pbk

Library of Congress Cataloging in Publication Data
Main entry under title:

Bottomley, A. Keith.
   Crime and punishment: interpreting the data
   Bibliography: p.
   Includes index.
   1. Criminal statistics—England.   2. Criminal statistics
—Wales.   3. Criminal justice, Administration
of—England.   4. Criminal justice, Administration
of—Wales.   I. Pease, K. (Kenneth)   II. Title.
   HV7415.B68 1986   364'.942   86–819
   ISBN 0–335–15390–9 (U.S.)
   ISBN 0–335–15389–5 (U.S. : pbk.)

Text design by Clarke Williams
Typeset by Colset Private Ltd, Singapore
Printed in Great Britain by St. Edmundsbury Press Ltd.,
Bury St. Edmunds, Suffolk

To the memory of
a dear father,
and to Judy.

Contents

Preface

Crime and punishment continue to be major subjects of private concern and public debate. Whether they merit this central position, in comparison with other issues impacting on the quality of contemporary social life, is not for us to say. It is also open to some doubt whether the reach of the criminal law is the right one, or whether it excludes some wicked actions and includes some inconsequential ones. However, in view of the perceived significance of crime and punishment as they now are, it seems obvious that discussion of them should be as well-informed as possible, with both the present state of our knowledge and the real extent of our ignorance fully acknowledged. Perhaps the currently fashionable view is that statistics in this area are meaningless. We believe, in contrast, that they provide a wealth of information of relevance to policy and practice, although the information is emphatically not susceptible to easy comprehension or accurate superficial readings. We would like to see a process of the rehabilitation of official statistics as *one* aid to understanding what is happening. This book aims to make a modest contribution to this process, by taking a constructive, albeit critical look at the information available in official sources which concern crime and the criminal justice process in England and Wales today, supplemented by material drawn from criminological research studies. Despite the lacunae in and deficiencies of the available data from such sources – many of which will become evident in the following pages – it is our belief that citizens should be aware of what the State does on their behalf in the area of crime and punishment. The publication and dissemination of regular statistics is one contribution to citizen awareness. It is right that the State should feel obliged to provide information of this sort for open debate and informed consent to, or challenge of, aspects of the policy response to crime, its victims and its perpetrators. However the provision of such information is of little use if the citizen feels unable to appreciate or respond to it.

We shall concentrate our attention upon the situation in England and Wales during the last 20 years or so, but will refer to selected comparative statistics from earlier times and other places, as space and the availability of data allow. To illustrate the particular pitfalls, but also the potential pay-off, of systematic comparative analysis, we have undertaken (see Chapter 5) a preliminary look at juvenile justice data from the three jurisdictions which coexist within the United Kingdom, and which operate rather different juvenile justice systems. In general, within the limits of our primary focus, our aim is to be as comprehensive and as comprehensible as possible. As the reader will see, there are some cases where merely being comprehensible reveals some aspects of the system which are troubling in their implications, and others which are equally reassuring or provocative.

Compared to the detailed theoretical and empirical studies that will be familiar to our colleagues within academic criminology, a deliberately wide-ranging survey of statistics of this kind can only skim the surface of many topics, and if we appear to gloss over some of the technicalities involved in the production and presentation of the statistics, this is probably because we really are glossing over some of the technicalities involved! Where we felt it unavoidable to sacrifice precision for clarity, we did so wherever we felt that the overall information pattern would not thereby be distorted. To those who find such imprecision unsatisfactory, we offer no apologies. We hope that the book encourages a movement towards fuller understanding and the more imaginative use and policy-directed interpretation of official data, in conjunction with the findings of research. We hope the book enables a wider audience to sample the possibilities of understanding official data on crime and punishment. The audience now could scarcely be narrower than the very few who currently patronize Her Majesty's Stationery Office with its invaluable – but overpriced – publications.

University of Hull,
University of Manchester.
July 1985.

Keith Bottomley
Ken Pease

Acknowledgements

Crown copyright material is reproduced in the following Tables and Figures with the kind permission of the Controller of Her Majesty's Stationery Office: Table 1.9, M. Hough and P. Mayhew *The British Crime Survey: First Report* (1983); Table 1.11, P. Stevens and C.F. Willis *Race, Crime and Arrests* (1979); Tables 1.12 and 1.13, R.V.G. Clarke *et al.* 'Elderly Victims of Crime and Exposure to Risk' *Howard Journal of Criminal Justice, 24* (1985); Table 2.3, J. Burrows and R. Tarling *Clearing Up Crime* (1982); Table 2.5, J.A. Ditchfield *Police Cautioning in England and Wales* (1976); Table 2.7, G. Laycock and R. Tarling 'Police Force Cautioning: Policy and Practice' *Howard Journal of Criminal Justice, 24* (1985); Tables 3.1 and 3.2, R. Gemmill and R.F. Morgan-Giles *Arrest, Charge and Summons*, Royal Commission on Criminal Procedure (1980); Tables 4.8 and 4.9, *Prison Statistics England and Wales 1983*; Table 6.2, L.T. Wilkins *Delinquent Generations* (1960); Fig. 2.1, *Criminal Statistics England and Wales 1983*; Fig. 6.2, R. Tarling 'Unemployment and Crime' Home Office Research and Planning Unit *Research Bulletin* No. 14 (1982); Fig. 6.3, Home Office Statistical Bulletin 7/85 'Careers of those born in 1953, 1958 and 1963'; Figs. 6.6, and 6.7, F. Gladstone 'Crime and the Crystal Ball' Home Office Research Unit *Research Bulletin* No. 7 (1979).

Grateful acknowledgements are also due to the following authors and publishers for permission to use material from their publications: Table 1.1, D.L. Philips *Crime and Authority in Victorian England*, Croom Helm (1977); Tables 2.1 and 2.2, D.P. Farrington and E.A. Dowds 'Disentangling Criminal Behaviour and Police Reaction' in D.P. Farrington and J. Gunn (eds) *Reactions to Crime: the Public, the Police, Courts, and Prisons*, Wiley (1985); Table 4.6, N.D. Walker, 'A Note on Parole and Sentence Lengths', *Criminal Law Review* (1981); Table 6.3, K. Pease 'Did the Falklands War Reduce Crime?' *Justice of the Peace, 147* (1983); Fig. 1.3, R. Litton and K. Pease, 'Crimes and Claims: the Case of Burglary Insurance', in R.V.G. Clarke and T.J. Hope (eds) *Coping with Burglary*, Kluwer-Nijhoff (1984); Fig. 4.1, G. Robertson 'Changes in the Use of the Criminal Provisions of the 1959 Mental Health Act' in T. Williams *et al.* (eds) *Options for the Mentally Abnormal Offender*, British Psychological Society (1984); Fig. 4.5, K. Pease and M. Sampson 'Doing Time and Marking Time' *Howard Journal of Penology and Crime Prevention, 16* (1977);

Fig. 5.1, *Children's Hearing Statistics 1982*, Scottish Education Department (1985); Fig. 5.2, C.J. Fisher and R.I. Mawby, 'Juvenile Delinquency and Police Discretion in an Inner-City Area', *British Journal of Criminology, 22*, (1982); Fig. 6.1, L. Lenke 'Drugs and Criminality in Scandinavia' in N. Bishop (ed.) *Crime and Crime Control in Scandinavia 1976–80*, Scandinavian Research Council for Criminology (1980); Fig. 6.4, I. Waller and J. Chan 'Prison Use: A Canadian and International Comparison', *Criminal Law Quarterly, 17* (1974).

List of Tables

xvi *Crime and Punishment: Interpreting the Data*

List of Figures

How Much Crime?
How Many Criminals?
How Many Victims?

It is impossible to give any accurate or straightforward answers to the questions posed in the title of this opening chapter. Not only does everything depend on what is meant by 'crime', 'criminals' and 'victims', but even if there were to be broad agreement on the definition and scope of these basic terms, it is very apparent that most of the extant methods of measuring the nature and amount of crime, criminality and victimization would be inadequate to the task. Accordingly, any reader who has turned to this book simply in the hope of finding the 'true facts' of the contemporary crime scene would be well advised to stop now, unless prepared to consider a rather more complex version that may initially disappoint but should ultimately provide a much better understanding of the issues surrounding attempts to answer these primary questions.

Our limited objectives in this chapter are, first, to examine relevant information from official statistics on the trends and patterns of recorded crime in England and Wales; second, to draw attention to the many problems of interpretation in any such examination; third, to compare, contrast and supplement this information with data deriving from surveys of crime victimization among the general public. Although we shall be concentrating primarily upon the apparently 'hard' data deriving from government statistical sources and criminological research studies, this should not be taken to imply that we believe that data of this kind exert a particularly strong influence upon the general public's understanding of crime. Any influence they may have is channelled through the far more powerful agencies, in the moulding of public opinion, of the news media. It is invariably distorted in the process. Furthermore, ordinary people's perception of crime is often significantly affected by their own direct or indirect personal experiences, which may or may not be congruent with the messages emanating from other sources of information. Nevertheless, despite the probable marginality of official and academic data on crime for most of the general public, no serious attempt to understand the subject can simply dismiss them out of hand, but must approach them critically and with caution, recognizing them as the proper starting point of any systematic analysis of crime in society.

The Official Picture of Crime

1. Recorded Crime Trends

The statistics which are traditionally used for the purpose of calculating the official 'crime rate' in England and Wales derive from the monthly police force returns to the Home Office of 'notifiable offences' recorded by the police.[1] There are currently about 70 different types of offence recorded in this way, grouped under the following eight headings:

1. Violence against the person
2. Sexual offences
3. Burglary
4. Robbery
5. Theft and handling stolen goods
6. Fraud and forgery
7. Criminal damage
8. Other

In general terms notifiable offences include all those offences known to the police for which a suspect, if apprehended and found to have a case to answer, could elect to be tried by jury. This right is a sort of official marker for more serious crimes, although in practice many examples of notifiable crimes are not events that most of us would regard as particularly serious. Thus, even before taking into account the large proportion of notifiable offences that are not reported to or recorded by the police (see below) it should be recognized that the distinction between notifiable and non-notifiable (or indictable and non-indictable) crime provides only a rough and ready picture of what might be regarded as 'serious' offences. Of particular note is the fact that the majority of motoring offences are excluded from the list of notifiable offences, with the exception of reckless driving and the theft or unauthorized taking of a motor vehicle. It often appears that what is classified as a notifiable offence is more the product of administrative and legal values and convenience than of a careful calculation of the relative social or personal significance of various kinds of illegal behaviour.

While information about notifiable offences is available from tables of offences known to or recorded by the police in *Criminal Statistics*, information about non-notifiable offences generally is not available. Information about the extent of non-notifiable and non-indictable offences is only available in the shape of statistics of *persons proceeded against*. Of all persons proceeded against, fewer than a quarter face charges for indictable offences, with well over half facing charges for non-indictable motoring offences. Thus, the official data on recorded offences exclude those offences of which the majority of offenders dealt with by the courts have been convicted! This single example shows the limitations of the official crime rate, which on its own is clearly inadequate as a 'social barometer' of trends in illegal behaviour.

Any official crime rate is more or less artifically constructed on the basis of a variety of administrative and legal considerations, which inevitably vary from time to time and between countries and regions. To say that a crime rate is artificially constructed is not the same as saying that it is arbitrarily constructed. The distinction between notifiable and other crimes is made deliberately so that an image of serious crime is not obscured by the inclusion of trivial offences, and so that court procedures may be scaled to the seriousness of the offence committed. All Western jurisdictions make distinctions between offences according to their seriousness for the purposes of police and court process. The way in which they do this gives important clues about their social values, and in this sense the organization of criminal statistics is a fruitful area of study for sociologists of law.

As it emerges from incidents reported to or discovered by the police and subsequently recorded by them, the crime rate is the product of a series of decisions taken by victims or witnesses of crime, by police officers, or by offenders who may make the police aware of earlier crime by admitting them together with the offence for which they are apprehended. Later in this chapter we will be considering some of the factors which may determine whether or not an offence is reported to the police, and in Chapter 2 we shall examine the ways in which the police deal with crimes that become known to them; but we shall begin by examining in broad outline the trends in recorded crimes. It will become increasingly evident that statistical products of this kind may reveal more about the changing attitudes and decision-making of those involved in the process than about any changes in offending behaviour itself. However much this may be so, the figures remain important as constituting the official 'facts' about crime on the basis of which the thrust of the 'fight against crime' is decided or justified.

In 1983, just under three and a quarter million notifiable offences were recorded by the police in England and Wales. Although this total was about 1% lower than the recorded total for the previous year, the general trend in recent years, and throughout most of this century since the First World War (with the exception of the decade 1945–55, immediately following the Second World War), has been one of steadily accelerating increase, as described by McClintock and Avison in their study *Crime in England and Wales* (1968):

> The simple answer to the question as to the extent of the recorded increase in indictable crime during the present century is that it rose from an annual level of one hundred thousand, in the first decade, to three hundred thousand in the late thirties, five hundred thousand in the mid-fifties and to more than a million by the mid-sixties. (McClintock and Avison, 1968, p. 17)

The annual rate of increase in recorded crime during the 1920s averaged 5%, but in the generally more affluent period from 1955–65 the rise in recorded crime was double this, at 10% a year. Examining trends in the crime rates of a country across an extended period of time is almost as hazardous as making comparisons between different countries. The substantial social, economic and technical changes in Britain during the past fifty years make the interpretation of crime statistics particularly difficult, but the ten-fold increase in the number of recorded offences seems to suggest that there have been changes relating to crime which reflect other social changes over the same period, and may be a direct consequence of them. Whether the change takes the form of increased opportunities for crime (notably the motor car), changes in attitudes towards crime (perhaps including the effects of trade unions on strategies for dealing with crime in the workplace) or changes in the inclination to commit crime (perhaps through a decline in respect for property) is difficult to decide. Purely for interest in reflecting the types of theft offence reaching the courts between 1835 and 1860, Table 1.1 is reproduced from Philips (1977). One can at least speculate on changes in opportunity, attitudes and inclinations which conspire to make the pattern revealed look so strange to us.

Table 1.2 shows the main trends in the number of notifiable crimes recorded by the police during the period 1963–83, divided into the main offence groups. Almost twice as many crimes were recorded in 1983 as 1973, and more than three times as many as in 1963. If the figures are examined on a yearly basis, it is possible to express changes in the recorded crime trends in terms of the average annual rate of change, but since the mid-sixties there has been so much fluctuation in the annual figures that this way of presenting the data is not very helpful. For instance, from 1963–73 the annual rate of increase was just under 6%, but in two of the years (1968 and 1972) the increase was around 1% and in 1973 there was a decrease of just under 2%. Similarly, from 1973–83, the annual average increase was still just under 6%, but the range extended from an increase of more than 18% in 1974 to decreases of 3% in 1978 and 1% in 1979 and 1983.

Between 1963 and 1983, by far the most rapid increase was in recorded criminal damage which showed a rise of more than 6000%. A substantial part of this statistical increase was caused by the decision, from 1977 onwards, to record all

TABLE 1.1 Black Country larceny committals 1835–60, divided into categories

Category of Larceny	Committed for Trial	
	No.	*%*
Theft from place of work	4,904	28.2
Larceny of clothing	2,996	17.2
Larceny of food or drink	1,438	8.3
Larceny from the person	1,304	7.5
Larceny of small domestic animals	925	5.3
Larceny of large domestic animals	331	1.9
Larceny of timber and fodder	321	1.8
Other simple larcenies	5,191	29.8
TOTAL	17,410	100.0

SOURCE: Philips (1977) Table 27, p. 178.

TABLE 1.2 Notifiable* offences recorded by the police by offence group, 1963–83
England and Wales   *Number of offences (in thousands)*

Offence Group	1963	1968	1973	1978	1983†	% increase 1963–83
Violence against the person	20.1	31.8	61.3	87.1	111.3	(454)
Sexual offences	20.5	23.4	25.7	22.4	20.4	(−0.5)
Burglary	219.1	287.1	393.2	565.7	813.4	(271)
Robbery	2.5	4.8	7.3	13.1	22.1	(784)
Theft and handling stolen goods	653.4	853.1	998.9	1441.3	1705.9	(161)
Fraud and forgery	54.4	74.5	110.7	122.2	121.8	(124)
Criminal damage**	6.9	12.2	52.8	306.2	443.3	(6325)
Other notifiable offences	1.1	2.1	7.8	3.5	8.7	(691)
Total	978.1	1289.1	1657.7	2561.5	3247.0	(232)

NOTE   *   In 1978 and earlier years known as indictable.
      **   Includes all criminal damage offences.
      †   The figures for 1983 are based on new counting rules introduced in 1980, which, together with certain legislative changes make them not precisely comparable to those for previous years. The main statistical trends are, however, not significantly affected.

SOURCE: Annual volumes of *Criminal Statistics England and Wales*, 1963 to 1983.

criminal damage offences, including those of value £20 and under (previously not included); but even when these are deducted from recent totals to make the comparison more accurate, the number of recorded offences of criminal damage in 1983 is still almost forty times as great as in 1963.[2] Yet as we will see later, so much criminal damage remains unrecorded that there remains scope for this offence to feature much more prominently yet in the statistics.

The next largest increases during this period (although much less than the increase in recorded criminal damage) were in offences of robbery and violence against the person. More than three times as many robberies were recorded in 1983 as in 1973, which in turn had three times more than in 1963. But even in 1983 the 22 100 offences in this category constituted less than 1% of all notifiable offences. The rate of increase in recorded offences of violence against the person slowed down a little between 1973 and 1983, when more than five times the number were recorded as had been recorded in 1963. However, offences of violence have never constituted more than 4% of the total of notifiable offences.

An important point to make at this stage is that despite its usefulness in breaking down the total number of offences into more meaningful categories, statistical grouping of offences can be misleading by its implicit suggestion of homogeneity within a category. This is particularly important when offences of hugely different degrees of seriousness are included within the same category. Many examples could be cited. In the category of criminal damage, the vast majority of offences are relatively minor acts of damage to personal or public property, but also included in 1983 were more than 17 000 arson offences, which can lead to long sentences of imprisonment for those found guilty. Likewise, offences of violence against the person range from assault and concealment of the birth of a child to murder and manslaughter. In recent years the Home Office has divided this category into 'more serious' and 'less serious' offences. This sub-division shows that 'more serious' offences of violence against the person have increased much more slowly than 'less serious' offences of the same type. For the whole period 1963–1983, the number of more serious offences increased by 123%, whereas the number of less serious offences increased by more than 500%; in 1983 the more serious offences constituted less than 7% of all recorded offences of violence, compared with 15% in 1963. This may suggest a real increase in slight violence, or a decreased tolerance of slight violence, so that offences of slight violence are increasingly reported to the police. There is currently no way of distinguishing between these alternatives.

Recognition of the general trends in the statistics of recorded crimes of violence is particularly important when one comes to discuss the 'murder rate'. Strictly speaking, this term is best avoided since it is invariably used incorrectly. 'Murder' is the verdict of a court of law in the trial of a suspected person. In this sense, there are only some 100–150 murders each year in England and Wales. However, official statistics now usually refer more broadly to offences of 'homicide', which include the legal/statistical categories of murder, manslaughter, (including 'diminished responsibility' by s.2 of the 1957 Homicide Act), and infanticide, and it is upon this statistic that our analysis must be based.

Compilation of official statistics relating to homicide in England and Wales used to differ from all other offences recorded by the police in that if the initial police classification of the offence was altered in the course of subsequent proceedings this was the basis for the official figures, whereas in all other offences the initial police classification was retained for official purposes. Since 1973 parallel statistics have been published showing the number of offences initially recorded as homicide by the police alongside those that were subsequently no longer recorded as homicide, which has averaged around 10–12% of those initially recorded as such. Table 1.3 shows the statistics for homicides 1963–83. Because of the relatively small numbers involved, fluctuations from year to year make it rather more difficult to identify and describe trends than is the case for most other offences. Misleading impressions can easily be created, depending on which years are chosen as the basis for any comparisons. In general terms it is clear from Table 1.3 that the number of homicide offences recorded by the police has gradually increased from 1965 to the present. Interestingly, before the early 1960s the average number of homicides recorded as known to the police had remained amazingly constant, at around 300 a year, for more than three decades.

Using the revised figure for offences currently recorded as homicide, in the 1960s the figure was usually around 300–350, in the 1970s it increased to more than 400 a year, and in the 1980s it has consistently been above 500. However, this rate of increase is much lower than that for all other offences of violence, keeping close to, or below, the rate of increase for the offences classified as 'more serious' by the Home Office. Between 1973 and 1983 the total number of homicide offences initially recorded by the police was just over 40% more than the total recorded in 1963–72, and almost identical to the increase in more serious offences of violence over the same period.

TABLE 1.3 Offences initially recorded by the police as homicide by current classification and per million of the population

England and Wales

Year	Offences initially recorded as homicide	Offences no longer recorded as homicide	Offences currently recorded as homicide		Outcome of cases decided by the Court to be homicide		
			No.	No. per million of pop.	Murder %	S. 2 manslaughter %	Other Manslaughter %
1963	307						
1964	296						
1965	325						
1966	364						
1967	414	60	354	7.3			
1968	420	60	360	7.4			
1969	395	63	332	6.8	29	21	45
1970	396	57	339	7.0	33	22	40
1971	459	52	407	8.3	27	22	45
1972	480	71	409	8.3	25	25	44
1973	465	74	391	8.0	26	26	45
1974	599	73	526	10.7	35	24	38
1975	508	65	443	9.0	26	23	49
1976	565	77	488	9.9	27	27	44
1977	484	66	418	8.5	32	27	39
1978	535	64	471	9.6	31	25	42
1979	629	83	546	11.1	36	26	37
1980	621	72	549	11.2	30	27	41
1981	556	55	501	10.1	36	23	40
1982	618	59	559	11.3	38	25	36
1983	553	47	506	10.2	36	25	36

SOURCE: Criminal Statistics, England and Wales.

Finally, to return to the initial distinction between 'murder' and 'homicide' statistics, Table 1.3 shows that only about one-third of those offences that are finally recorded as homicide result in a court verdict of murder, with a quarter resulting in a finding of s. 2 (diminished responsibility) manslaughter, and a further 40% in a simple manslaughter verdict. No easy answer, therefore, can be given to the question of what is a country's murder rate, without considering the basic terms in a much more precise fashion than is commonly the case. It is perhaps worthwhile restating and developing this point because it illustrates some of the problems in interpreting criminal statistics generally. For a death to be classified as homicide, it has got to be known to have occurred. This typically, but not invariably, means that a body has to be found. Virtually all killings where the body remains undiscovered are not classified as homicide. Where a body exists, it has to be judged to have been done to death by someone else. Who knows how many homicides get no further than the enigmatic 'open verdict' of a coroner? Once in court, a murder is decided to have happened on the basis of evidence given in court, evidence which is clearly not available in all those cases of killing which don't reach court, and which fails to satisfy the jury in some of those cases which do reach court! Figure 1.1 illustrates part of the process in a simplified way. Does the reader still think it is sensible to ask about the country's murder rate?

Burglary offences constituted one quarter of all recorded offences in 1983, totalling 813 400. This was more than double the number recorded in 1973, and this appears to indicate a steady increase in a type of crime which understandably gives rise to deep concern among members of the public (see below). Apart from the important evidence, to be discussed later, concerning changes in the reporting and recording of this offence, it should be noted that only about half of the burglaries recorded involve dwelling houses, of which a significant minority (21% in 1983) were attempted burglaries or completed burglaries in which nothing was taken. In 13% of recorded burglaries in a dwelling, the value of the property stolen was under £25, with a further 18% involving the loss of property worth £25 but under £100. These statistics are not intended to give the impression that the seriousness of a burglary is to be measured only or even primarily in terms of the monetary value of the stolen property, but are given to counterbalance common misperceptions and fears surrounding this particular offence.

Offences of theft (including 'handling stolen goods' or 'receiving' as it used to be known) have always constituted a majority of all notifiable crime recorded by the police. In 1983 more than half of all notifiable offences were in this category; in 1963 two-thirds of all indictable offences were theft or receiving stolen property. The rate of increase in these offences has been slightly lower than that for all notifiable offences; between 1978 and 1983 the annual average rate of increase was only 3%, compared with an average of 7% a year between 1973 and 1978. In 1983 almost half of all the offences in this group involved either theft from or unauthorized taking of a motor vehicle, but in 1963 the comparable figure (including the then non-indictable offence of taking a motor vehicle without the owner's consent) was only 27%. Other social and technological changes are reflected in the drop in the proportion of thefts from automatic machines and pre-payment meters to only 2% of the total in

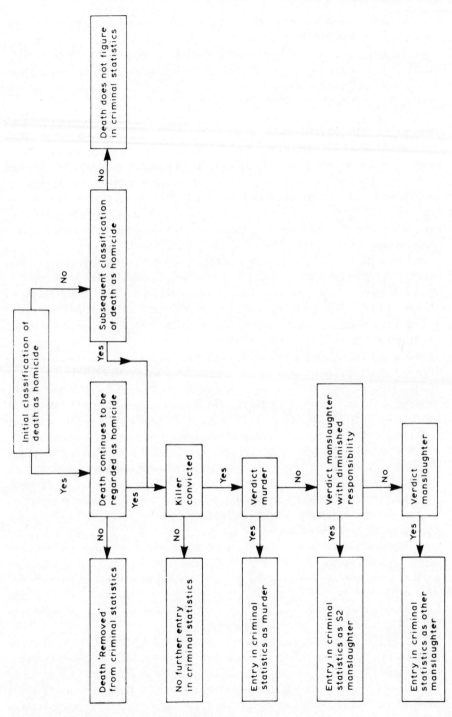

FIGURE 1.1 *Murder verdict: 'from corpse to statistic'*

1983 (compared with 8% in 1963), and the increase in recorded thefts from shops, which in 1983 constituted almost 1 in 7 of all thefts, compared with only 1 in 12 in 1963. Despite inflation, the face value of property stolen in the majority of thefts remains surprisingly low; thus, in 1983 more than a third of recorded offences involved theft of property worth less than £25, and in a further quarter the value was from £25 up to but not including £100.

Trends in recorded sexual offences during this period were very different from those of any other offence group. Between 1963 and 1973 the number of recorded offences increased steadily by 25%, but there then followed a steady annual *decrease* from 1973 to 1981, levelling off in 1982–3. As a result, the total number of sexual offences recorded in 1983 was slightly lower than it had been twenty years earlier. In 1963 recorded sexual offences constituted some 2% of the total, but by 1983 the proportion had dropped to 0.6%. In most years approximately three-quarters of recorded sexual offences involve females as the victim, although in 1982–3 it was slight increases in offences against males (together with the offence of 'gross indecency with a child', that became a notifiable offence for the first time in 1983) that halted the steady decline of the previous decade. Recorded offences of unlawful sexual intercourse with girls under the ages of 13 and 16 decreased quite sharply in the eleven years 1973–83, by 45%, to just over 3000 in 1983. Recorded offences of indecent assault on females dropped by just over 18% during the same period to just under 11 000 in 1983. However, the small but critically important category of recorded rape increased substantially during the period. In 1963, only 422 offences of rape were recorded by police forces in England and Wales; by 1973 the figure had reached 998, and it continued to rise (unlike any other sexual offence) throughout the next decade so that by 1983 a total of 1334 rapes were recorded, representing an increase of more than 200% upon the 1963 figure. Interpretation of this trend is more than usually fraught with difficulty, as the reporting and recording of rape is particularly susceptible to changing attitudes and expectations on the part of victims and the police, together with factors in society at large and in the administration of justice. Indeed, attempting to measure the 'true' incidence of sexual offences, especially those involving young children or women economically dependent or otherwise powerless *vis-à-vis* the offender, poses almost insuperable problems. However, in view of the importance of this most serious of sexual offences, in personal and social terms, and the irresponsibly sensational way in which the media may treat it, there is a particular need for a calm appraisal of available evidence and the development of a relevant criminological research tradition. Whether the development of such a literature will emerge from the women's movement is as yet open to conjecture, although that literature has already made an inestimable contribution in locating the offence in terms of general definitions of gender roles.

This brief survey of trends in official criminal statistics for the last twenty years has highlighted a few of the salient features, and raised a number of issues to which further attention will be paid in later parts of this book. So far, despite references to 'crime rates', most of the statistics have been presented simply as numbers from which proportionate changes have been calculated. Many commentators would claim that this method of presentation seriously distorts an analysis of trends in recorded crime. According to such a view, crime should be expressed in relation to the number of people available to commit crime. At the crudest level, this means expressing crime statistics in relation to population statistics. There is merit in such a view, and it is now becoming almost a matter of routine for crime and punishment statistics to be expressed as a rate per 100 000 population. This appears to be the only way of making meaningful comparisons between countries or between regions within a country. When the total population of a country has remained fairly static, as in England and Wales during the last two decades, presenting crime statistics in this way actually makes very little difference to the apparent trends – whichever way you look at it recorded notifiable crime has increased approximately threefold during this period. Expressed in terms of a number per 100 000 population, there has been an increase from two and a quarter thousand to over six thousand. Rather more importance must be given to correcting for population rates in longer historical analyses, as in McClintock and Avison's study of crime in England and Wales from 1901 to 1965. During this period the population increased from 32½ million to nearly 48 million, and the number of crimes recorded by the police from 81 thousand in 1901 to more than a million. In simple numbers this is a 14-fold increase in recorded crime. Expressed as a rate per 100 000 population, it represents less than a ten-fold increase, from a rate of 249 (1901) to 2374 (1965) (see McClintock and Avison 1968, p. 23).

Although it may often be desirable, even necessary, to express crime statistics in relation to population statistics, it is important to be cautious of too ready and uncritical an embrace of this approach. To start with, a crime rate per head of population should not be confused with an offender rate. The first represents the number of crimes per head of population. The second represents the number of people committing crimes per head of population. These are quite different. Not all crimes recorded are committed by separate individuals. Many offenders will have committed several offences each. Likewise some offences will have been committed by a group of people acting together. To express crimes per head of population obscures these differences. Strictly speaking, if crimes are to be expressed as a proportion of anything, it should be as a proportion of things people do, not as a proportion of people available to do things. We should beware of easily reaching the conclusion that 'people commit crime, therefore more people can be expected to commit more crime', so that if the ratio between crime and population is unchanged then there can be nothing which requires an explanation. It can be seen at once that underlying such an assumption is an emergent theory about rates of offending, and possibly about rates of victimization, which leaves itself wide open to a series of supplementary questions such as whether all members of a population are to be regarded as equally 'at risk' of offending, and, if not, whether crime rates should be expressed in relation to population weighted by relevant demographic variables (and who is confident that the relevant variables are known) rather than in relation to a population total that has little theoretical substance. For example, should those under the age of criminal responsibility be excluded? Should young people be given an extra weighting? What significance should be attached to the gender composition of the population, in view of gender differences in known offending rate? Indeed, given the change in the pattern of crime opportunities, should one adjust for social changes like the number of cars registered, or the number of cars registered corrected for the number of young males in the population, given their particular propensity for taking cars without their owners' consent! The motor car is arguably the most criminogenic device yet invented, and to fine tune estimates of the crime rate without reference to it is rather like adjusting incidence of the diseases of childhood by child population while ignoring developments in public health measures. Some would argue that in any case adjusting crime rates by population changes or anything else gives a spurious impression of accuracy to statistics subject to a host of distorting influences in their construction. Arguments such as these are proper restraints on statistical enthusiasm. Statistical techniques may all too easily be used as apparent aids to knowledge when they are either of limited value, or positively harmful in creating a false impression of sophistication in an analysis that fails to confront the basic issues in their use. Nevertheless, population-corrected crime rates are useful supplements to simple aggregations of crime, provided that they are seen as the beginning of a potentially valuable line of enquiry rather than as foreclosing the debate about the complex relationship between crime and population characteristics. Yet it should be emphasized that there are some purposes for which correcting for population composition is simply wrong. For example, let us consider decisions on police force strength. It is by no means obvious that police strength should be linked to numbers of notifiable crimes, but insofar as crime statistics are relevant to police strength at all, it is the absolute number of crimes, not the number of crimes per head, which is relevant. To police a football match, you need to know the absolute amount of likely trouble, not the proportion of the crowd which will be involved. The size of the crowd is relevant in judging likely trouble, but it would be a foolish policeman who sent more of his men to police a crowd of 2000 where 10% were likely to cause trouble than to police a crowd of 20 000 where 5% were likely to cause trouble! For other purposes, population-linked crime statistics are helpful. Estimating the likely effect of demographic changes on crime requires their use, although, as noted earlier, many complications attend their use. The most fundamental point to be made is that intended use is central to all decisions about criminal statistics and their manipulation.

2. Known Offenders

If official data on the nature and extent of crime have serious limitations, the same is true to an even greater extent of official data on known offenders. Not only is such information necessarily restricted to offences recorded by the police, but it relates only to that proportion of those offences which are officially 'cleared up' by the police. A detailed examination of the processes that lead to the statistic of 'cleared-up' crime will be found in Chapter 2, but there are two points that demand emphasis at the outset in any discussion of known offenders. First, only a minority of notifiable offences recorded by the police are subsequently cleared up: between 1963 and 1983 the annual clear-up rate fluctuated somewhat, but following a peak of 47% in 1973 there has been a steady decline to a low point of 37% in 1982 and 1983 (see Table 1.4). However, because of the substantial rise in the number of recorded offences the actual *number* of offences cleared up increased from 422 000 in 1963 to well over a million in

TABLE 1.4 Clear-up rates for notifiable offences recorded by the police, by offence group, 1963–83

Offence group	1963	1968	1973	1978	1983
Violence against the person	87	82	82	77	75
Sexual offences	80	77	78	76	73
Burglary	38	36	37	32	30
Robbery	43	39	46	30	24
Theft and handling stolen goods	39	38	43	40	37
Fraud and forgery	86	84	82	84	69
Criminal damage (excluding < £20 value)	56	40	39	30	26
Total offences cleared up %	43	42	47	42	37
(no. in '000s)	(421.9)	(540.3)	(772.1)	(997.7)	(1143.3)

SOURCE: Annual volumes of *Criminal Statistics England and Wales*.

1981–3. The second important point to note about the clear-up rate is that it varies considerably between the different offence groups, so that whereas only about 3 in every 10 recorded burglaries are cleared up by the police every year, more than 7 out of every 10 recorded sexual offences and violence against the person are cleared up. As a consequence, basic information is available for a much higher proportion of those responsible for recorded offences against the person than for offences against property. Does that mean that we can generalize more confidently about sexual and violent offenders than about burglars? It does not. When assault takes place by someone who isn't a stranger, the police find out who did it at the same time that they find out that it was done. This is also true for predatory sex offences by non-strangers, and for consensual sex offences, where only the arrival of the police simultaneously reveals the crime and identifies the offenders. However, to say that identified offenders are typical of all such offenders in these categories is very much another matter. Why do friends and acquaintances identify a person as a criminal? It would be stretching credulity to say that the process was random. In consequence, the image of violent offenders and sex offenders we obtain from official statistics is not necessarily more generalizable than the image of known burglars, despite the higher clear-up rates of the former crimes.

For official purposes an offence can be counted as cleared up when a suspect has been proceeded against, whatever the eventual outcome of those proceedings (see Chapter 2 for further details of what counts as cleared up). By virtue of the fact that some suspects may be charged with more than one offence, or have other offences 'taken into consideration', or be subject to the counting rule that they only appear once in the statistical tables (for their most serious offence), the number of persons recorded as proceeded against each year is usually about half of the number of offences recorded as having been cleared up. In recent years there has been a substantial growth in the cautioning of offenders, as an alternative to more formal processing in the courts, and so routine information about known offenders covers those who have been officially cautioned by the police as well as those who have been found guilty by the courts of indictable offences. These data form the basis of our analysis of the characteristics of known offenders.

Table 1.5 shows that less than half of all known offenders are adults aged 21 and over, and there has been little change in this pattern throughout the period 1963–83.[3] However, since 1963, the proportion of known offenders who are juveniles (under the age of 17) has declined, with a corresponding increase in the young adult offender group, aged 17 but under 21, from about 1 in 6 of the total to almost a quarter in 1983.

There is considerable variation in the extent to which offenders from each age group are involved in the different types of offence. Table 1.6 shows the detailed picture for 1983. Juveniles feature particularly in offences of burglary, theft and criminal damage, but hardly at all in fraud and forgery or motoring offences – in which more than 7 out of 10 offenders are aged 21 or over. Young adults are prominent in robbery and violence against the person, as well as burglary and criminal damage; there is no type of offence in which they do not figure significantly. In addition to offences of fraud and indictable motoring offences, adults contribute particularly to sexual offences and violence against the person, but are under-represented in offences of burglary and criminal damage.

Another way of examining the relationship between age and known offending is to present the data according to the incidence of known offending per 100 000 population in each age group. This also provides a useful way of comparing patterns of known offending among males and females. Table 1.7 shows that the rate of known offending for males doubled between 1963 and 1983; for females it increased almost threefold. Throughout the 1960s and (perhaps significantly) until the raising of the school-leaving age from 15 to 16 in 1972, the peak age of offending for males was 14; from 1973 onwards it has always been 15. For females, on the other hand, the peak age of known offending has remained at 14 throughout the period. A further difference between males and females is that for girls aged between 13 and 15 the known offender rate is significantly higher than at other ages, with that for 16–18

TABLE 1.5   Persons found guilty or cautioned for indictable offences by age group, 1963–83

England and Wales

Year	Total no. (in '000s)	Aged 10 years and under 17	Aged 17 years and under 21	Aged 21 years and over
		%	%	%
1963	(233.2)	35.5	17.3	47.3
1968	(292.2)	30.9	20.5	48.7
1973	(428.2)	36.5	20.7	42.7
1978	(519.0)	34.1	20.8	45.1
1983	(574.5)	29.2	23.6	47.2

Source: *Criminal Statistics England and Wales.*

TABLE 1.6   Persons found guilty or cautioned by type of offence, age group, and sex, 1983

England and Wales

Offence group	Total no. (in '000s)	Aged 10 & under 17	Aged 17 & under 21	Aged 21 & over	Total Males	Total Females
		%	%	%	%	%
Violence against the person	(58.5)	19	29	52	91	9
Sexual offences	(9.3)	22	18	59	99	1
Burglary	(84.7)	38	30	32	96	4
Robbery	(4.2)	24	33	45	95	5
Theft and handling stolen goods	(311.7)	36	21	43	76	24
Fraud & forgery	(27.2)	7	21	73	78	22
Criminal damage	(14.4)	35	28	37	93	7
Motoring offences	(30.3)	6	23	71	97	3
(others)	(35.4)	(3)	(23)	(74)	(89)	(11)
Total (%)	100	29	24	47	83	17
no. (in '000s)	(575.9)	(167.9)	(135.5)	(271.1)	(479.6)	(94.9)

SOURCE: *Criminal Statistics England and Wales, 1983.*

TABLE 1.7   Persons found guilty or cautioned, for indictable offences per 100 000 population in age group by sex and age, 1963–83

(a) *MALES*   No. per 100 000 population

Age	1963	1968	1973	1978	1983	% increase 1963–83
10	1551	1402	1704	1679	1305	−16
11	2069	2113	2719	2667	2153	4
12	2764	3026	3979	3931	3246	17
13	3572	3881	5414	5377	4784	34
14	4066	4689	6899	7056	6584	70
15	3083	4205	7559	8636	8249	168
16	2608	3843	6770	7894	7747	197
17	3113	4312	7129	7752	7549	142
18	2830	4127	6415	7496	7550	167
19	2481	3496	5280	6219	6706	170
20	2283	2958	4422	5192	5948	161
21 < 25	2011	2347	3089	3576	4224	110
25 < 30	1367	1745	1897	2269	3225	136
30 < 40	784	983	1262	1463	1559	99
40 < 50	432	520	673	838	953	121

TABLE 1.7 *contd*

(a) *MALES*   No. per 100 000 population

Age	1963	1968	1973	1978	1983	% increase 1963–83
50 < 60	205	247	349	447	486	137
60 & over	76	93	126	182	185	143
Total	1040	1280	1811	2125	2276	119

(b) *FEMALES*

Age	1963	1968	1973	1978	1983	% increase 1963–83
10	139	146	284	385	302	117
11	242	279	553	724	595	146
12	373	493	974	1225	1080	190
13	512	711	1341	1576	1699	232
14	603	798	1450	1762	1893	214
15	415	714	1282	1736	1780	329
16	324	563	898	1345	1317	306
17	336	547	854	1090	1080	221
18	349	435	749	1014	1015	191
19	283	366	609	857	921	225
20	224	312	527	733	836	273
21 < 25	237	278	445	624	670	183
25 < 30	186	254	329	466	517	178
30 < 40	152	199	281	372	33	120
40 < 50	132	153	187	274	243	84
50 < 60	93	121	148	204	168	81
60 & over	39	48	59	97	75	92
Total	154	202	310	434	421	173

SOURCE: *Criminal Statistics England and Wales.*

year-olds considerably lower; in contrast, for males aged 16–18 the offending rate has tended to be significantly higher than for older age groups or for those aged 13 years or younger. Thus, in each sex the age distribution of offending displays a distinctive pattern: the female rate has a relatively short 'peak' between the ages of 13 and 15, with a substantial decline in the late teens, followed by a continual but rather shallow decrease for the remainder of the age span; in contrast, the male rate has a rather wider 'peak', almost a plateau, between the ages of 14–18, but from the late 20s onwards there is a very rapid decrease in the known offending rate, so that for men in their fifties and sixties the rate is only about double that of women of the same age, whereas the overall average difference between the male and female offending rate in recent years has been 5:1. It is this difference between the sexes which is both well-known and little understood. In 1963, the rate of male offending was almost seven times greater (in official statistics) than that of females; by 1983, this difference has narrowed to the 5:1 ratio specified above. Another way of describing the gender difference is to note that by the age of 28, 33% of males and only 6% of females have acquired a conviction for a standard list offence (yet another of the ways of identifying more serious offences currently in use; see Home Office 1985b). Many theories have been put forward to explain this, of which some concentrate on factors that might influence male/female behaviour differences and others factors that might explain why and how the actions of the agents of criminal justice might 'bias' the statistics to understate female involvement in crime, arguing that changes in the official statistics may stem from changes in attitudes towards female offending by victims, witnesses and the police, rather than from changes in the behaviour itself. Be that as it may, we have already noted that between 1963 and 1983 there was a doubling in the rate of known male offending, compared with a virtual three-fold increase for females. However, there were considerable differences between the sexes in the rate of increase within different age groups. For example, throughout the period under consideration, there was no significant increase in the rate of known offending of boys aged 10–12 years, whereas for girls of the same age the rate of offending more than doubled. Similarly, in the age group 14–17, although the rate for boys in 1983 was almost twice that of 1963, for girls the increase was almost four-fold. For males and females aged 21 or over, the rates of increase over the same period were, for all practical purposes, identical. Figure 1.2 shows some of these patterns diagrammatically.

A final feature that distinguishes known offending among males and females is the different types of offence in which the official statistics suggest each sex indulges. Within the overall 5:1 ratio the sex ratios for some of the main offence groups in 1983 are set out below:

Motoring Offences (indictable only) 30:1
Burglary 25:1
Robbery 20:1
Criminal Damage 13:1
Violence against the Person 10:1
Fraud and Forgery 3:1
Theft and Handling 3:1

Alternatively, the proportion that each of the above types of offence constitute of the total recorded for each sex can be compared. More than three-quarters of all known offences by females involve theft or handling stolen goods, compared with just half of the male offences; and whereas 1 in every 7 of the male offenders are convicted or cautioned for burglary, this is so for only 1 in every 25 female offenders. Only 1% of female offenders are convicted for indictable motoring offences, in contrast with 6% of male offenders. Finally, whereas just 6% of known offences by females involve violence against the person or robbery, these constitute 12% of male offences.

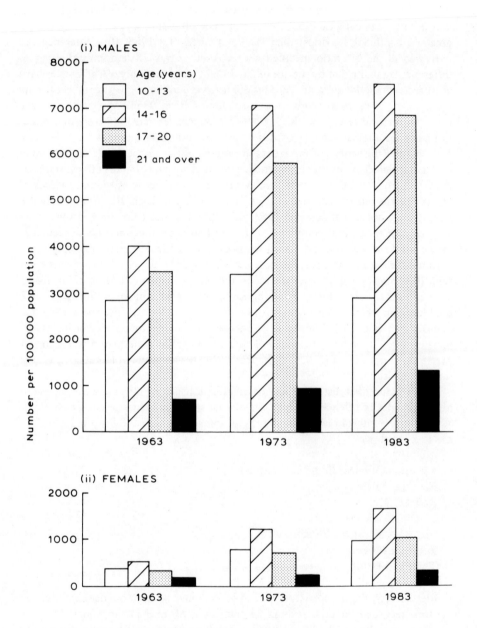

FIGURE 1.2   *Persons found guilty or cautioned for indictable offences per 100 000 population, by age group and sex, 1963, 1973 and 1983.*

However interesting and tantalizing information on known offenders may be, this part of the chapter must end on a note of caution and scepticism. Official statistics provide only the barest information on offenders proceeded against, their age and sex (and occasionally their race – see below). Additional information on the personal characteristics and social background of offenders has to be derived from research studies, usually based on relatively small samples of offenders selected at a particular time or place within the criminal justice process. The most ambitious and impressive study to look at a quite large sample over a long period is that undertaken by Donald West and David Farrington (see West 1982). This gave extensive and valuable information about characteristics of recorded offenders and others. This study has the crucial advantage of selecting its sample before the sample became enmeshed in the criminal justice process. No amount of information about known offenders can tell us anything for certain about those responsible for recorded offences that are not cleared up or about the much larger number of offences that never become known to the police. It would be very unwise to extrapolate from the little knowledge we have about the people who are known to the criminal justice system to the much greater number (probably) of those who are unknown. The processes whereby offences and offenders are discovered and officially documented are neither random nor arbitrary, and there are no good grounds for automatically assuming that those who escape discovery, or if discovered escape official record, are likely to share the characteristics of those who are not so fortunate.

From Behaviour to Crime Statistics

In the first part of this chapter we have presented an image of crime and criminals which is to be gained from annual criminal statistics for England and Wales. Routine statistics of this kind earn their keep by presenting an image of a social issue which can inform concern or policy. However, as has been made clear earlier, there are various ways of presenting the data which change the image – for example the linking of demographic changes, such as those in age and gender, with rates of crime. Thus, even assuming that the police come to know of and record crimes, how to interpret changes in crime rate is by no means a simple matter, depending as it does on a host of changes in inclination, temptation and opportunity to commit crime. But of course the police do not always come to hear about crime, and when they do, they by no means always clear it up. It is not possible to generalize from what the police record as crime to what the public suffer by way of crime. In this part of the chapter we will deal generally with the phase up to and including report to the police. We will also deal with the patterns of non-report, and with the separate issue of crime fear. In the next chapter we will be concerned with the statistics of, and research about, the ways in which the police record and clear crime.

Let us consider first the process by which an action becomes a crime statistic. The first threshold to be crossed, and one too easily overlooked, is the recognition of an action as a crime. A great deal of behaviour takes place which could be charged as assault, but which is more likely to be regarded as part of life's hurly-burly. As Rossi *et al.* (1974) point out, the line between manly sport and crime is a thin one. Indeed, many assaults are televised each year with no real thought of them as crimes. They take place on soccer pitches, with policemen a few yards away on the touchline. Many of these assaults end in a handshake between assailant and victim. At worst, they end in the suspension of the offender from a few games by the Football League authorities. Yet some of these assaults are of such brutality as to end the playing career of the victim, as happened in a Second Divison game a few days before this passage was written. Further, journalists and television commentators distance assaultive behaviour from the idea of crime by using euphemisms. They refer to players who frequently assault others as 'hard', 'uncompromising', or 'physical'. This tendency to draw the boundaries of crime much more narrowly than the criminal law permits is not restricted to the playground, the pub and the sports field. In the study of occupational crime, it can be seen both that much fraud and theft are seen as perks of a job rather than crime, and that this is a perception shared with those who are their victims and employers, who seem content to live with a degree of loss which does not get out of hand, and to deal by means other than the criminal law with transgressors (Ditton 1977, Henry 1978, Mars 1982 and Duff 1985).

There is another reason for failure to recognize an event as a crime, and that is that no-one, other than its perpetrator(s), is in a position to recognize it as such. Many corporate crimes fall into this category. For example, in the pharmaceutical industry, often no-one is in a position to assess whether clinical trials have been falsified to advance the marketing of a new drug (Braithwaite 1984). Illegal drug use is another type of criminal behaviour of which this is true, as are sexual offences like incest.

When some action is thought of as crime, what determines whether the police or another prosecuting agency becomes aware of the event? Certain kinds of crime are dealt with because the police or some other enforcement agency themselves come to be aware of the event. The Inland Revenue Investigation Department, the Factory Inspectorate, the Customs and Excise, the Department of Health and Social Security Inspectorate, and so on, are examples of enforcement agencies in whose domain crime is typically revealed by activities of the agency rather than the report of the victim. With these important exceptions, the way in which events are made available for inclusion in criminal statistics is through citizen report, most often victim report. It is primarily through surveying victims of crime both reported and unreported that insight has recently been gained into the reasons which victims give for reporting crimes, and thus how the image of crime is filtered through the medium of victim report.

Images of crime

The reason for gathering routine statistics is to monitor a state of affairs which is of social concern. The metaphor traditionally used is that of the social barometer. Criminal statistics purport to give an image of crime. It is, as we have suggested, an image of crime which is seriously distorted. Is there any way of getting closer to the 'reality' of crime? Two ways have been tried. The first involves asking a sample of people what crimes they have committed. Such approaches are known as self-report studies of crime. The second approach involves asking a group of people what crimes they have suffered. These two methods have different advantages and disadvantages, although both rely on representative sampling. Self report studies can pick up victimless and private crimes like drug abuse and breaches of health and safety legislation, whereas victim surveys will not. Self report studies can pick up offences of murder and manslaughter, while not many victims of murder seem willing to be interviewed! Self report studies may pick up offences against children too young to be sensibly included in victim surveys. Both types of study rely on people telling the truth and not locating a crime incorrectly in time, since typically experiences are asked for which took place during the past year, five years etc. However there is less reason to lie if you are a victim than if you are an offender. Someone who has committed an offence may not tell the interviewer because he does not trust the interviewer to keep quiet. He may keep quiet because he is ashamed of what he has done. Conversely he may claim offences he has not committed if he feels that he will gain kudos thereby. This sort of problem has led to the use of extremely elaborate systems in self report studies to ensure the obvious confidentiality of answers, and the recognition of that by interviewees (see Belson, 1968). Perhaps because of the particular difficulties and disadvantages of self report studies, recent years have witnessed an increasing reliance on and preference for victim surveys, despite their necessarily partial coverage of crime. This tendency has reached the point at which victim surveys are now known generally as crime surveys. The only victim survey which has employed national coverage of England and Wales is known as the British Crime Survey. The first report of the survey was published in 1983 (see Hough and Mayhew, 1983). A separate analysis of the data from Scotland has also been published (Chambers and Tombs, 1984). It is thus obvious that data on trends in crime, as reflected in victim surveys, cannot yet be supplied. The earliest local victim survey in England was done in 1976 (Sparks *et al.*, 1977) and more recent local surveys have been done in Merseyside (Kinsey, 1984) and the Midlands (Farrington and Dowds, 1985). Useful data are likley to emerge from local surveys. National surveys show wide variations in crime and crime report between parts of the country. Local patterns of crime clearly pose distinctive problems in responses to crime by local authorities and police forces. However, because it will feature so centrally in what follows, a brief description of the British Crime Survey should be given.

The data analysed in the following pages is taken from the England and Wales sample of the survey. This involved the interview of one person aged 16 or above in each of 11 000 households in England and Wales. A further 5000 households were sampled in Scotland. The sampling frame was the Electoral Register, so that the more people on the Electoral Register in a household, the more chance there was for a household to be selected. However, it was possible to correct for this and other imbalances by weighting the data appropriately. All people involved in the survey were given the main questionnaire, which included background information and screening questions to see if respondents or the household generally had fallen victim to crime (the screening question took the form 'Since 1st January 1981 has anyone done X to you' where X was an ordinary language approximation to the legal definition of an offence such as burglary or robbery (see Hough and Mayhew, 1983 p. 8). Whenever an offence was mentioned, the respondent filled in a victim form for each separate offence suffered which included details about its perpetrators and consequences. All respondents who filled in victim forms and two in five of those who did not, also completed a follow-up questionaire detailing their lifestyle, including their contacts with the police and their own offending behaviour. (In this sense, the British Crime Survey was also a self report study. However, the levels of admission of crimes was so low as to invite scepticism about the results of this part of the survey).

In short, the British Crime Survey provides much of interest in clarifying who suffers crime. Already, four major reports have been generated using its findings (Hough and Mayhew 1983, Southgate and Ekblom 1984, Maxfield 1984 and Gottfredson 1984) and more are envisaged (see Hope 1984). A second sweep of the British Crime Survey has now been completed and some of its preliminary results have just been published (Hough and Mayhew, 1985). This survey seems likely to be a periodic, if not regular, complement to conventional criminal statistics in the future.

Because victim surveys have been such a recent development in this country, it is not yet possible to use them to reveal trends over time in crime suffered, to compare with the trends in recorded crime described earlier in this chapter. However, for one offence it is possible to show some interesting changes over a reasonable period in both crime recorded and crime suffered. The crime is burglary. It is worth looking at burglary as an example of the kind of insight which victim surveys may come to afford in time.

Trends in reported and recorded burglary
In a Home Office publication, Crime Prevention News (issue 2 1982) we read 'A nationwide prevention campaign to combat the steep increase in domestic crime, particularly burglary, is to be launched by the British Insurance Association on 15th March . . . to focus public attention on the ever-increasing risk of being burgled' (p. 1). Certainly the number of domestic burglaries recorded in criminal statistics increased during the period covered by this book. For present purposes, the crucial period is 1971–81. The number of recorded domestic burglaries increased from 204 560 in 1971 to 349 692 in 1981. There are two simple and obvious ways in which this increase in officially recorded burglaries could have come about. The first is that the increase really did occur and that a constant proportion of the burglaries which happened were reported and recorded. The second is that the increase did not occur, but that more of the burglaries suffered were reported to and recorded by the police.

Among the regular data-gathering exercises which are undertaken by the Government's Office of Population Censuses and Surveys is the General Household Survey (GHS) which samples households and asks questions about household expenditure, practice and experience. The survey included a question about burglary in 1972, 1973, 1979 and 1980. Households were asked about burglaries suffered during the twelve months preceding interview. The conclusion reached in the survey report of 1981 was 'overall, in the total period covered by the GHS questions on this topic, there was almost no change . . . in the incidence of burglaries in private house-holds' (Home Office, 1982 p. 75). This seems to suggest that the 50% increase in burglaries during the 1970s just didn't happen. Can official statistics really be so misleading? In a last desperate defence of the recorded burglary figures, one could point out that most of the interviews for the 1980 General Household Survey were conducted during 1979, and Criminal Statistics show the sharpest rise in recorded burglaries in 1980, so it is just possible that the contrast between Criminal Statistics and GHS would have been less stark if the last survey had happened later. However the first British Crime Survey published in 1983 was based on interviews carried out in 1982 and inviting recall of events in 1981. Comparison with the GHS yields estimates of the rate of burglary within 1.3% of each other. This surely clinches the view that the increase in burglary during the 1970s was indeed almost completely illusory.

There are two types of change which may account for the increase in recorded burglary with a constant actual rate of burglaries. The first is a change in the proportion of burglaries reported to the police. The second is a change in the proportion of reported burglaries recorded as such. Can the GHS shed any light on whether it is a change in public reporting or police recording practice underlying the observed pattern? The GHS showed no changes between 1972 and 1980 in the proportion of victims of burglary reporting the crime to the police. Unless burglary victims are lying, this makes it reasonable to think in terms of changes in police recording practice. This point will be developed in the next chapter.

If we were to rely on Criminal Statistics to understand the trends in burglary during the 1970s, we would miss the most dramatic trend of all. This is the change in the loss incurred in the average household burglary. Although burglary loss information is included in Criminal Statistics, adjustments in the way in which it is presented make it impossible to get an idea of change across the decade. However the picture may be supplemented by information from the British Insurance Association and this is presented as Figure 1.3.

It will be seen that the losses from burglary have increased enormously, even when corrected for inflation. Thus the really major discernable trend during the 1970s was an increase in burglary losses suffered by insurance companies. How can the trends be reconciled? It could simply be that the average value of house contents increased over the decade, although it is difficult to produce any analysis of this kind which can yield such a sharp increase. The explanation could be – but is not – an increase in the proportion of households covered by insurance. In fact, that increase is very modest. It could be the increased availability of new for old policies, which impression (in the absence of available statistics) suggests was sharp during the decade. This would increase the amounts claimed and the incentive for fraudulent claiming (see Litton and Pease, 1984). The point here is not which of these alternatives, if any, is the correct one. It is merely that the consideration of data from the British Insurance Association, the British Crime Survey, the General Household Survey and Criminal Statistics, taken together, offers a much more complete, albeit more complex, picture of what the burglary problem might be.

Reporting a crime to the police

The decision to report a crime to the police is arguably the most important single decision in the entire criminal justice process. Only reported crimes are available for official record. Crime report also triggers the process of criminal investigation. Crime

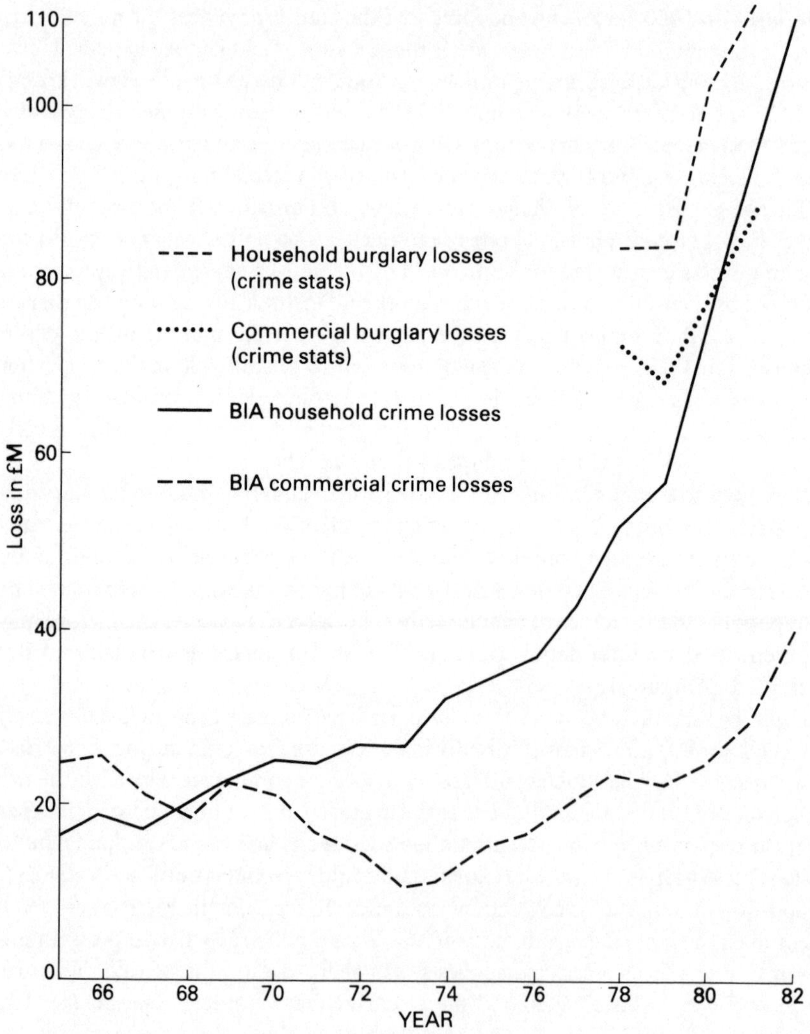

FIGURE 1.3 *BIA household and commercial crime losses 1965–81 (UK) and burglary losses recorded in criminal statistics (England and Wales) 1977–80.* (N.B. All sum adjusted to 1980 prices.)

SOURCE: this analysis first appeared in Litton and Pease (1984).

trends, patterns and prevalence have traditionally been taken from statistics of recorded crime, rather than of crimes suffered. The failure to report crime precludes victim support. It renders problematic the evaluation of crime prevention initiatives (Skogan, 1984). It prevents accurate areal analysis of crime (Brantingham and Brantingham, 1981). On the other hand failure to report sometimes has good consequences. For example a degree of self-imposed restraint by victims will serve to limit the wasteful use of police resources. Insofar as offences occur within families and between acquaintances, report to the police may well create resentments which are socially divisive. Further, even were complete report to be judged desirable, it would prove impossible to achieve, because of informal processes which lead to the under-recording of events reported to the police as crimes (see Chapter 2). To summarize, there are both advantages and disadvantages in the under-reporting of crime. How one is to judge the balance of advantage and disadvantage depends crucially upon the nature of the filter which the decision to report a crime represents. Suppose that the crimes which went unreported were trivial and left their victims unruffled. In this case, the disadvantage of non-report set out above would be less crucial. If, on the other hand, more serious crimes went unreported, actions based upon official statistics would be more seriously flawed. A particularly troubling pattern of non-report would be one in which particular social groups did not report serious crimes because of their hostility towards the police. In such a case, the resource savings yielded by non-report may be thought illusory when set against the alienation from the police which such hostility would reflect.

What does the British Crime Survey tell us about crime reporting? Table 1.8 shows the percentage of crimes of different types which are reported to the police. It shows the distribution both of offences which are reported and those which are unreported. In other words, it shows what the image of crime would be if based upon all crime rather than just reported crime. It is clear that certain crime types, notably threats to kill, assault and vandalism, would loom much larger in statistics of all crime. *Relatively*, theft of motor vehicles would be seen as less frequent. Overall, Table 1.8 makes it clear that the scope for increase in officially recorded crimes by changes in victim report are enormous. However, it should not be concluded that anything that could be called 'the crime problem' corresponds more closely to crime in general than to reported crime alone. Unreported incidents were generally the less serious ones in terms of the value of goods stolen, damage done and injury caused. When an offence was not reported, the victim was asked why this was so. These reasons are presented as Table 1.9. It is clear that the most frequent single reason for non-report is the triviality of the offence, but a substantial number of reasons are to do with perceived police impotence or disinterest. The Hough and Mayhew (1983) report correctly emphasized the triviality aspect of the results. Nonetheless, there does appear to be a significant problem here. Another way of presenting the data would be to say that more unreported offences stayed unreported for reasons *other than* their triviality. Offence triviality has been widely canvassed as the most important reason for non-report (Gottfredson and Hindelang 1979, Skogan 1984). However, the British Crime Survey data clearly need further analysis to enable confident conclusions of this kind to be made. In the 1984 sweep of the Survey, victims were asked directly to rate the

TABLE 1.8   Distribution of frequent offences in British Crime Survey 1982 by police knowledge of offence

British Crime Survey, 1982   *Numbers (in '000s)*

Offence	Known to police		Unknown to police		Total	
		%		%		%
Wounding	49.8	(3.9)	69.7	(2.3)	119.5	(2.7)
Assault/attempted assault	148.8	(11.7)	413.9	(13.4)	562.7	(12.9)
Robbery/attempted robbery	20.5	(1.6)	23.6	(0.8)	44.1	(1.0)
Theft/attempted theft from the person	48.8	(3.8)	107	(3.5)	155.8	(3.6)
burglary/attempted burglary in dwelling	189.5	(14.9)	96.1	(3.1)	285.6	(6.6)
Theft in a dwelling	10	(0.8)	45	(1.5)	55	(1.3)
Car theft	93.4	(7.3)	5.5	(0.2)	98.9	(2.3)
Theft from car	143.4	(11.3)	320.9	(10.4)	464.3	(10.7)
Cycle theft	52.9	(4.2)	29.9	(1.0)	82.8	(1.9)
Theft from outside the home (including milk bottles)	97.0	(7.6)	363	(11.8)	460	(10.6)
Other theft	143.8	(11.3)	467	(15.1)	610.8	(14.0)
Criminal damage to a motor vehicle (over £20)	34.1	(2.7)	138.7	(4.5)	172.8	(4.0)
Criminal damage to a motor vehicle (£20 or under)	29.5	(2.3)	392.8	(12.7)	422.3	(9.7)
Criminal damage to the home (over £20)	35.0	(2.8)	46.3	(1.5)	81.3	(1.9)
Criminal damage to the home (£20 or under)	102.0	(8.0)	210.8	(6.8)	312.8	(7.2)
Threat to kill	73.0	(5.7)	354.9	(11.5)	427.9	(9.8)
Total	1271.5	(100)	3085.1	(100)	4356.6	(100)

Total unweighted n = 4465

seriousness of the offences committed against them. Analysis of these ratings will give some additional insight into problematic non-report. Another useful addition in 1984 was the request for reasons for reporting a crime, which may of course not be the opposite of reasons given for not reporting one.

Feelings that the police are impotent, which loom quite large in the reasons for not reporting crime in the 1982 survey, may reflect dislike of the police or realism. Garofalo (1981) working in the United States finds this reason to be independent of

TABLE 1.9   Reasons for non-report to the police, British Crime Survey 1982

	Personal offences %	Household offences %
Too trivial; no loss or damage	38	49
Police could do nothing	16	34
Inappropriate for police; dealt with matter ourselves	13	5
Fear/dislike of the police	6	1
Inconvenient	5	2
Police would not be interested	3	9
Fear of reprisals	2	<1
Reported to other authorities	3	2
Other specific answers; vague answers	21	10

Question: 'Did the police come to know about the matter?' If no, 'Why not?' (Multiple answers allowed)

Weighted data; unweighted n = 1,695 (including incidents which occurred in 1982)

SOURCE: Hough and Mayhew, (1983), Table 3, p. 11.

attitudes towards the police. Working in London Sparks *et al.* (1977) reached the same conclusion. Table 1.10 shows the data of relevance from the 1982 British Crime Survey. It shows that those victims who thought the police in general did a good job did not more often report a crime committed against them than did those who felt the police did a poor job. There *is* a significant association between police rating and report, it is not a simple one with good rating and report going together. In fact interpretation of Tables like 1.10 is particularly difficult. Specifically, those people who report offences to the police may have their view of police quality changed by their contact with the police which eventuates from their report. Some of those people who used to think the police did a good job may change their minds when dealing

TABLE 1.10   Report to the police by judgement of the quality of police work, British Crime Survey 1982

Rating of Police	Offence came to Police Notice				Total
	Yes		No		
Very Good	416.6	(35.5)	842.3	(30.0)	1258.8
Fairly Good	596.1	(50.8)	1533.1	(54.6)	2129.3
Fairly Poor	103.0	(8.8)	249.2	(8.9)	352.1
Very Poor	58.2	(4.9)	183.7	(6.5)	241.9
Total	1173.8	(100)	2808.3	(100)	2982.1

Unweighted n = 4278

with them as a victim. Some of those who used to think the police did a poor job may be unexpectedly impressed. The picture will be clearer after the 1984 survey, where extra information can be brought to bear on the problem. As of now, there is no reason to suppose that the judgement of police impotence as a reason for victim non-report is anything other than the result of a victim's realistic assessment of the situation.

For comparison with criminal statistics, the full usefulness of the British Crime Survey has yet to be realized, since it is comparison of trends which enable an overall view of whether the apparently remorseless rise in recorded crime is matched by a comparable increase in crime suffered. Whatever the relationship between trends, information gained should be used, not as a stick with which to beat published statistics on recorded crime or complacency if the trends coincide. Nor should it be used to provide a better barometer of social health. Rather it should be used intelligently to yield a better understanding of the dynamics of the process by which events that happen to people get shrunk and distorted into recorded crime statistics, an understanding which we can use to change the process in pursuit of agreed social goals.

Reporting to the Police: The case of race

It was noted earlier that very little information about offenders exists in official statistics, beyond the basics of age and gender. A partial exception to this is offender race. Statistics produced by the Metropolitan Police (Home Office 1983) purported to show that where the victim of a crime against the person is able to classify the ethnic appearance of the offender, that offender is black in a higher proportion of cases than would be expected given the ethnic composition of the population. At first sight, this suggests that black offenders are more given to committing crimes against the person. Before reaching that conclusion, let us consider the alternative possibility that white people have a lower threshold of report to the police when victimized by a black person. This would generate a higher rate of report of offences against whites by blacks, and would give the impression of personal offences being committed by black people in a disproportionately large number of cases. Table 1.11 is taken from Stevens and Willis (1979). It shows that an explanation along these lines is likely to be correct. It will be noted that the degree of injury inflicted in recorded crimes of violence differs according to race. The proportion of white victims of 'coloured' attackers who suffered no injury was over twice as high as the proportion of victims who suffered no injury in other types of encounter. This strongly suggests that the Metropolitan Police data are a function of different thresholds of report by crime victims, with white victims seeming more ready to report crimes which left them uninjured when the offender was not white. Crow and Cove (1984) likewise present data suggesting that black people convicted of property offences have stolen less that white people convicted. It seems, then, that it is especially dangerous to reach conclusions about offender race from statistics on recorded crime.

Fear of crime

One of the central concerns of the British Crime Survey has been to characterize crime as a rare event. A much quoted passage of the report reads:

TABLE 1.11   Attackers and victims in reported crimes of violence by degree of injury (MPD 1975)

Degree of injury	White attacker White victim (n = 6 521)	White attacker Coloured victim (n = 643)	Coloured attacker Coloured victim (n = 937)	Coloured attacker, White victim (n = 3 616)
	%	%	%	%
Fatal	2.8	2.8	1.9	0.5
Serious	8.9	7.6	11.8	3.9
Slight	66.5	68.4	63.4	45.8
None	21.8	21.2	22.8	49.8
TOTAL	100.0	100.0	99.9	100.0

SOURCE: Scotland Yard, special tabulation, from Stevens and Willis (1979), Table 6, p. 37.

The survey showed that the statistically average person age 16 or over can expect:
   a robbery once every 5 centuries (not attempts);
   an assault resulting in injury (even if slight) once every century;
   the family car to be stolen or taken for a joy ride once every 60 years;
   a burglary in the home once every 40 years.
Of course, it is somewhat artificial to express the risks in this way, since different types of people face very different risks; nevertheless the device shows that the risks of these fairly serious crime are fairly small ones. (Hough and Mayhew, 1983, p. 15)

From one perspective, the problem of crime is predominantly its effect on the quality of life: the avoidance of soccer grounds on Saturday afternoons and inner city areas in the evening; the time and money expended in protecting oneself against the risks. A repeated finding of victim surveys is that the elderly are less at risk of becoming a personal crime victim than the young (Hough and Mayhew, 1983) but more fearful (Maxfield, 1984). Why is this? It could be that the fearful old withdraw from public places and are for that reason not victimized, or alternatively it could be that the elderly would not be victimized as much as young people even if they went out more often. The choice between these alternatives is much aided by the analysis of Crime Survey data by Clarke, Ekblom, Hough and Mayhew (1985). Table 1.12 and 1.13 show rates of victimization in the evening by age, gender and the number of evenings spent out per week. Table 1.12 contrasts victimization experiences of those who travel riskily and those who do not. Table 1.13 contrasts experiences of those who went to risky places and those who did not. It will be seen that the lower rate of victimization of the elderly holds up in both tables. Thus, the socially active elderly are less prone to street crime than even the socially inactive young. It could, of course, be argued that the elderly are more street wise. They know how to plan their route, avoid risky places and so on. However, the more probable explanation remains that the fearful old have much less reason to be fearful of crime than others, (although fear of the *consequences* of victimization, were it to happen, may well be better-founded). While fear of crime is taken to be an important social problem in its own right, it

TABLE 1.12   Risk per 1000 of evening 'street crime' victimization, by age, sex, and number of evenings out, comparing those who travelled 'riskily' and 'non-riskily'

	1,2 evenings out			3+ evenings out		
	Young	*Middle*	*Old*	*Young*	*Middle*	*Old*
	Risk per 1000					
Men: non-risky	42	10	–	71	20	3
Men: risky	107	14	10	104	6	5
Women: non-risky	10	5	–	18	14	–
Women: risky	33	10	4	32	8	35
Total	37	9	2	61	15	11
	Unweighted nos.					
Sample	1046	1983	627	1098	871	195
Victims	64	44	4	104	20	4

NOTE   Respondents were given a score of 2 whenever they went out on foot or by public transport (bus, taxi, train, underground) and a score of 1 if they went out by any other mode of travel. Scores were summed and divided by the number of evenings out, to give a continuous variable ranging from 1 to 2. This was then dichotomised to give an even distribution: 'non-risky' = anyone scoring 1.5 or less; 'risky' = anyone scoring over 1.5.

SOURCE: Clarke *et al.* (1985), Table 5, p. 7.

TABLE 1.13   Risk per 1000 of evening 'street crime' victimization, by age, sex, and number of evenings out, comparing those who went to 'risky' and 'non-risky' places

	1,2 evenings out			3+ evenings out		
	Young	*Middle*	*Old*	*Young*	*Middle*	*Old*
	Risk per 1000					
Men: non-risky	55	7	5	83	3	6
Men: risky	70	17	–	85	23	2
Women: non-risky	12	3	1	7	20	29
Women: risky	23	14	5	29	5	–
Total	38	8	2	62	14	11
	Unweighted nos.					
Sample	1056	2004	635	1119	884	200
Victims	65	44	4	106	20	4

NOTE   'Non-risky' = people who did not go to pubs, clubs, discos or parties on any night out; 'risky' = all other people.

SOURCE: Clarke *et al.* (1985), Table 4, p. 6.

cannot be addressed by official criminal statistics. Skogan and Maxfield (1981) portray a complex picture in which fear is embedded, a picture in which physical disorder, vicarious victimization, and incivility are responded to. As Maxfield (1984) points out:

> Further research should . . . not focus on levels of fear, or on who is afraid. Understanding the reasons underlying the attitudes of most fearful groups is more important. While some research at the national level will continue to be informative, smaller scale studies in inner cities, especially neighbourhoods where crime and fear are most acute, is especially needed. (Maxfield, 1984, p. 44)

A theme is emerging from the material so far in the chapter. It is that any reference to official statistics at the front end of the criminal justice system needs information from elsewhere to make any sort of sense. Given that this is so, it may be reasonable to ask whether official statistics of the kind currently prepared are useful, and if so, how they should be modified to serve their proper uses most efficiently. The British Crime Survey offers a challenge to conventional statistics. It is too early to speculate about how statistics on recorded crime and survey data on crime will come to complement and supplement each other. That survey material will change what are taken as the purposes of statistics on recorded crime seems beyond question.

Endnote:
Availability Of British Crime Survey Data
The British Crime Survey is itself a form of criminal statistics. It represents a revolution in criminal statistics in that the data on which it is based is readily available to anyone with access to a mainframe computer (or with access to anyone with access to such a computer)! The Economic and Social Research Council's survey archive in Wivenhoe Park Essex keeps the data tape from the 1982 survey, and the intention is that data from subsequent surveys are to be lodged there too. While the Home Office Statistical Department has always been ready to do special runs of data included in Criminal Statistics, the direct access to data and the ways in which it is possible to manipulate it gained by that direct access, is a significant development. In a real sense the Crime Survey demystifies the picture of crime. Categorization by offence title provides one instance of this. In the real world, people do not suffer from assaults, they suffer from being hit on the nose or pushed to the floor. They do not suffer from burglaries, they suffer from returning to a house with a broken window and a video recorder missing. Offences cover a multitude of sins! A burglary can range from an event with no loss and no damage to an event of great loss and much damage. Both of these events would be categorized as burglary in Criminal Statistics. In the British Crime Survey, one can see how people suffer in ways which can be linked to ordinary experience. Table 1.14 provides an example of this. It shows the kinds of hurt suffered during assaults. It brings the events of the crime to specific life in a way that a sheer number of assaults cannot. This may also be a significant point in reducing fear of crime. When one reads a statistic about assaults, the image of assault may or may not correspond to the average assault suffered. The British Crime Survey tells us

TABLE 1.14   Injuries sustained in assaults, British Crime Survey data, 1982

	No.	*%*
None	259	45
Bruises/black eyes	231	40
Scratches	40	7
Cuts	42	7
Knocked out	1	0
Total Injury Elements	573	100

(Total unweighted n = 296)

what the average assault really is like. Looking at the survey data contained in Table 1.14, we venture to suggest that the image which the word assault conjures up is more severe than the image implicit in that table. It may yet be that this sort of comparison represents the greatest service of the British Crime Survey.

Notes

1. The terminology was first used in 1979; before that year they were referred to as 'indictable offences'. The classification of indictable offences is very similar to the later one, except that it includes some additional offences, e.g. betting and gaming, firearms and certain extra motoring offences. For a list of both groups see Appendices 2 and 3, *Criminal Statistics England and Wales 1983*.
2. Between 1977 and 1983 the number of recorded offences of criminal damage under the value of £20 has remained very consistently around 170 000 a year.
3. If non-indictable offenders are included in the category of known offenders they outnumber indictable offenders 3 to 1, and their age distribution is very different: in 1983 less than 2% were juveniles, and more than 80% were aged 21 years or over.

2

Police Work and Criminal Statistics

The police are perceived to exert a major influence upon the early stages in the production of criminal statistics. It is easy to understand why. The official crime rate is based upon crimes '*known to the police*'; in addition, the proportion of known crimes that are 'solved' each year are referred to as the police '*clear-up rate*' or 'detection rate'. This choice of words carries the clear implication that 'clearing-up' crimes is a direct outcome of police work. Despite the plausibility of this traditional image linking police work and crime statistics, it is necessary to disentangle the respective contributions of members of the public (as victims, complainants or witnesses), the police, and the circumstances in which crime incidents typically occur. Only after this is done will the exact nature of the police role in the production of conventional criminal statistics become available for sensible debate.

In this chapter we shall examine the role of the police at three crucial stages in what can be called the 'social construction' of official statistics. This phrase sounds like sociological jargon of the worst kind. In fact it is a useful shorthand to describe the process whereby complex events are filtered through a set of people with their own aims and preoccupations, to emerge as a set of statistical 'facts' about crime. The three stages to be covered are:

i) the recording of crimes reported to or discovered by the police;
ii) the detection or 'clearing-up' of crime; and
iii) the choice whether to ignore, caution or prosecute known offenders.

At each of these stages in the criminal process we will conclude that the influence of the police is considerable, although not always quite what is commonly imagined. The topics dealt with in this chapter by no means exhaust the full extent of police influence upon official statistics of crime and law enforcement; Chapter 3 will further document the decision-making process involving the police, as it traces the progress of suspects from the initial intervention by the police, through the pre-trial and trial stages to conviction or acquittal.

The Recording of Crime by the Police

There is now a widespread realization that there exists a huge 'dark figure' of undiscovered and unreported crime. As for those notifiable offences which go to make up the official crime rate, readers familiar with any of the recent criminological investigations into the discovery of crimes will be aware that the major way in which crime incidents come to the attention of the police is report by members of the public, especially those who have been the victims. It results much less from the activity of the police themselves uncovering offences. Studies in Britain have shown that between 77% and 96% of crimes recorded by the police are initially reported to them by members of the public, and are not the consequence of direct or indirect initiatives on the part of the police (McCabe and Sutcliffe 1978; Mawby 1979; Steer 1980; Bottomley and Coleman 1981; Hough and Mayhew 1983; Farrington and Dowds 1985). Looking at hitherto unpublished data from the 1982 British Crime Survey as an example, 53% of offences which the police came to know about did so through victim report, 38% through the report of another citizen, 4% because the police were there, 1% were discovered by the police, and 4% came to police notice in other ways. Although this somewhat underrepresents police relevance (because the victim does not know of all police knowledge about offending) it gives a rough idea of the preponderance of citizen report as a means by which the police come to learn of offences.

What is perhaps less well known than the 'dark figure' of *unreported* crime is the much more shadowy 'grey figure' of *reported but unrecorded* crime, i.e. reported crimes which do not subsequently appear in police returns to the Home Office which form the basis of official statistics of crimes recorded by the police. There are a few brief and rather confusing references to this in the annual *Criminal Statistics: England and Wales*; thus, in the volume for 1983, we find:

> The process of recording an offence starts when a person reports to the police that an offence has been committed or when the police otherwise discover evidence of an offence . . . The police make an initial examination of the facts to determine if there is *prima facie* evidence that the law has been broken. The information then available is not complete but it gives some indication of whether a particular offence has been committed. A crime report is usually made out for incidents that appear to involve a notifiable offence, the main exception is that in some forces a crime report is not used for offences of criminal damage where the damage is less than £20 in value. (Home Office 1984b, para 2.3)

> Many offences are either not reported to the police or not recorded by them. However, some evidence of the extent of under-recording of certain offences is available from the results of the British Crime Survey and the General Household Survey. The extent of under-recording for different offences varies according to a number of factors including the type, circumstances and severity of the offence, whether a suspect is known to the victim, the ease with which a report can be made and insurance claim requirements. Offences recorded therefore form only a proportion, and for many offences a small proportion, of the total number committed. (Home Office 1984b, para 2.5)

Despite the frequent reference to *under-recording* in the second paragraph quoted above, the discussion fails to distinguish between non-reporting and non-recording, serving only to perpetuate the confusion. The British Crime Survey (BCS) does not suffer from the same fault. It provides the most systematic, if somewhat tentative, evidence to date on this issue, reaching the conclusion that:

> . . . it would seem from a comparison of survey results with *Criminal Statistics* that, of the incidents which were known to them, the police recorded as separate notifiable offences about two-thirds of incidents which involved property loss or damage, and rather less than half of those involving violence. (Hough and Mayhew 1983, p. 12)

It was estimated that the statistic of domestic burglaries *recorded* by the police was about 70% of the survey figure of such burglaries *reported* to the police. On the other hand, for offences of theft of motor vehicles and thefts in dwellings the BCS estimates actually showed *fewer* incidents reported to the police than appeared in *Criminal Statistics*. The interesting explanation offered for this discrepancy concerns the possibility of different recording practices for burglary (which involves trespass as an essential element) and theft in a dwelling, (which does not). The classification of the offence committed when something is stolen from a house depends upon who you think did it. If it was a family member or guest, the offence is theft in a dwelling. If the offender was trespassing, the offence is burglary. Thus 'some of the incidents which the BCS classified as burglary may well have been classified by the police as the lesser offence of theft in a dwelling, perhaps where the credibility of the complainant was judged by the police to be low' (Hough and Mayhew 1983, p. 13; for a similar example, see Bottomley and Coleman 1981, pp. 88–90).

These findings of the nationwide British Crime Survey can be compared with those of earlier research. For example, in their detailed crime victimization survey of three London boroughs in 1972, Richard Sparks and his colleagues estimated that only about one-third of all the offences that had been reported to the police appear to have found their way into the police statistics (Sparks, Genn and Dodd 1977, pp. 156–7). They also found considerable variation in police recording practices, not only according to offence type but also among the different boroughs surveyed. Non-recording was highest for reported assaults and thefts from the person, and lowest for burglaries and theft from dwellings. When variations in police recording practices were added to variations in the public's reporting of crimes, the total effect upon the official statistics was very considerable:

> Our data suggest that the proportion of incidents reported to the police by victims is lowest in Brixton and highest in Kensington; the proportion of reported incidents which become reported as crimes also appears to be highest in Kensington, but appears substantially lower in Hackney than in Brixton . . . This means that the police statistics present different patterns of crime in the three areas from those which emerge from our survey estimates. It also means, however, that the relative rates of crime also differ. (Sparks, Genn and Dodd 1977, p. 157)

The same survey showed that Brixton and Kensington had about the same overall crime rates (as reported by respondents interviewed) but the *officially recorded* crime rate for Brixton was only three-fifths of that found in Kensington.

For a slightly different angle on the problem of estimating and explaining police recording practices we can refer to the findings of studies that have focused directly on the way police respond to crime complaints from members of the public and what happens to such complaints after an official crime report has been filed. McCabe and Sutcliffe (1978) were among the first to publish detailed research of this kind, based upon their observation of police work in Oxford and Salford. In the Salford sub-division less than half of the 367 complaints/allegations (that may have been defined as 'potential crimes' by the complainants) resulted in any offence being recorded by the police, ranging from only 11% of reported 'domestics' and 'disturbances' to more than three-quarters of the reported breaking and enterings. At the two Oxford stations less than 3 in every 10 reported incidents resulted in offences being recorded, ranging from only 2% of 'domestics' to 60% of the breaking and enterings (McCabe and Sutcliffe 1978, pp. 55–56). However, after official crime reports had been made out, only a very few offences in either area were subsequently written off as 'no crime' (namely 2% in Salford, 6% in Oxford), with some of the difference between the two forces being due to variations in the operational handling of incoming calls from the public;

> . . . clearly the initial write-off within each month will depend to some extent upon the recording policy and practice in the area. Where crime reports are filed only after a fairly full investigation, the no-crime rate should be low. But this cannot account for all the variation between one police area and another. There may be differences in policing to be taken into account . . . (McCabe and Sutcliffe 1978, p. 73)

Latest confirmation of the potential significance of apparently trivial handling procedures comes from the fascinating Nottinghamshire case study by Farrington and Dowds, in which it was found that police switchboard procedures in Nottinghamshire differed from those in the adjacent Leicestershire and Staffordshire forces. In Nottinghamshire a telephone call might be put directly onto a crime complaint form and given a crime number, rather than being logged for initial investigation; as a result, a significantly higher proportion of telephone calls were recorded as crimes – until the procedure was changed in January 1983 in an effort to bring down the county's embarrassingly high crime rate (Farrington and Dowds 1985, pp.63–65; see below for further discussion of this study).

The research of David Steer in Thames Valley, written up for the Royal Commission on Criminal Procedure (see Steer 1980), confirmed the important filtering role of uniformed police officers in respect of the definition and recording of incidents as crimes, as a result of which 'comparatively few complaints that reach the CID officer fail subsequently to be recorded as crime' (Steer 1980, p. 55). In samples drawn from the Oxford division in 1974, Steer found that about 8% of offences initially recorded as known to the police were written off as 'no crime', with an additional 1 or 2% suspected of being 'no-crimed' by the investigating officers (Steer 1980, pp. 58–9). Bottomley and Coleman (1981) reported a 'no-crime' rate of 11% for their Northern

City research sample in 1972, but with a significant decline to 4% by 1978 for the corresponding city centre division (following amalgamation into a larger county force), which was very much in line with the national figure for England and Wales in that year of 3% (Chartered Institute of Public Finance and Accountancy (CIPFA) 1978; Bottomley and Coleman 1981, pp. 60–64). For 1983, the national 'no-crime' rate was 6.6%, varying from 1% in South Wales to 19% in the London MPD (CIPFA 1984).

Despite the different perspectives and methods that have been adopted for studying how the police do or do not record incidents as crime, there has been considerable agreement concerning the main types of factor that appear to influence police practices. To begin with, the reported 'crime' may turn out on further investigation to have been the result of a mistaken belief on the part of a complainant (e.g. missing property may turn up, having been misplaced rather than stolen), or it may have been a deliberately false or malicious report by someone wishing to waste police time, to cause trouble for an obvious suspect, or reflecting mental disturbance. The incident may not have all the necessary ingredients to count officially as a crime, or alternatively there may not be sufficient evidence against a person suspected of having committed an offence in circumstances where if there is no offender there is no offence (e.g. *attempted* offences, handling stolen property etc.). A significant minority of cases that are eventually 'no-crimed' by the police are ones in which the complainant no longer wishes to proceed with the allegation or give evidence against the accused person – particularly common in crimes against the person, where victim or offender may be related or acquainted. Thus, in a Scottish study of sexual assaults, 24 of the 44 no-crimes were recorded by the police as 'complaints withdrawn'. However, the authors warned against always taking this label at its face value, 'the term "complaint withdrawn" was often misused by the police to describe cases where the complainant was left with no option, and where it appeared that cases would have been marked groundless or unsubstantiated anyway' (Chambers and Millar 1983, p. 43). It is interesting and may turn out to be important that the British Crime Survey 1982 showed that, for offences where the victim sees the offender and knows him/her, the victim is less satisfied with both uniformed and CID officers than is the case when the offender is not known to the victim (previously unpublished result). The difference is not statistically reliable and so nothing should be made of it. However if the same result emerges from the 1984 survey, it will become worth speculating whether the victims of offenders known to them may feel pressured by the police to sort out their own problems.

This leads into perhaps the largest group of cases which are not recorded by the police because they choose to exercise their discretion not to count an incident as worth recording as a crime, for various (and often questionable) reasons ranging from a subjective assessment of its relative triviality (especially if no personal victim has been involved), through the blameworthiness, assessed by the police officer, of the participants in the exchange within which the crime occurred (Chatterton 1983), to the perceived likelihood of its having been committed by a child or children under the age of criminal responsibility, or, perhaps most questionably, due to police assessment of the chances of its being cleared up or their view of the appropriate boundaries for intervention in conflicts within families, between neighbours or amongst various minority groups.

The extent to which these and other factors influence police decisions is likely to vary from area to area and from officer to officer, particularly since little official guidance exists to encourage consistency or provide principled justifications for conventional practices. What may appear to an outsider to be a relatively straightforward matter of assessing the ingredients of an alleged incident (as well as the 'moral character' of the incident's reporter!) is also complicated by the internal significance attached to the likelihood of detection and the subsequent impact upon official clear-up rates (see below). The nature of the decision-making process is also altered if a *person* has been reported as an alleged offender, and not just an *event* reported as a possible offence, with a consequent overlap between 'no-crime' situations and 'refused charges' (see Bottomley and Coleman 1981, pp. 71–73; Ashworth 1984, pp. 16–17). The operational imperatives for the police officer may vary according to his position in the hierarchy and according to tensions between uniformed and CID officers. These imperatives do not invalidate what is said elsewhere in this chapter, and they are not discussed here. However, any intention to change practice in this area must take into account the local and national working culture of the police, ably described by Chatterton (1976, 1983), and by Holdaway (1984), or be doomed to failure.

Even if police officers wished to use no discretion in their recording practice, it would be impossible for them to live up to their aspiration. In the Home Office handbook for police returns for criminal statistics 'Counting Rules for Serious Offences' many classifications cannot be made without a highly subjective approach. Some examples are given below: these are chosen for their clarity, so as to exclude discretion, yet even they reveal the possible ambiguities. For example the general rules for offences of violence against the person:

> Where there are any specific intended victims one offence should be counted in respect of each intended victim . . . Where there is no specific intended victim one general offence should be counted.
>
> An occasion is usually a 24 hour period. However the circumstances of an offence may make it obvious that a longer period is to be preferred.

And for sexual offences:

> 1. Buggery is committed twice on the same occasion. Count one offence.
> 2. Buggery is committed on two separate occasions – victim willing – count one offence
> victim unwilling – count two offences if each incident is reported separately.
> 3. Buggery is committed by a man with his wife several times over a period of years, without her consent, before she reports the incidents – count one offence – when reported.

And for recording offences as separate *tics* (i.e. "taken into consideration"):

Forces should consider whether the circumstances of the case and the details available give sufficient grounds to believe that the offence happened, was not recorded and is not part of a series . . . No hard and fast rule can be given as to what level of detail is sufficient. This of necessity is left to police judgements in consideration of circumstances of the case, the offender, past experience etc.

The last words in this section can appropriately be left to McCabe and Sutcliffe:

The decision to accept or reject a report that a crime had been committed is an essential part of the discretion exercised by all police officers but particularly by those of the lowest rank who are in closer contact with the community. Our experience in police stations and on patrol taught us to accept this discretion as part of the relationship between police and people and as a reflection of the relativity of criminal incidents which, for their definition, depend upon the perceptions of victims, observers, police officers, magistrates and other agents of social control. Generally speaking, offences that most of us would call serious were, in our experience, treated as such by the police officers to whom they were reported. Trivial offences were or were not ignored according to local tradition and practice, the strength or weakness of the complainant, perhaps the outlook of individual police officers and so on. It seems to be true that decriminalization of trivial offences has taken place to differing degrees in different places; and the process begins with the recording of an offence, not, more visibly, with the failure to prosecute an offender. But, as with all discretionary practices, there are areas of anxiety. (McCabe and Sutcliffe 1978, p. 85)

A Digression Upon the Criminal(?) County of Nottingham

The potential significance of police recording practices for rates of officially recorded crime has already been established. The links between the discovery, recording, and detection of crime is illustrated dramatically in the recent analysis by Farrington and Dowds (1985) of events in the (apparently) chronically wicked shire of Nottingham.

In 1981 Nottinghamshire had the highest serious crime rate of all areas in England and Wales, greater even than that of London or the deprived Northern conurbations. Nor was this a single year's statistical fluctuation. In every year since 1975 the crime rate of Nottinghamshire had been far higher than seemed reasonable given the nature of the area. It had always vied with London and Liverpool as the most criminal area of England and Wales, with a crime rate around twice that of adjoining areas Derbyshire, Staffordshire and Leicestershire. The untangling of the reasons for this by David Farrington and Elizabeth Dowds provides one of the most fascinating examples of how important it is to include an understanding of police procedures if you want to understand crime rates. They began by carrying out a local crime survey in Nottinghamshire, Staffordshire and Leicestershire. They found that there was indeed a higher rate of crime in Nottinghamshire but the difference only accounted for between one quarter and one third of the difference in levels of recorded crime. Further, the pattern of crime suffered and the pattern of crime recorded were similar in the three study areas. The explanation for the major part of the difference between the counties obviously lay elsewhere.

The police discover crimes in a variety of ways (see Bottomley and Coleman 1981, and below in this chapter). A crime victim may telephone the police, hail a patrol car or call at a police station. A witness, friend or relative may inform the police in these ways. The police may come upon crimes being committed or discover they have been committed in the course of their investigations into other offences. The pattern of discovery was quite different in Nottinghamshire from that found in the other counties studied, and this is presented as Table 2.1.

Most strikingly, one quarter of all crimes came to light in Nottinghamshire when offenders admitted them. In contrast, this was the means of discovery in 4% of crimes in Leicestershire, and 8% of crimes in Staffordshire. Other studies have generated figures very much lower than the Notts quarter. Farrington and Dowds speculate 'The high incidence of crimes originating in admissions in Nottinghamshire may mean either that more admissions were made by apprehended offenders (perhaps because Nottinghamshire's interrogation procedures were more intensive) or that Nottinghamshire police were more likely to record such admissions as crimes (or both)'. We are told that Leicestershire had a policy of not recording crimes originating in admissions, and this may explain why there were so few of them in Leicestershire. Also, both Leicestershire and Staffordshire seem to have applied more demanding criteria for accepting that a crime had occurred than did Nottinghamshire. In Leicestershire and Staffordshire crimes would not usually be recorded unless either stolen property was discovered or the name or address of the victim was known. These criteria were not always satisfied in Nottinghamshire. Also, the system of continuation sheets used in Nottinghamshire (and Staffordshire) facilitated the recording of multiple crimes admitted during questioning (Farrington and Dowds 1985, pp. 58–59).

The other major reason for the high level of recorded crime in Nottinghamshire was that county's greater tendency to record trivial offences. Table 2.2 shows that as far as offences of stealing or handling were concerned, the amount stolen was much smaller in Nottinghamshire than in the other counties. The effect of more admissions to the police and the recording of more trivial offences, when added to the rather

TABLE 2.1   How crimes were discovered

	Notts.		Leics.		Staffs.	
	No.	%	No.	%	No.	%
Police, directly	19	(2.3)	17	(5.2)	26	(6.7)
Police, on admission	211	(25.4)	14	(4.3)	30	(7.7)
Public call at station	143	(17.2)	103	(31.3)	108	(27.7)
Public telephone call	340	(41.0)	178	(54.1)	203	(52.1)
Public call to patrol	111	(13.4)	9	(2.7)	20	(5.1)
Other	6	(0.7)	8	(2.4)	3	(0.8)
TOTALS	830	(100)	329	(100)	390	(100)
Rate per 100 000 pop.	84.3		38.6		38.6	

SOURCE: from Farrington and Dowds (1985), Table 7, p. 58.

TABLE 2.2   Value of stolen property

	Notts.		Leics.		Staffs.	
	No.	*%*	*No.*	*%*	*No.*	*%*
£1 or less, nothing	167	(25.0)	38	(4.5)	43	(15.4)
£2–£10	154	(23.1)	50	(16.6)	57	(20.4)
£11–£25	79	(11.8)	33	(10.9)	48	(17.1)
£26–£50	67	(10.0)	51	(16.9)	35	(12.5)
£51–£100	66	(9.9)	43	(14.2)	34	(12.1)
£101–£250	67	(10.0)	37	(12.3)	26	(9.3)
£251–£500	41	(6.1)	30	(9.9)	21	(7.5)
Over £500	27	(4.0)	20	(6.6)	16	(5.7)
TOTALS	668	(100)	302	(100)	280	(100)

SOURCE: from Farrington and Dowds (1985), Table 8, p. 59.

higher real crime rate in Nottinghamshire, served to explain all the differences in recorded crime rate. Perhaps Robin Hood's shire is not so wicked after all.

There is a paradox here. The work of Farrington and Dowds provides a telling demonstration of the unreliability of criminal statistics as indicators of criminal behaviour. What price the social barometer? However, it also shows that sense can be made of these statistics and that the way in which they can be interepreted also gives some indicators as to what it is fair to do or what it is good policy to do. For example, the acceptance of the admission of an offence without independent evidence of the offence having been committed is revealed as an important factor, and one which appears to make a noticeable difference to what is recorded as crime. That surely provides a guide to better practice. Better in what respect depends upon one's policy aim, but the information is not without meaning. The point being laboured here is that to deny criminal statistics any meaning (there are lies, damned lies, statistics and criminal statistics) is a mistake. The Nottinghamshire example reveals meaning in the statistics of recorded crime. It's just that the meaning is not the obvious one.

Attention should be drawn here to the work of econometricians in the field of criminal justice. For example, Carr-Hill and Stern (1979) produce evidence to suggest, *inter alia*, that size and expenditure of police forces play 'important and independent roles in the determination of the offence rate and the clear-up rate' (p. 256). Whatever the truth of their particular assertions (and they have been the subject of bitter attack – see for example Monica Walker 1981), they do perform the extremely valuable function of teasing out relationships and possible causal linkages between variables of interest which they distinguish with rare ingenuity. Discussion of the work of Carr-Hill and Stern is largely outwith the scope of this book, but it is highly recommended for numerate readers with plentiful supplies of aspirin and wet towels for use when their head starts to hurt!

Crime Detection and 'Clear-up' Rates

Apart from the recorded crime rate itself, perhaps the most commonly used (and equally commonly abused) official statistic relating to crime is the police 'clear-up' rate. Just as there has always been the temptation, rarely resisted, to use the official crime rate as a kind of index of the nation's moral health, so there is a seemingly irresistible urge to interpret trends in the proportion of recorded offences that have been 'cleared up' as an index of police effectiveness, with direct implications for community fears about the number of undetected criminals remaining at large. On neither count is such reliance upon the clear-up rate justified. At the simplest level, choices made about what crimes to record will result in changes in how successful you are in clearing up what you do choose to record. As will be noted in Chapter 7, differences in reconviction rates between offenders given different sentences are largely (but probably not wholly) a product of the offenders not the sentences. In the same way, judicious selection of what to record can yield widely different clear-up rates. In Northern Ireland during the 1970s there was a dramatic decline in clear-up rates. One interpretation of this is that it represents an increase in public confidence in the police during the period, the public now being more prepared to report difficult-to-solve offences. The meaning of the clear-up rate is so elusive that perhaps it should be called the unclear-up rate. Chatterton (1983) describes with telling examples how organizational imperatives work to ensure that many crimes with a low potential for producing a prisoner and a number of other offences to be taken into consideration, remain unrecorded.

The basic data about trends in the official clear-up rate in England and Wales between 1963 and 1983 were set out in the previous chapter (Table 1.4, p. 13). It was noted that despite a gradual decline in the proportion of offences cleared up in the last ten years, from 47% (1973) to 37% (1983), the actual *number of crimes* detected by the police during this period increased by about 50%. This pattern was very similar to an earlier trend between the mid-50s and the early 60s, when the clear-up rate dropped from 49% (1955) to 39% (1965), at a time when the number of offences recorded as known to the police was increasing by an average of 10% each year (see McClintock and Avison 1968, pp. 92–94). So, before embarking upon any more sophisticated analysis and interpretation of the data, it is necessary to emphasize that for certain purposes the starting point ought to include at least a recognition of the *numbers* behind the percentages. A simple exercise such as comparing the annual number of crimes cleared up to the current operating strength of the police force invariably shows a steady increase in the number cleared up per police officer, whether in the 1950s and 60s or in the 70s (McClintock and Avison 1968, Burrows and Tarling 1982).

However, any approach to the understanding of clear-up rates that focuses on direct links between police manpower and the detection of crime is founded upon question-able assumptions about the nature of criminal activities and the tasks of detection that face the police in their routine response to these activities. A proper grasp of the complex processes that ultimately produce these statistics must begin with an appreciation of the circumstances surrounding different types of crime, especially the typical relationship and interaction between offender and victim, and a related awareness of the variety of ways in which crimes are actually recorded as cleared up by the police. The discussion that follows will concentrate upon these two dimensions, in an attempt to untangle at least some of the strands in the interpretation of police clear-up rates. We will be left with the clear impression of significant variation between police force areas. Hence, we will proceed to a consideration of the extent to which variations between different forces may be due to factors largely outside police control (such as the types of crime in particular areas) or to factors intrinsic to police detection work but not directly amenable to change via the injection of material resources *per se*.

Variations between offences

The immediately striking feature of any tabulation of the clear-up rate, by offence group, is the wide variation that exists between different categories of offence, and the stable pattern of these differences over considerable periods of time. In particular, recorded crimes against the person, of a violent or sexual nature, have a high clear-up rate (currently about 75%) which is usually more than double that of property crimes like burglary and theft. As most crimes against the person are in the Home Office's less serious category (see above, Chapter 1), this difference cannot be explained primarily through the proposition that the majority of such offences arouse wide-spread public concern and media attention, resulting in the investment of extensive police resources for their detection – this is true of only a handful of the most serious offences in any police force area each year. The main explanation lies in the fact that in a large number of offences against the person the offender is known to the victim, and can thus be immediately identified for the purposes of police apprehension. Even in those cases where the offender is not known to the victim prior to the offence, it is often possible for a clear description to be provided to the police leading to the subsequent identification of the suspect(s). However, where the offender is a total stranger and the offence is committed in circumstances that make personal identification difficult, then the clear-up rate drops much closer to that for offences of dishonesty (McClintock and Avison 1968, p.108). By contrast, in most property offences there is no direct contact between victim and offender, so that any suspicion that falls on a person does so more indirectly through circumstantial evidence.

The other important feature to note is that there are some offences (often hidden within a larger group) which are automatically cleared up by virtue of having become known to the police. They include some sexual offences, such as indecency between males, unlawful sexual intercourse with underage girls, and incest; property offences, such as handling stolen goods, theft by an employee and shoplifting; and various others such as drug trafficking, frauds and causing death by dangerous driving. Most of these offences are not, indeed cannot, be recorded as known to the police *unless a suspect is also known*, hence their virtually automatic 'detection', and subsequent appearance in the clear-up rate statistics at or near the 100% level! It is easy to see how the 'detection rates' for these offences can inflate the overall statistics so that, for example, the already modest clear-up rate for the category of theft and handling stolen goods would be substantially reduced by the exclusion of shoplifting and handling (Bottomley and Coleman 1981, p. 97).

Chatterton (1976) categorized the types of investigation leading to arrests. He found that in only 24% of cases was the activity leading to arrest police-initiated. Otherwise the arrest occurred predominantly because the offender was named or the police were there and detained someone. It is clear from Chatterton's analysis that type of clear-up varied according to crime type. The point being made here is not intended in any way to denigrate the work of the police in bringing to book those guilty of the offences listed above, but merely to emphasize the fact that whatever credit is due should be for the initial *discovery* of the 'offence-cum-offender', and *not* for the separate 'detection' (or clearing-up) of such an apparently large proportion of recorded offences, which, as we have seen, is inevitable in the circumstances.

Any meaningful interpretation of clear-up rates must therefore begin by distinguishing the contribution of different offences to the overall total, in the knowledge that in some instances no *separate* issue of detection arises once the offence itself has been discovered and recorded by the police, and in other offences the task of detection is considerably eased by the victim's ability to identify the guilty party.

The discussion can now be extended to examine the situation facing the police in clearing the offences to which neither of the circumstances distinguished above applies.

Methods of 'clearing-up' crime

There are a number of different ways which lead a crime to be recorded as cleared up: broadly, an offence is said to be cleared-up if a person has been charged, summonsed or cautioned for the offence, if the offence is admitted and is taken into consideration by the court or if there is sufficient evidence to charge a person but the case is not proceeded with, because for example the offender is under the age of criminal responsibility, or is already serving a long custodial sentence for another offence or because the victim is unable to give evidence. (Home Office 1984b, para 2.25)

Regrettably, the official statistics do not give a breakdown of the clear-up rate according to these categories, and we have to rely on research studies for information about the extent to which the different routes to clear-up are used. The most comprehensive and recent study is that of Burrows and Tarling (1982) for the Home Office Research and Planning Unit, which was based on national data for 1974–77, made available by HM Inspectorate of Constabulary. The other studies that will be referred to here were carried out in single (mainly urban) forces by researchers. What their studies lose in representativeness they make up for in level of detail of local police practices and procedures. The charging or summonsing of an offender represents the commonest mode of clear-up. Burrows and Tarling (1982, Appendix B) found that 54% of crimes cleared by the police each year were cleared in this way. A further 10–12% were cleared when an offender was cautioned. This was quite close to the finding in Bottomley and Coleman's study of Northern City, in which 61% were

TABLE 2.3   Methods by which crimes were cleared up by the police, by offence group, 1977. (28 forces, England and Wales)

| Type of Offence | Method of Clearance | | | |
	Charge/ Summons	T.i.c.	Caution	Otherwise without proceedings
Violence against the person	83	1	6	11
Sexual offences	62	10	19	9
Burglary	43	33	5	20
Robbery	86	5	4	6
Theft and handling stolen goods	51	25	15	9
Fraud and forgery	50	45	2	3
Criminal damage	75	8	7	10
Other indictable	74	8	4	14
Total	53	26	11	11

SOURCE: Burrows and Tarling (1982), Table 6, p. 20.

cleared by charge or summons, and a further 9% by caution (Bottomley and Coleman 1981, p. 140).

Considerable attention has been paid by researchers to the second most frequent method of police clearance, namely by offences being 'taken into consideration' (t.i.c.) by the court when an offender has been convicted of other similar offences. John Lambert was the first to document this in his Birmingham study of 1967, in which he found 44% of a sample of recorded property offences to be cleared by being 'taken into consideration', including as many as two-thirds of detected thefts from cars and houses (Lambert 1970, p. 43). In Northern City, it was found that, for all offence groups combined, exactly one-quarter of detected crimes were cleared up by being t.i.c., but there was wide variation between different types of offence, with this method not featuring at all in cases of violence or sexual offences, but accounting for 58% of detected fraud and forgery cases, 39% of burglaries and 24% of shoplifting and handling stolen goods (Bottomley and Coleman 1981, Table 5.1, p.96). Burrows and Tarling also reported that 25–27% of all crimes were cleared by the t.i.c. method, but with considerable variation between offence groups (see Table 2.3). The rank order of frequency of t.i.c. clearances by offence group was very close to that found in Bottomley and Coleman's study, with violence and sexual offences at or near the bottom, fraud/forgery and burglary at the top, and theft/handling stolen goods near the middle.

These research studies also provide confirmation of one of the important features of the Nottinghamshire case study of Farrington and Dowds (1985, discussed above), namely the considerable extent to which offences cleared by t.i.c. only came to light during the questioning of those suspected of other offences. In Bottomley and Coleman's study more than half (54%) of the offences cleared by t.i.c. first became known to the police at the questioning stage, including as many as three-quarters of the shoplifting and handling cases and two-thirds of the frauds (Bottomley and Coleman 1981, p. 99). From their survey, Burrows and Tarling reported an identical proportion of 54% of all t.i.c. clearances involving offences not previously known to the police, including almost three-quarters (73%) of offences of fraud and forgery, and more than half (57%) of thefts and handling stolen goods. Interestingly, although offences of violence against the person, sexual offences and robbery are not as likely as other offences to be cleared in this way, when they were, the vast majority had not previously been known to the police (Burrows and Tarling 1982, Table 7, p. 23).

The clear message that emerges from practically all recent empirical studies of police work in the detection of recorded crimes is that the police are rarely faced with the classic situation of detective fiction, that of the search for the unidentified perpetrators of known offences. The majority of crimes are cleared up either as a result of direct information about the identity of the offender provided by the victim at the time when the crime is first reported to the police or because they are automatically solved in the very process of crime discovery or because they are admitted during questioning for another offence.

Rob Mawby's analysis of successful detection methods in Sheffield, in which he provides a rather broader classification than the formal clearance categories discussed above, confirms that a majority of offences (58–62%) 'were cleared up because evidence given to the police led them directly to the offender . . . the vast majority of crimes cleared up in these areas were done so because of knowledge of the situation provided by members of the public' (Mawby 1979, p. 112). This still left 4 out of 10 offences cleared up by *indirect* methods, this overall proportion hiding a range of proportions for different offence types, from 70% of housebreakings cleared up to 6% of offences of violence. He also discerned some intriguing patterns linking the detection rate, the reporting agent and the detection method: some offences had high detection rates but low levels of police involvement in the discovery and detection stages, e.g. shoplifting, meter thefts, fraud, violence and sexual offences; other offences had low detection rates, but high rates for police discovery and detection by indirect methods, e.g. thefts of/from cars, breaking and entering (other than dwellings) (Mawby 1979, pp. 126–7). Similarly, in the Thames Valley police force area, David Steer found that the proportion of cases in which the offender was caught red-handed or in which from the outset there was little or no question about the identity of offenders ranged from 47% to 71%, with most of the remaining cases accounted for by the indirect method of detection, by the interrogation or interviewing of a suspect at a police station following arrest for other offences (see Steer 1980, pp. 71–78 and 96 ff). His conclusions, taken together with those of Burrows and Tarling, lead him to provide a realistic assessment of police detection work in the following terms:

> In about three-quarters of all cases, the business of detecting offenders, though it may have required patience and application by the investigating officer, was relatively straightforward. Only in one-eighth of the cases described was there really strong evidence of the importance of local police knowledge or of that indefinable sixth sense by which officers are somehow able to feel that they are dealing with the guilty party

. . . . As important as their skill in the initial identification of suspects was the ability of police to extract from those who had been identified the names of those who had participated with them in the commission of the offence . . . It was therefore in the interview room that the skill and application of police officers was perhaps at its most important in the discovery of offenders. (Steer 1980, pp. 115–116)

Burrows and Tarling concur:

to label that a detection was achieved by indirect means suggests to the detective that such a detection is interpreted as being less satisfactory than others. It appears to belittle the value of two of the most common strategies by which such clearances are achieved, interrogation and the searching of the premises of those in custody; this is particularly threatening when, arguably, it is in the conduct of interrogations that detectives display a special skill not exercised by all police officers. (Burrows and Tarling 1982, p. 21)

Variations between forces
Having outlined some of the basic components of the process of clearing up crime, the final question to be addressed in this section concerns the explanation of variation between the clear-up rates of different police force areas. Addressing this question will serve to bring together some of the implications of the earlier discussion, and should enable some conclusions to be reached about the legitimacy of the clear-up rate in comparing the performance of police forces.

Published statistics of the clear-up rates of different police forces in England and Wales are not very readily available. (The only place where these details appear to be collected together is in the publications of C.I.P.F.A. Statistical Information Service, *Police Statistics: Estimates/Actuals*). However, the invaluable research of McClintock and Avison in the 1950s and 60s (when there were almost three times as many forces as there are today), revealed a huge national variation in clear-up rates, varying between 28 and 80% in 1955 and 21 to 74% in 1965. Although *urban* forces generally had lower clear-up rates than *rural* forces, there was a greater range of rates among urban forces than among rural forces (McClintock and Avison 1968, pp. 98–105). They stated that 'it can reasonably be assumed that some of the extreme variations in detection rates can only be accounted for in terms of variations in police practices in enforcing the criminal law and recording crime' (pp. 101–102), and linked variation in clearance rates to the indirect and 'automatic' detection methods discussed above, with the suggestion that changes in the use of interrogation for this purpose may occur as a result of key personnel changes. They called for the sort of research into the police detection process that subsequently occurred in the 1970s, and recommended that serious consideration should be given to the calculation and regular publication of 'relative detection rates':

Because of the differences in police practice as regards additional offences charged or taken into consideration by the courts or in cautioning offenders, it is suggested that it would be useful for the purpose of comparing detection rates of different forces to exclude those offences that are cleared up by 'indirect methods' both from the total of crimes known to the police and from the total of crimes cleared up. This would give what might be described as a 'net' figure for crimes known to the police and a 'net' figure for detection; the percentage of the latter to the former may then be described as the 'estimated relative detection rate'. (McClintock and Avison 1968, p. 115)

Almost two decades later, we are still having to manage with the traditional form of clear-up rate. The amalgamation of police forces into larger units has resulted in a slight reduction in the variation of clear-up rates together with a gradual decline in the overall rate. *Criminal Statistics England and Wales 1983* presented some tantalizing data on variations between types of force, with a caveat and some tentative interpretations:

> Comparisons of clear-up rates for individual police forces tend to be misleading because of differences in the circumstances of offences between areas and variations in recording practice ... The Metropolitan areas [MPD, City of London, W. Midlands, Merseyside, Greater Manchester W. Yorkshire, S. Yorkshire and Northumbria] are shown separately and it is seen that there is considerable variation between them even though they all have a high incidence of offences per head of population. The Metropolitan Police District and the City of London have generally lower clear-up rates than the other forces; this is thought to be mainly because of differences in recording practice. (Home Office 1984b, para 2.27)

More specifically, in 1983, for all indictable offences, over 80% of police forces in England and Wales had a clear-up rate of between 35 and 49%; two forces (City of London and MPD), had a rate of less than 20%; Surrey and Hampshire had rates of 30% and 33% respectively; and four forces (Dyfed-Powys, Gwent, Cheshire and North Wales) had clear-up rates of between 50 and 56%. For offences of burglary in a dwelling, one metropolitan force had a clear-up rate of less than 10%, two metropolitan forces had rates of 45–50%, with 70% of all forces having clear-up rates of between 25 and 39%. The average clear-up rate for offences of violence against the person was much higher, with four (non-metropolitan) forces clearing up over 90%, and more than three-quarters having clear-up rates of 75–90%. Five of the six forces with rates below 75% were from Metropolitan areas, of which the lowest two cleared up 45–54% of their recorded crimes of violence (Home Office 1984b, Fig. 2.8 p. 31; CIPFA 1984, Table 13 S).

The early speculations of McClintock and Avison about possible explanations for variations between forces, and more recent interpretations of the kind offered, albeit tentatively, by the authors of *Criminal Statistics* have been tested. Burrows and Tarling (1982) review previous research. They conclude 'with one or two exceptions, the level of crime was not found to be significantly related to any measure of investigative performance' and that 'taken as a group the demographic and socio-economic factors considered ... had little effect in explaining differences in clearance rates' (Burrows and Tarling 1982, p. 3). Evidence on the relationship between police resources and clear-up rates was rather more conflicting, with some studies finding a correlation between high clearance rates and lower numbers of recorded crimes per officer.

The primary aim of the Burrows and Tarling study was to see whether investing more resources in the police would be likely to result in an increase in the clear-up rate. A necessary first step was to see whether the clear-up rate, as presently constructed, was the most appropriate index of police performance in the investigation and detection of crime, in view of research evidence that variations in clear-up rates could be largely attributed to different strategies of crime detection and procedures for recording clearances. The main conclusion of this initial stage of the study was that 'the clear-up rate is a remarkably robust measure', so that although excluding crimes cleared by some of the indirect measures did alter the overall clear-up rates, most of the alternative measures correlated highly with the existing statistic. Furthermore 'notwithstanding extremely wide differences between forces in the methods used to clear crime, and in their other strategies, the analysis suggested these tend to have more of a random impact on force rates, rather than producing extensive bias' (Burrows and Tarling 1982, p. 7).

For their central analysis of the determinants of the clear-up rate, Burrows and Tarling used data from the statistical returns of all police forces in England and Wales in 1977 (with the exception of the MPD and the City of London). The extent to which a force was urban was *not* significantly related to the clear-up rate, nor were social variables generally found to be strongly related to it. The most important single factor that emerged from the analysis was the *'crime mix'* of an area, i.e. the proportion of recorded offences in groups with an above average clear-up rate, such as violence, sexual offences, fraud, shoplifting and handling stolen goods:

> 'Crime mix' was always the most highly related variable, regardless of which other variables accompanied it. This factor, then, appeared to be the most important determinant of the clear-up rate, while the crime rate was not a significant influence. (Burrows and Tarling 1982, p. 10)

Among the factors that might explain the remaining variance, the authors suggested differences between forces in the arrangement for investigating crime and in the way crimes come to the notice of the police; but with regard to the primary objective of the research it was concluded:

> The principal implication of these results is that the remedy for declining clear-up rates is not to be sought solely in increased police manpower. The clearance of most routine crime, as various research studies have shown, derives from the help supplied to the police by the public, rather than from the efforts of the police. (Burrows and Tarling 1982, p. 14)

Cautioning of Offenders

Having discussed the extent to which police practices and policy influence the recording of crime and the ways in which it is cleared-up, the final section of this chapter examines the extent to which police forces in England and Wales exercise their discretion to caution offenders. The caution is a formal, recorded, warning to an offender by a police officer. Typically the cautioning officer is of the rank of inspector, but the style and content of the warning varies greatly. A caution may, in theory, only be given when sufficient evidence exists for the case to be brought to court, the offence is admitted, the victim agrees for the case to be dealt with as the police see fit, and the offender (or parent/guardian) agrees for the case to be dealt with in this way. In cautioning an offender the police act as important 'gate-keepers' of the criminal justice system by diverting many offenders, both young and old, from the more formal and potentially stigmatizing court appearance – although at the same time dragging some into the ever-widening net of state intervention. There are those for whom cautioning replaces no official action rather than a court appearance (see Farrington and Bennett 1981, and below, Chapter 5). In this respect, it is far from clear that cautioning has achieved its intended aim of reducing offenders' contact with criminal justice in general, and the courts in particular – certainly not to the extent implied by a surface reading of cautioning statistics. The relevance of this debate for analysing trends in juvenile justice will be considered in more detail in Chapter 5.

The first official statistics on cautioning in England and Wales appeared in 1954, with figures for each police force published in *Supplementary Statistics*, until 1973. Then, for six halcyon years, from 1974 to 1979, the single annual volume of *Criminal Statistics: England and Wales* carried detailed information on police cautions, by offence, age, sex and police force areas, together with summary tables and interpretation in the introductory comments to the volume. Since 1980 the invaluable summary tables and commentary have been retained and expanded in the shorter 'popular'(?) volume of *Criminal Statistics*, but some of the more detailed analyses of cautioning have been relegated to Volume 4 of the Supplementary Tables.

In the late 1950s and early 1960s the *number* of people cautioned for indictable offences increased rapidly each year, with the figure almost doubling in the five years 1954–58 (from 10 000 to 20 000) and reaching 25 000 by 1962. However, in view of the equally rapid increase in the annual number of recorded crimes and persons proceeded against, the *proportion* of known offenders cautioned by the police during this period remained steady at around 11–12% (McClintock and Avison 1968, p.157). (The cautioning *rate* is the number of offenders cautioned expressed as a percentage of the number found guilty or cautioned).

The end of the 1960s saw a dramatic change in the situation, especially as far as the cautioning of juveniles was concerned, partly due to the anticipated implementation of the 1969 Children and Young Persons Act. Ditchfield described the changes in the pattern of juvenile cautioning (for indictable and non-indictable offences) as follows:

> The number of cautions given in 1968 for juvenile offenders – 33 703 – was actually slightly less than the number given in 1960, but one year later in 1969 the number given had risen by as much as a third, accounting for the whole of the increase in cautioning in that year. This meant that the proportion of all cautions given to juveniles increased by 8%, from 53% to 61%, compared with a rise of only 4% over the whole of the previous 8 years. Then in 1971, when the 1969 Act came into force, there was another large increase in cautioning, again by about one third, and the proportion of total cautions given to juveniles reached 66%. (Ditchfield 1976, pp. 6–7)

Table 2.4 and Figure 2.1 show the broad trends in the cautioning of offenders (aged 10 years and over) during the last 21 years. Almost all the significant changes occurred between 1968 and 1971, but they were mainly restricted to juvenile offenders. The proportion of 14–16 year-olds cautioned practically doubled, with a more than 50% increase in the proportion of 10–13 year-olds. Farrington and Bennett's (1981) analysis of changes in the official processing of juveniles in London after the introduction of the juvenile bureau scheme suggested very strongly that the increase in cautioning between 1968 and 1970 was accompanied by a widening of the net of arrested juveniles. For 10–13 year-olds there was a degree of diversion from court appearances, but this was not the case for 14–16 year-olds (for further discussion see Chapter 5).

The pattern of cautioning for adults hardly changed at all, and remained very stable throughout the entire period, with only 4% of males aged 17 and over cautioned each year, and with the proportion of adult females cautioned staying around 8–10% until a modest rise to 12% in 1983. For juveniles, the rate of increase in cautioning has slowed during the last decade, while still growing steadily, so that by 1983 three-quarters of all boys dealt with were cautioned, as were 90% of girls of the same age. As the total number of known offenders in this youngest age group has declined in recent years, especially for boys, the increase in the cautioning rate has been accompanied by a decrease in the numbers cautioned by the police. Consistent across all the comparisons is the gender difference: the cautioning rate for females is significantly higher than for males – which does not necessarily imply any gender bias on the part of the police, but may be related to the types of offence and previous criminal history of females, compared with males (see below, for further discussion).

TABLE 2.4   Trends in cautioning for indictable offences: 1963–83

| | *Offenders cautioned as a percentage of those found guilty or cautioned* | | | | | | | |
| | *MALES* | | | | *FEMALES* | | | |
	TOTAL	*All Ages*	*10–13*	*14–16*	*17 years & over*	*All ages*	*10–13*	*14–16*	*17 years & over*
	%	%	%	%	%	%	%	%	%
1963	10	10	27	14	4	15	40	23	8
(nos. in '000s)	(24.1)	(19.3)	(9.2)	(5.4)	(4.7)	(4.7)	(1.7)	(1.1)	(1.9)
1968	12	11	38	18	4	18	52	29	10
(nos. in '000s)	(34.9)	(27.2)	(13.4)	(7.6)	(6.2)	(7.7)	(2.7)	(2.0)	(3.0)
1973	21	19	63	33	4	32	83	58	10
(nos. in '000s)	(90.8)	(69.3)	(34.5)	(25.7)	(9.1)	(21.5)	(9.8)	(7.3)	(4.4)
1978	21	18	64	34	4	31	85	57	9
(nos. in '000s)	(103.0)	(74.1)	(33.7)	(30.5)	(10.0)	(28.9)	(12.8)	(10.5)	(5.6)
1983	21	18	74	42	4	34	90	68	12
(nos. in '000s)	(114.9)	(82.7)	(32.0)	(37.5)	(13.1)	(32.2)	(12.0)	(13.1)	(7.2)

SOURCE: *Criminal Statistics, England and Wales*, annual vols. 1963–83.

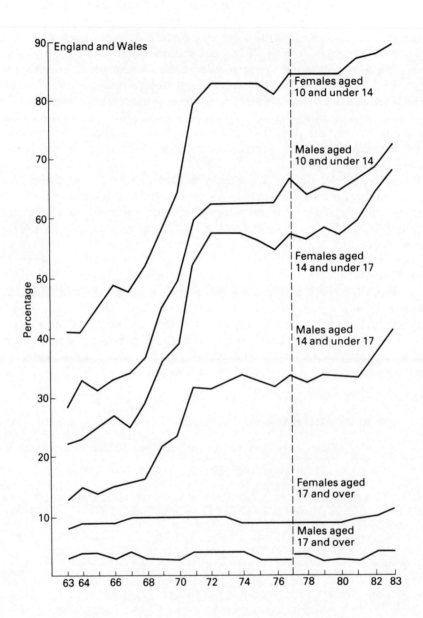

FIGURE 2.1   *Offenders cautioned for indictable offences* as a percentage of offenders found guilty or cautioned for indictable offences by age and sex.*

* 1963–76 not adjusted for the Criminal Law Act 1977 nor the change in counting of proceedings.
SOURCE: *Criminal Statistics England and Wales 1983*, Fig. 5.2, p. 72.

An important and controversial feature of the development of cautioning that is not revealed by these data is the extent to which variations exist between police forces in different parts of the country. McClintock and Avison drew attention to this in their analysis of cautioning during the period 1954–62. Their findings present a useful backdrop for later research during the period with which we are mainly concerned. At a time when there was little variation from year to year in the national cautioning rate, wide differences were discovered between police force areas:

> In 1962, for example, there were 4 forces which did not caution any offenders for indictable offences, and at the other extreme there were 4 forces cautioning more than 4 out of 10 offenders including one cautioning more than half the known offenders. Even if one accepted as a reasonable variation around the national average of about eleven per cent a range from 5 to 20 per cent, this still leaves 54 out of 124 forces either above or below this wide range. (McClintock and Avison 1968, pp. 208–9)

To complicate the picture further, many forces showed considerable change within their own practices during the eight-year period studied. 49 out of the 124 forces substantially altered their cautioning practice, with 21 cautioning fewer offenders at the end of the period, and 28 cautioning more:

> An examination of the individual variations according to type of police area does not indicate any particular high or low cautioning rates as being related to the different sizes of urban areas, even to differences between urban and rural areas. Almost all types of area showed a range of less than 5 per cent to more than 30 per cent. (McClintock and Avison 1968, p. 210 Table 7.12)

For the country as a whole McClintock and Avison found considerable variation in the use of cautioning according to offence type. For sexual offences, 32% were cautioned, 12% for thefts, and 4% for offences of violence; but even when the type of offence was taken into account discrepancies between forces remained. Similarly, differences occurred in relationship to the age of offenders, and an interesting analysis revealed three groups of police forces: first, those whose cautioning rates for all age groups were *above* the national average, as was the case in 11 large and 27 small towns; second, those whose rates for all age groups were *below* the national average, as in the MPD and six very large counties; and third, 6 large cities whose cautioning rate for juveniles was higher than average but for adults lower than average (McClintock and Avison 1968, p. 213). Even today it is difficult to disagree with the conclusions they reached on the basis of research more than twenty years ago.

> From a close study of the individual variations in cautioning rates between forces and within forces, and over a period of time, it can be stated that there is no agreed national policy on the extent to which the police can legitimately exercise their discretion not to prosecute. The variations are too great to be explained in terms of differences in types of crime, or sex and age of offenders in the different local areas. (McClintock and Avison 1968, p. 210)

The research surveys of Ditchfield (1976) and Laycock and Tarling (1985) provide conveniently spaced assessments of cautioning practices in the intervening period, enabling us to find out whether the sort of variation identified by McClintock and Avison has continued, and to consider possible explanations for any variation that does persist.

Ditchfield analysed the cautioning rates for indictable offenders, both juvenile and adult, in the 46 police force areas in England and Wales in 1973 (excluding the City of London). As far as adults were concerned the areas with the highest rates of cautioning tended to be rural (e.g. Suffolk 20%, Wiltshire 17%, Dorset and Bournemouth 14%), whereas the lowest were mainly urban, with Liverpool and Bootle, Manchester and MPD cautioning very few, and Bradford, Durham and Teeside cautioning only 1% of adult offenders. The picture was slightly more complicated for juveniles. The lowest rates were still to be found in the urban areas of Teeside (16%) and Hull (24%), but apart from those two forces, there was not as much difference between the remaining urban areas and the rest of the country, in contrast with the situation before 1969 when urban forces cautioned significantly less than other forces (Ditchfield 1976, pp. 13–14). In the light of these findings Ditchfield felt able to conclude:

> Consequently the 1969 [Children and Young Persons] Act . . . has established a more even pattern of juvenile cautioning between police forces – at least between urban and rural areas. Cautioning of adults, on the other hand, remains more dependent on the type of area being considered, and the policies of individual forces. (Ditchfield 1976, p. 13)

Before examining the evidence as to how far the variations were due to the different kinds of offenders and offences which police forces had to deal with, and how far to different prosecution policies, the findings of Laycock and Tarling's study of trends in cautioning between 1974 and 1982 will be considered. The clear conclusion to emerge from their research was that:

> disparities in cautioning rates, though still large, have in fact over the years decreased . . . the difference between force rates has narrowed steadily, although not dramatically, during the period. The reduction in the range has been caused by both an increase in the minimum rate and a decrease in the maximum; there is evidence of convergence towards the average. (Laycock and Tarling 1985, p. 82)

Nevertheless, as they readily admit, substantial differences in overall cautioning rates between forces continue, as does the gulf between cautioning rates of adults and juveniles. The latest statistics, for 1983, show that variation in the cautioning rate for indictable offences (excluding those of three forces, which are stated to be 'artificially high because of incorrect recording practice' (!)), ranged from 9% to 37%; for juveniles, the ranges were 37 to 68% (males) and 62–89% (females); and for adults (17 years and over) the ranges were 0–13% for men and 0–32% for women (Home Office 1984b, Table 5.6 p. 90). Certain forces tend to appear either at the top or bottom of the rank ordering right across the age and sex categories: thus, Bedfordshire, Notting-hamshire, Staffordshire and Northamptonshire have generally high cautioning rates, whereas the MPD, Cumbria, Cleveland, Leicestershire and South Wales appear consistently at the bottom of the list, with very low cautioning rates. Despite there being a tendency for the cautioning rates of some forces in more rural areas to be above average and those of the metropolitan areas to be below average, the national pattern is one of considerable complexity that cannot sustain any simple generaliza-tion about urban and rural links with cautioning rates. In order to progress towards a deeper understanding and fuller explanation of variations between areas, many more factors than geography and age must be taken into account.

It has long been recognized that, in addition to cautioning being used more frequently for minor than for more serious offences of all kinds, there is a marked and consistent difference between the cautioning rate for different types of offence. Certain sexual offenders are likely to be cautioned much more than average (especially those admitting unlawful sexual intercourse with teenaged girls, and the less serious cases of indecent assault) as, to a lesser extent, are those committing offences of theft (especially shoplifting) and handling stolen goods; on the other hand, the cautioning rate for offences such as robbery, fraud, violence and burglary tends to be consistently below the general level. Ditchfield's recognition of the importance of the offence variable led him to analyse the relationship between the cautioning rates of police forces and the proportion of shoplifting and minor thefts in the total of recorded offences. He discovered that 'over police areas as a whole, this variable proved to have a very strong relationship with both adult and juvenile cautioning rates; in general, the larger the proportion of these two offences, the higher the cautioning rate' (Ditchfield 1976, p. 16). Although he also examined other factors which might have influenced the cautioning rate, such as the number of known offenders/1000 population, the density of population and the clear-up rate, any association that was found was attributable to the variable's high correlation with the crime pattern of an area, and not to any independent influence they had: 'It was clear, therefore, that the pattern of crime was the most important variable in determining the level of cautioning' (p. 18).

This conclusion has not been seriously challenged by later research. However, Ditchfield conceded that crime patterns only accounted for about half of the actual variation in cautioning rates between forces, so that most of the remaining variation was likely to be a result of differences in prosecution policies. Two policy-related features that may explain some of the remaining variation are (i) the rate at which courts in different areas award conditional or absolute discharges, and (ii) the proportions of first offenders and recidivists cautioned or prosecuted by different police forces.

The proposition that all police forces may be faced with a similar proportion of minor offenders for whom there is a choice between a police caution or prosecution followed by court discharge, seems a fairly simple and not implausible explanation of differences in cautioning rates – in other words rates of cautioning should be high in areas where rates of discharge are low and vice versa, because the same group of offenders is being distributed between the two alternatives differently in different areas. In the 1960s, studies by Sebba (1967) and Somerville (1969) provide qualified support for this sort of reasoning. In the first detailed study of the cautioning of adults, Steer (1970) found no evidence for such a relationship, although his analysis of data from the 120 police forces in England and Wales in 1966 confirmed that quite a strong relationship of the kind predicted was found for juveniles – 'there appears to be a strong likelihood that juvenile offenders who have committed a first or minor indictable offence either receive a caution from the police or a discharge from the court' (Steer 1970, p. 21). Pursuing the same line of enquiry, Ditchfield analysed this relationship for all police force and court areas in 1973, and found clear evidence that 'the larger the proportion of offenders cautioned, the smaller the proportion of offenders discharged – whether as a proportion of those found guilty at court or as a proportion of all known offenders. This is true both for juveniles and for adults' (Ditchfield 1976, p. 19). Another feature that emerges from his data (see Table 2.5) is that the high cautioning/low discharge rate areas tended to be more rural, whereas the low cautioning/high discharge rate areas tended to be urbanized and industrial. Possible explanations suggested for apparently different policies and practices in urban and rural areas included the readier access to courts, which often sit daily in large cities but much less frequently in country towns, and/or a belief on the part of the police that, especially in a situation of high rates of recorded crime the courts are in a better position to adjudicate on appropriate disposals than are the police (Ditchfield 1976, p. 25).

Analysis of the statistics for 1983 suggests that, just as there has been a significant reduction in the range of cautioning rates, there has also been a weakening of the

TABLE 2.5   Proportion of known offenders cautioned, and proportion of offenders found guilty at court who were discharged, 1973

(%)

POLICE FORCE	JUVENILES		ADULTS	
	Cautioned	*Discharged*	*Cautioned*	*Discharged*
Devon and Cornwall	68	13	13	7
Suffolk	63	19	20	5
Wiltshire	63	14	17	6
Bedfordshire & Luton	61	16	10	6
Nottinghamshire	58	16	8	8
Cumbria	56	19	6	9
Thames Valley	53	22	6	9
Manchester	52	30	0	28
Metropolitan Police District	48	30	0	14
Liverpool & Bootle	46	21	0	10
South Wales	36	31	2	12
Kingston-on-Hull	24	30	8	11
AVERAGE (ENGLAND & WALES)	51	20	7	9

SOURCE: Ditchfield (1976), Table 13, p. 19.

relationship between cautioning and court discharge rates. Table 2.6 shows that the average court discharge rate of the ten police force areas that caution the highest proportion of offenders of all ages is no different from that of the areas that caution the lowest proporton of offenders. The only slight support for Ditchfield's 1973 findings is that the few areas that exhibit the high caution/low discharge pattern or its converse, also follow the urban/rural pattern he identified, with Wiltshire, Devon and Cornwall and Norfolk in the former category, and the MPD, S. Wales, Greater Manchester in the latter. Similarly, a more detailed breakdown of the rates for juvenile offenders, by sex and police force area, shows no evidence of a systematic relationship, with the average court discharge rates of the areas that caution lower proportions of offenders being just 2% below that of the high caution rate areas. It seems clear, therefore, that the proportion of all offenders found guilty or cautioned who are either cautioned by the police or discharged by the court does in fact vary from area to area; thus, in the case of male juvenile offenders, this combined proportion varied from three-quarters of those in Northamptonshire and Bedfordshire to less than half in Cleveland and the MPD; in the case of female juveniles, it varied from over 90% in Nottinghamshire, Northamptonshire and Hampshire to less than 80% in Leicestershire, W. Yorkshire and the MPD.

This declining association between discharge rates and cautioning rates may indicate that net-widening rather than diversion is increasingly taking place. Alternatively, it may be that courts have forgotten how trivial the most trivial offenders are! They just sentence on what they get, taking their line on discharges from the population appearing before them, and grant a particular proportion of discharges consistent with the court's 'culture'. The implications of these alternatives are entirely different, and in this case, the available statistics being unusable to distinguish between the alternatives, further research really *is* necessary!

The study by Laycock and Tarling (1985) was designed to investigate further the role of police differences in the explanation of cautioning variation. It was conducted in the context of renewed concern expressed by, among others, the members of the Royal Commission on Criminal Procedure (1981). It was part of a consultative process that ended with the introduction of new guidelines for cautioning (Home Office 1984a, Home Office Circular 14/1985). A questionnaire and request for relevant policy documents were put to all Chief Officers of Police in England and Wales. The work confirmed the importance of an offender's criminal history for the decision whether to caution. Information gathered from 9 forces shows that there was a fairly close relationship between the proportion of all offenders who were first offenders and a force's cautioning rate (see Table 2.7). The police forces with higher cautioning rates were (except for Nottinghamshire) also those with the higher proportion of first offenders, and there was much less variation in cautioning practice for first offenders, of whom more than two-thirds were cautioned in all forces. In contrast, column D shows that there was considerable variation in the cautioning of recidivists, broadly in line with the stated policies of the forces concerned. We can see, therefore, that some of the overall variation is due to significant differences in policy and practice regarding the cautioning of second and subsequent offenders.

A further factor that has been put forward as a possible influence on cautioning

TABLE 2.6 Police cautioning and court discharge rates, by police force areas, 1983

	ALL AGES			JUVENILES – MALE			JUVENILES – FEMALE	
POLICE FORCE	Cautioned %	Discharged %	POLICE FORCE	Cautioned %	Discharged %	POLICE FORCE	Cautioned %	Discharged %
Bedfordshire	37	15	Northamptonshire	68	21	Nottinghamshire	89	34
Nottinghamshire	33	14	Bedfordshire	67	24	Northamptonshire	88	28
Staffordshire	32	15	Nottinghamshire	66	24	Devon and Cornwall	86	25
Northamptonshire	31	13	Devon and Cornwall	64	15	Hampshire	86	34
Wiltshire	30	9	Hampshire	64	19	Bedfordshire	84	40
Devon and Cornwall	29	8	Thames Valley	63	19	Norfolk	83	36
Hampshire	28	12	Sussex	62	20	Staffordshire	82	34
Norfolk	27	9	Norfolk	61	17	West Mercia	82	30
Thames Valley	27	10	West Mercia	61	24	West Midlands	81	33
West Mercia	27	13	Staffordshire	60	24	Sussex	80	26
Surrey	20	6	Cheshire	47	22	Durham	72	31
Lancashire	19	14	Gwent	47	29	Cheshire	71	40
Cheshire	17	11	South Yorkshire	46	21	Cleveland	71	21
Cleveland	17	10	West Yorkshire	45	19	N. Wales	71	37
Greater Manchester	17	17	Greater Manchester	44	27	South Yorkshire	70	34
Humberside	17	11	Humberside	44	23	West Yorkshire	69	28
Leicester	17	8	South Wales	44	31	Gwent	69	49
Cumbria	15	10	Cumbria	41	18	Cumbria	68	39
South Wales	15	16	Metropolitan Police District	41	20	Metropolitan Police District	69	31
Metropolitan Police District	9	14	Cleveland	37	17	Leicestershire	62	33
Average (England & Wales)	21	13	Average (England & Wales)	52	21	Average (England & Wales)	77	33

SOURCE: *Criminal Statistics, England and Wales.*

TABLE 2.7   Proportion of juveniles cautioned and the proportion of first offenders
and recidivists cautioned in selected police forces

Police force	Proportion of offenders cautioned	Proportion of offenders who were first offenders	Proportion of first offenders cautioned	Proportion of redidivists cautioned
	%	%	%	%
	A	B	C	D
Norfolk	67.5	68.2	84.2	31.7
Suffolk	62.5	76.4	73.0	28.3
Nottinghamshire	60.1	46.2	94.1	31.0
Essex	59.7	60.3	88.6	15.9
Hampshire	56.3	61.9	81.3	15.7
Greater Manchester	48.3	56.0	77.4	11.2
Merseyside	46.6	52.8	69.9	20.5
Cheshire	45.0	54.2	69.0	16.6
Metropolitan Police	37.3	47.1	70.9	7.5

SOURCE: Laycock and Tarling (1985), Table 1, p. 86.

practices is the extent to which different police forces proceed against suspected offenders by way of a written summons to appear in court as opposed to physical arrest and the laying of a formal charge (see Chapter 3, below). It is generally believed that cautioning is an option that is only available for those who have been summonsed or reported for summons. However, in research for the Royal Commission on Criminal Procedure, Gemmill and Morgan-Giles (1980) found that the relationship between summons, arrest, charge and caution was not quite so straightforward as had been assumed. In a comparison between the towns of Bootle and Barnsley, although similar proportions of juveniles were cautioned, in Bootle all of them had first been charged, whereas in Barnsley they had previously all been warned for summons (Gemmill and Morgan-Giles 1980, Table 3.16 p. 22), showing that a caution is a live option for juveniles whatever method is chosen for initial process. Similarly, Laycock and Tarling's analysis of the relationship between summons rates and cautioning rates for all police forces in England and Wales showed that there was a modest positive relationship in the case of adults, but no reliable relationship for juveniles (Laycock and Tarling 1985, p. 88).

   The extent to which other procedural differences between forces contribute to the explanation of variation in cautioning practice is difficult to establish, and requires more comparative study of the kind piloted by Tutt and Giller (1983). They placed 15 forces studied along a line from the 'welfare' to the 'justice' approach to police decision-making about juveniles, reflecting different penal philosophies and typically associated with different organizational structures for consultation and level at which a decision is taken. A direct link between orientation, procedures and cautioning rate was difficult to establish in the case of juveniles because 'whatever decision-making structure is adopted, a large proportion of first time offenders coming to the notice of the police will receive a caution' (Tutt and Giller 1983, p. 593). They admit that the evidence is inconclusive:

> Clearly, there is no simple correlation between police procedures and the level of cautioning. Thus, the West Midlands Constabulary which adopts a predominantly 'justice' approach cautions males under 17 at precisely the national average (i.e. 47%) whereas Derbyshire, which appears to have a 'welfare' approach cautions the same group at a lower than national average rate (i.e. 43%). Alternatively, Devon and Cornwall and Greater Manchester have specialist bureaux and yet the former cautions at a rate much higher than the national average (i.e. 62%) whereas the latter is considerably lower (i.e. 35%). (Tutt and Giller 1983, p. 594)

As these researchers conclude, no single factor is likely to account for all variation in police cautioning. Some can undoubtedly be laid at the door of differences in types of crime committed, some to the varying proportion of first offenders, and some perhaps to explicit policy choices, whether deliberately or incidentally impacting on the rate of cautioning. This suggests that there may be scope for reducing disparities by the introduction of national guidelines for cautioning and agreed criteria for prosecution. More research is needed to keep track of the rapidly-changing scene concerning prosecution arrangements and the mushroom growth of instant cautioning schemes. The fact of net widening must be addressed squarely, as the Home Office has accepted in Circular 14/1985, and a serious attempt made to investigate the extent to which it is occurring. Above all, in the face of established attitudes and working practices, the basic principle of equality of treatment must be constantly reaffirmed, although the fact that the very essence of cautioning involves discretionary judgements about *people* suggests that justice and the caution make difficult bedfellows:

> While the interaction between organisation, offence and offender variables needs to be explored further, the perception and attitude of police officers towards juveniles and their crimes, developed in the local working context, may be an equally if not a more important determinant of the production of differing cautioning rates . . . If some element of 'natural justice' is to be preserved in the juvenile justice system, it would seem reasonable to hope that juveniles committing similar offences in different police force areas would at least have a similar opportunity and likelihood of receiving a caution even if the methods by which they were processed by the police were dissimilar. (Tutt and Giller 1983 p. 595)

Endnote

At this stage in the book, we have dealt, in as much detail as space allows, with the information routinely available about events classified as crimes, and about the relationships which these might have with the population of events which are candidates for such classification. We have tried to offer insights into how the translation from the event to the classification occurs, and some of the more obvious policy issues which can or could be informed by an understanding of how this happens. In the last section of this chapter, we have moved from the event as the unit of analysis to the person. However you might feel about the processes of crime report, record and clearance, there emerges from those processes a set of people who are then dealt with by agents of the state. In the next three chapters of the book, arguments about how people got where they are will be placed on one side. Instead we will concern ourselves with information about the paths they tread through prosecution, sentence, punishment and freedom.

3

The Criminal Process: from Suspicion to Conviction

There are a variety of paths by which persons suspected by the police of having committed a crime may be brought to court for trial. Figures 3.1 and 3.2 are diagrammatic illustrations of the stages from the reporting of a crime , through pre-trial and court proceedings, to final verdict.

The quality and comprehensiveness of statistical information about the criminal process is very variable. For several important topics, regular data are not available for the whole of the period upon which we are focusing, and it will be necessary to draw upon evidence from research studies – ranging from the studies of bail and remands in custody in the early 1960s to the invaluable research studies commissioned by the Royal Commission on Criminal Procedure (1981). For purposes of presentation and analysis the stages will be treated separately. Nonetheless, one of the main conclusions to emerge from research into pre-trial processes and court decision-making is the close links between the different stages. A decision or course of action taken at one point can influence or even determine what happens at subsequent stages. Although it is well-nigh impossible to establish, this is no doubt a two-way street, with the anticipated events in the courtroom influencing earlier decisions. For instance, the police decision to charge is based upon the existence of a *prima facie* case, but this standard must surely be informed by the fate of earlier decisions to charge upon reaching court.

Summons or Arrest

Those who are suspected by the police of having committed an indictable offence may be required to appear at a magistrates' court either in answer to a written summons, or

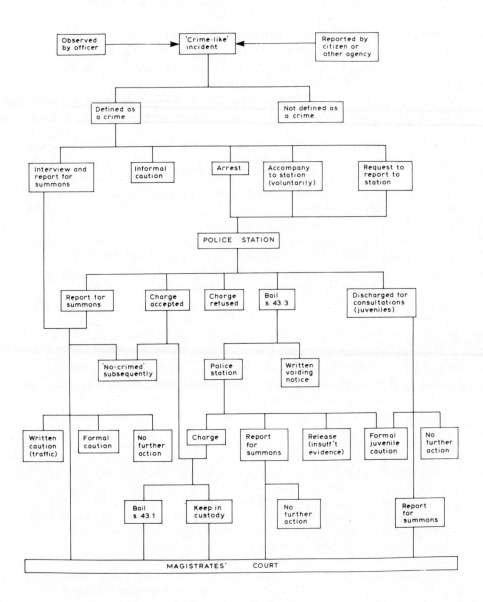

FIGURE 3.1   Paths to court: from crime to court appearance

SOURCE: Adapted from Gemmill and Morgan-Giles (1980), Fig. 2.2, p. 14 and Ashworth (1984) Fig. 2, p. 13.

having been arrested and charged. Published information on the extent to which these alternative ways of initiating criminal proceedings have been used during the last two decades is surprisingly incomplete, but from the data that are available a clear trend is apparent. In 1963, 33% of those appearing in magistrates' courts for indictable offences were summonsed, ranging from more than half of those suspected of violence and sexual offences, to just one fifth of those suspected of burglary and robbery. In contrast, 60% of those appearing for non-indictable (excluding motoring) offences were summonsed. The proportion of indictable suspects summonsed dropped slowly but steadily throughout the 1960s. When regular statistics appear again, in the late 1970s, the trend is again downwards, from 24% in 1978 to 21% in 1983. The proportion of non-indictable suspects summonsed had dropped slightly below 60% by the end of the 1960s, but has increased in recent years from 58% in 1980 to 62% in 1983. Thus, even from the fragmented evidence available, it is clear that there has been a major shift in the means by which police prefer to bring accused people to court.

Despite the curious reluctance to publish systematic information about the use of summons and arrest in the 1970s, the Home Office Statistical Department did release some tantalizing data to Gemmill and Morgan–Giles, in connection with their research for the Royal Commission on Criminal Procedure, showing the proportion of persons brought to court by summons, for each police force area in 1976. In the case of adults, of whom 17% were summonsed in the whole of England and Wales, the range was from zero in Cleveland to 72% in Derbyshire, with 7 forces summonsing more than 40% and 7 forces less than 5%. In the case of juveniles, of whom 61% were summonsed in the whole country, the range was from 3% in Greater Manchester to 98% in South Yorkshire (Gemmill and Morgan-Giles 1980, pp. 1–2 and Appendix A). The authors commented as follows on the question of urban-rural differences:

> Generally rural forces are more inclined to use summonsing than are urban forces, but this is not invariably the case. The police in rural Cambridgeshire, for example, only rarely summons adults, while the forces in the largely urban Metropolitan Counties of South and West Yorkshire use the summons procedure respectively for over one third and very nearly one half of those who appear in court for indictable offences . . . Such variations in the use made by police forces of arrest and summons could be said to undermine somewhat the argument that arrest is *per se* the most suitable method of bringing adult offenders before the courts. (Gemmill and Morgan-Giles 1980, p. 2)

For a proper appreciation of the variety of ways in which the police may initially proceed against suspects, the Home Office statistics are deficient not only in their incompleteness but because, as Gemmill and Morgan-Giles point out, they describe only the method by which accused persons finally *arrive at court* and not the method by which they are intercepted by the police in the first instance. Between initial police contact and court appearance there are many possible paths (for a suspect), so that not all arrested persons are subsequently charged (although they may be summonsed) and many of those arrested and charged may not be kept in police custody until the court hearing (Gemmill and Morgan-Giles 1980, pp. 10–11). The need to make such distinctions was highlighted by the research survey, for the Royal Commission on Criminal Procedure, in four police force divisions for the month of October 1978. Relevant data are presented in Tables 3.1 and 3.2. Large differences were found in the proportions summonsed in each of the four divisions studied; however, these were broadly in line with the differences shown by their 'parent' forces in the 1976 national survey – e.g. Bootle is part of Merseyside which summonsed just 2% of adults and 11% of juveniles in 1976, whereas Wrexham and Barnsley are in forces (namely North Wales and South Yorkshire) which summonsed very high proportions of adults (53% and 37% respectively) and juveniles (93% and 98%). Perhaps more surprising, however, is that a large majority of both adults and juveniles summonsed

TABLE 3.1   Paths followed to court: adults

	Lancaster %	Bootle %	Wrexham %	Barnsley %
Summonsed without arrest	9	1	31	7
Arrested and then summonsed	18	3	7	40
TOTAL summonsed	27	4	38	47
Charged and bailed	45	68	38	31
Charged and kept in custody	28	28	24	22
TOTAL charged	73	96	62	53
Total brought to court	100	100	100	100
(No. brought to court)	(158)	(219)	(103)	(254)

SOURCE: Gemmill and Morgan-Giles, Table 3.3, p. 18.

TABLE 3.2   Paths followed to court: juveniles

	Lancaster %	Bootle %	Wrexham %	Barnsley %
Summonsed without arrest	24	–	74	46
Arrested and then summonsed	48	13	16	53
TOTAL summonsed	72	13	90	99
Charged and bailed	12	68	5	1
Charged and kept in custody	16	19	5	–
TOTAL charged	28	87	10	1
Total brought to court	100	100	100	100
(No. brought to court)	(25)	(54)	(19)	(84)

SOURCE: Gemmill and Morgan-Giles (1980), Table 3.6, p. 20.

had initially been arrested, except in Wrexham where less than a quarter of those summonsed had been arrested.

Detention or Freedom Before Trial

1. Police Bail

The data in the lower half of Tables 3.1 and 3.2 lead conveniently into the next important stage in consideration of the initial processing of suspects by the police – namely, the extent to which those who have been arrested and charged by the police are kept in custody until their first court appearance or are released on bail by the police, either direct to court or to report again to the police station at a future date. In the Gemmill and Morgan-Giles survey of selected police forces about a quarter of the adult offenders appeared in court having been held in police custody (ranging from 22% in Barnsley to 28% in Lancaster and Bootle); for juveniles, the picture was more varied, with none appearing in police custody in Barnsley but almost a fifth in Bootle. National statistics for the period 1978–83 show that 13–14% of all offenders appearing in court for indictable offences had been arrested and held in police custody, with almost two-thirds (62–65%) arrested and bailed to court by the police. Of those appearing for non-indictable offences (excluding motoring) less than 1 in 10 had been arrested and held in police custody, with about one third arrested and bailed by the police. The proportion of those arrested for indictable offences who are held in custody by the police until their first court appearance varies according to the nature of the offence; it is highest for those charged with robbery, next for those charged with burglary, sexual offences and drunkenness; and lowest for offences of theft, handling stolen goods and most summary offences (see Table 3.3).

These data do not show what proportion of all cases had, at an earlier stage, been bailed by the police to report back to the police station on a specified date (under s. 43(3) of the Magistrates' Courts Act 1980, formerly s. 38(2) of the Magistrates' Courts Act 1952). There is little evidence on the use of this provision. Two of the studies carried out for the Royal Commission on Criminal Procedure provide some information, even though its primary focus of interest lay elsewhere. Softley's (1980) sample of 218 suspects observed at police stations in 1979 included 49 suspects (22%) who were bailed under s. 38(2) as it then was, or were told to come back to the station; of the rest, 1% were cautioned, 11% were released unconditionally, 22% were reported for a decision whether to prosecute, and 44% were charged. Of the 49 bailed by the police, 21 were eventually released unconditionally, 4 were cautioned, and 24, almost exactly one half, were prosecuted. It seems clear that this form of police bail is being used as part of a sifting procedure to select those suspects to be prosecuted. It is thus a procedure *anticipating*, not *following*, the relevant prosecution decision. Confirmation of the use of this particular form of bail as a delaying/sifting procedure for many who are not ultimately prosecuted or even formally cautioned is provided by Gemmill and Morgan-Giles' finding that about one third of the adult suspects who were not finally brought to court had been initially bailed by s. 38(2) (Gemmill and Morgan-Giles 1980, p. 21). Examination of the data in their study reveals that, for

TABLE 3.3   Persons proceeded against at magistrates' courts who had been arrested and charged, and held in police custody, by offence group. 1978–83

Offence Group	Persons held in custody by police until first court appearance					
	Percentage of persons arrested and charged					
	1978	1979	1980	1981	1982	1983
Indictable						
Violence against the person	20	20	18	19	19	18
Sexual offences	26	26	23	24	27	27
Burglary	30	30	28	27	26	27
Robbery	62	60	61	59	56	57
Theft and handling stolen goods	13	13	12	12	13	12
Fraud & forgery	21	19	18	18	18	18
Criminal damage	17	16	14	15	16	15
Drugs offences	17	17	17	10	12	17
Motoring offences	–	14	12	13	13	14
Other	–	40	33	40	40	39
Total	–	18	17	16	18	18
Summary (other than motoring)						
Assault on police	13	14	13	14	14	14
Drunkenness	22	19	19	25	28	25
Other	–	11	10	12	12	12
Total	–	16	˙16	20	22	20
Summary Motoring						
Driving while unfit	14	14	11	13	14	9
Other	–	14	12	12	13	13
Total	–	14	11	12	14	10
GRAND TOTAL	18	18	16	17	19	18
(nos. '000s)	(565.1)	(592.2)	(650.7)	(653.9)	(671.1)	(689.9)

SOURCE: Adapted from *Criminal Statistics, England and Wales* 1983. Table 8.3, p. 178.

adult males, s. 38(2) bail procedure was used in 8–17% of cases compared with police bail to court procedure (s. 38(1), now s. 43(1)) of from 27 to 57%. In only half of the s. 38(2) cases was the suspect ultimately brought to court (Gemmill and Morgan-Giles 1980, Appendix B pp. 45–51).

2. Court Bail and Remands in Custody

Surprisingly little attention has been paid to the extent to which *the police* grant bail to those arrested and charged with offences. The paucity of statistical data is a consequence of this neglect. An honourable exception to the general neglect is to be found in the work of Bottoms and McClean (1976). Much more attention has been focused on the extent to which people are granted bail by *the courts*, on being remanded. (The term 'remanded' refers to a court decision on a defendant whose case has been adjourned; a remand may be in custody or on bail, although the word is often misused as applying only to custody). Even this interest emerged rather tardily during the 1960s, and it was not until 1977 that Criminal Statistics began to provide reasonably adequate data on this stage of the process – probably as a result of the passing of the 1976 Bail Act and the recognition of the significant contribution which untried prisoners made to the continuing problem of prison overcrowding.

The two main situations in which the question of court bail, or remand in custody, arises, are (i) during summary trial, when the case has to be adjourned, and (ii) on committal for trial to the Crown Court. Since the end of the nineteenth century, statistics have been published showing the proportion of those committed for trial in custody to a higher court. In the late 19th and early 20th century, about three-quarters of all those committed for trial were detained in custody. After the First World War the proportion granted bail slowly increased until it had reached almost 60% by the outbreak of the Second World War. For twenty years after the war, the proportion granted bail on committal for trial remained at around the pre-war level and did not begin to rise until the 1960s, reaching 70% before the end of that decade. By 1975 the proportion of persons committed for trial and granted bail reached 80%. After reaching a peak of 84% in 1977, it has levelled off slightly for the last five years at around 80–81%.

Comparable information on the proportion of persons granted bail or remanded in custody in the course of summary trial was not available during most of the period since 1963. A number of research studies were carried out in the 1960s and early 1970s which, despite some local variations, indicated that about two thirds of those remanded by magistrates during summary trial were granted bail (Bottomley 1970, King 1971, Zander 1971, Bottoms and McClean 1976). A Home Office study by Simon and Weatheritt (1974), of the effects of the 1967 Criminal Justice Act upon the use of bail and custody by London Magistrates' Courts, showed that there had been a significant increase in the granting of bail between 1966 and 1969, by which time perhaps only a quarter of all defendants could expect to be remanded in custody for all the time before their trial (Simon and Weatheritt 1974, Table 7 p. 41).

Regular information about the use of bail and court remands began to be published in *Criminal Statistics* in 1977 and has continued to appear with some modifications every year since then. In 1983 about half (49%) of all those appearing in magistrates' courts for indictable offences were remanded (i.e. their cases were adjourned, at the request of either the defence or the prosecution). This represents a slight increase from the late 1960s and 1970s, when the proportion of defendants remanded was between 40 and 45%. Of those remanded, the percentage detained in custody at any time by the court has gradually decreased in recent years from 18% (1978) to 15% (1983). Within the overall average, the proportion remanded in custody in each offence group has varied considerably, from half of those accused of robbery and 25–30% of those accused of burglary and sexual offences, to 12–13% of those accused of violence, fraud and criminal damage, and only 1 in 10 of those facing charges of theft and handling stolen goods (Home Office 1984b, Table 8.5 p. 180). Many of these differences in court bail decisions reflect (and are probably directly influenced by) police decisions on bail and the way defendants are brought to court; those summonsed or bailed by the police are very much more likely, if remanded by the court, to be granted bail than are the minority of defendants arrested, charged and kept in custody by the police. Thus, in 1983, 96% of those remanded by magistrates after being summonsed were granted bail, as were 97% of those remanded after being arrested and bailed to court by the police, whereas only 48% of those remanded after being arrested and held in custody until first court appearance were bailed by the court (Home Office 1984b, Table 8.6 p. 181). Hardly any of those who have previously been bailed by the magistrates are committed for trial in custody but, conversely, a quarter of those committed for trial after having been held in police custody until their first court appearance and subsequently remanded in custody by magistrates were granted bail. People who have pleaded guilty or who have been convicted by a magistrates' court may be *committed for sentence* to the Crown Court, if the magistrates feel that a more severe sentence than they have power to impose is merited. About two thirds of these are committed in custody, which is perhaps understandable given the expectation of a longish custodial sentence that underlies such commitals. Precise details of other post-conviction pre-sentence remands in custody by magistrates or the Crown Court are not available in *Criminal Statistics*, but the combined effect is reflected in the *Prison Statistics* category of 'convicted but unsentenced' prisoners (see Chapter 4).

To anticipate our story somewhat, the ultimate link in the criminal process chain is that which connects the outcome of court proceedings to the paths along which defendants have reached their destination. Indeed, it was the discovery of an apparent relationship between court outcome and pre-trial bail/custody status that provided a major stimulus to research and then reform of the bail system in both North America and the United Kingdom in the 1960s. In 1983, for England and Wales, we find that the acquittal rate in magistrates' courts of those bailed by magistrates is consistently higher than that of those remanded in custody; and, for those tried in the Crown Court, the acquittal rate of those committed for trial on bail was four times that of those remanded in custody (21% compared to 5%). Similarly, at both magistrate and Crown Court levels, the chances of receiving a custodial sentence (if convicted) are very much higher for those previously remanded in custody than for those who had been granted bail; for example, at the Crown Court, 68% of those committed for trial in custody received a custodial sentence, compared with 42% of those committed for trial on bail (Home Office 1984b, Tables 8.6 and 8.11). We are wary of concluding that there is a direct causal link underlying these relationships (see Bottomley 1973, pp. 88–93) but would nonetheless stress the need to be aware of the possibility of influences from one stage of the penal process to the next.

Before concluding our discussion of police and court bail, one final statistic merits passing mention. This is the one which appears to measure the 'success' or 'failure' of bail decisions in ensuring a defendant's appearance at trial. For obvious reasons, the appearance or non-appearance for trial of the accused is and has always been a major concern of the police, the public and of court staff. The rate of bail absconding is a clear sign (although by no means the only one) of a degree of failure at this point in the criminal process. On this criterion, bail decisions during the last few years must be regarded as having been quite successful In 1983, only 3% of people bailed by the police failed to turn up in court on the due date to answer accusations of having committed indictable offences – although 11% of those bailed for drunkenness failed to turn up! Of those granted bail by magistrates, only around 4% of those charged with indictable offences abscond, with again a slightly higher percentage of non-indictable and motoring offence cases (Home Office 1984b, p. 176 and Table 8.12). Thus, at one level, despite the large majority of people being granted bail, the system seems to be working quite well in terms of its primary objective. Nonetheless, the police would argue that other objectives are served which require seeking remands in custody. These include the prevention of further crimes by the defendant if bailed, and the prevention of interference with witnesses. Measuring the extent to which these objectives are achieved by current bail/custody practice is self-evidently a quite different matter, requiring information which it would be difficult or impossible to gather in a satisfactory or reliable way.

Visible and Invisible Mistakes

The discussion of the proportions of people who had been released on bail who turn up at court or abscond brings to the fore the problems of deciding on criteria of success in criminal justice, or indeed in anything else. Whenever a choice lies between two alternative courses of action, it is possible to make one of two different mistakes. For instance, when you toss a coin you can call heads when it comes down tails, or you can call tails when it comes down heads. In this example, both mistakes are visible. Another example may serve to show that it is not always the case that both mistakes are visible, because of the action taken. A dilemma which most motorists in a cold climate face is whether to change the anti-freeze in the car radiator during the autumn. There are two possible errors here. The first occurs when you don't change the anti-freeze and you should have. This error comes to your notice as a ruined engine sometime during the winter. The other error occurs when you do change the anti-freeze and the replaced anti-freeze would have seen the winter through without problem. You can make this error. However you can never know you have made it. Likewise, in the discussion of bail decision-making earlier, there are two possible mistakes, only one of which is recognizable as a mistake. You can give bail to someone who then fails to show up at court, or you can deny bail to someone who would have shown up at court. Although you know how often the first kind of mistake is made, you can never know when the second kind of mistake has been made. Unfortunately many decisions in criminal justice are like changing the anti-freeze! One kind of mistake is visible, the other invisible. They are usually decisions about custody. For example, we know the number of people reconvicted after release on parole licence, but not the number of people who would not have been reconvicted had they been released on licence.

One qualification to the foregoing should be entered. Information about invisible errors is available if the balance of decisions made shifts. For example, if suddenly anti-freeze increased tenfold in price, fewer people would change it in the autumn, and the fate of the people who used to change it in the autumn and now don't would give information about the rate at which the invisible error was being made. In the same way, changes in the proportion of bail decisions made may yield some information about the extent to which people had been refused bail who would not have absconded. However, because of some inherent difficulties in research like this, for most practical purposes invisible errors stay invisible.

Why does the identification of invisible errors matter? We surely have enough trouble with the mistakes we know about, without scratching round for more. It matters because we must be wary of making judgements of success on the basis of the observed frequency of only one type of error. More generally it matters because the less often you make one kind of error, the more often you make the other. The more often you unnecessarily change anti-freeze, the less often you ruin your engine through lack of anti-freeze. If you guess a coin will come down heads all the time, you will never make the mistake of saying tails when you should have said heads. The cost of this is that you will say heads a lot of times when you should have said tails! In the same way, if you seek to minimize the number of bailees who fail to turn up at court, you will increase the number of those remanded in custody who would have turned up in court had they been bailed. This may be reasonable if you regard it as much more important to avoid one kind of mistake. In a classic study of people judged to be too dangerous to release from detention, it became clear that psychiatrists minimized the chance of someone being released who was dangerous at the cost of the continued incarceration of many people who were not dangerous (Steadman and Cocozza 1974). Whether you judge that reasonable depends upon your judgement of the relative importance of the two kinds of mistake. What is unforgivable, hence this section, is not even to recognize the invisible error!

Choice of Court Venue

Most defendants who appear in magistrates' courts accused of indictable offences have a choice of being tried by magistrates in the lower courts or opting for trial by judge and jury in the Crown Court. Some of the more serious offences can only be tried on indictment in the higher courts, but the rest are what is now called 'triable either way', which may be tried summarily, if magistrates and defendant agree.

During the last twenty years there has been a tremendous increase in the business of the criminal courts. Much of this involves proceedings for non-indictable offences, especially motoring, but there has been a dramatic rise in the number of persons proceeded against for indictable offences. In 1963, less than a quarter of a million people were proceeded against for indictable offences; by 1983, the number had increased to over 600 000. Luckily, as far as the swift administration of justice is concerned, the vast majority of defendants, when they have a choice, elect to have their cases dealt with by the magistrates, and as a result only a small proportion of indictable offenders appear for trial at the Crown Court. In 1963, only 10% of all those accused of indictable offences were tried at a higher court (Quarter Sessions and

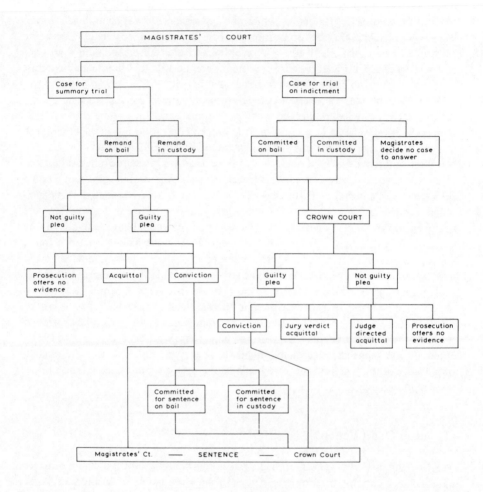

FIGURE 3.2   *Paths from first court appearance to sentence*

SOURCE: Adapted from Ashworth (1984) Fig. 2, p. 13.

Assizes as they then were called). The proportion of indictable offenders whose cases were heard at the higher courts has steadily increased over the last two decades, despite legislative attempts such as Part III of the Criminal Law Act 1977 to redistribute some of the work of the Crown Court, so that by 1983 one in six (16%) of all those accused of indictable offences appeared at the Crown Court – totalling 95 000 persons, compared to 22 000 in 1963.

Table 3.4 shows the dispositions of all defendants aged 17 and over proceeded

TABLE 3.4   Defendants aged 17 and over proceeded against at magistrates' courts
for indictable offences, 1973–83

	Total number proceeded against ('000s)	Number of defendants ('000s)			
		Proceedings discontinued etc.	Tried Summarily	Committed for trial (no.)	(%)
1973	280	2	232	47	(17)
1978	364	3	289	72	(20)
1983	448	5	350	93	(21)

SOURCE: extracted from *Criminal Statistics, England and Wales, 1973*. Table 6.3, p. 110.

against at magistrates' courts for indictable offences between 1973 and 1983. In the
last five years, the proportion committed for trial at the Crown Court in the different
offence groups varied from some 95% of those facing charges of robbery, 40% of
those accused of burglary, and one third of alleged sexual offenders, to less than a
quarter of those accused of violence against the person, one in seven of those accused
of theft, and only a few per cent of those accused of indictable motoring offences
(Home Office 1984b, Table 6.4 p. 111).

The decision about court venue has great personal and practical significance for
very many defendants. It is surprising that there are so few research data about the
way in which this crucial decision is made. In their study of a large sample of
defendants in Sheffield in 1971–72, Bottoms and McClean found that almost four-
fifths opted for summary trial, 4% elected trial on indictment, and the remaining 17%
were facing charges that had to be tried at the higher court. In other words 'where the
defendant had a choice he opted for summary trial in 95% of the cases' although the
remaining 5% of cases represented more than one fifth of all higher court cases
(Bottoms and McClean 1976, p. 78). The main reason for defendants electing
summary trial was 'to get it over with' and avoid any further delay – a reason given by
60% of defendants – with almost a quarter expecting to get a lighter sentence. Of the
minority who elected trial by jury, half expected a fairer trial, 29% acted on their
solicitor's advice, and 14% believed they had a better chance of acquittal (Bottoms
and McClean 1976, pp. 91 and 95). Similar reasons were reported in a survey carried
out for the James Committee (1975): more than half of the defendants chose summary
trial in order to have the case dealt with quickly, and almost half felt they had a better
chance of a light sentence. The main reasons that influenced those choosing trial on
indictment were that 'the case is gone into more thoroughly, given a better hearing'
(57%), 'there is a jury to listen to the case' (46%), on solicitor's advice (40%), and the
defendant has a better chance of being acquitted (30%) (see Home Office 1975,
Appendix C pp. 141–146 and Gregory 1976, ch. 3). There is also, of course, a strong
link between choice of trial on indictment and an intention to plead not guilty – even
though, in the event, the plea may be changed to one of guilty at the last minute
(Home Office 1975, p. 142; Baldwin and McConville 1977).

Legal Aid

Before investigating how much waiting time is typically involved in a case that goes to the higher court, and the validity of the belief in a better chance of being acquitted by a jury than by magistrates, this seems an appropriate point to examine recent trends in the provision of legal aid.

Legal aid is neither a fizzy drink for barristers nor artificial insemination by solicitor. It is the provision, under certain circumstances, of help with the financial costs of legal representation. Legal aid statistics provide an approximate guide to the extent to which defendants in various types of court proceeding may be legally represented, and legal representation in turn directly affects decisions of many kinds, including bail, choice of plea, chances of acquittal and sentence. Furthermore, it is important to monitor legal aid, because of its implications for public expenditure and the work of the legal profession – to say nothing of its role in enabling justice to be seen to be done. The basic framework for the present legal aid arrangements in criminal proceedings was established by Part IV of the Criminal Justice Act 1967, following the recommendations of the Widgery Committee (Home Office 1966). A rapid growth in the provision of legal aid had already begun in the early 1960s, with the proportion of people appearing for trial and sentence at the higher courts granted legal aid doubling from 30% in 1960 to over 60% by 1966 (Borrie and Varcoe 1971 p. 7). Table 3.5 shows the increase in applications for legal aid between 1969 (when the present statistical series started) and 1983. In that 15 year period the number of legal aid applications more than trebled. The proportion of those applying for legal aid for indictable proceedings in magistrates' courts increased from less than one quarter in 1969 to well over three-quarters in 1983; in juvenile court proceedings, there was an increase from 4% (1969) to 42% (1983). Legal aid applications for trial or sentence at the Crown Court remained at around the 95% level for the whole period. The extent to which applications were *granted* varied according to the type of proceedings: 90% of applications for summary trial of indictable offences were granted, and slightly more of applicatons for criminal proceedings in juvenile courts. 99% of applications relating to committal proceedings and trial at the Crown Court were granted, but only 6 out of 10 applications for the trial of non-indictable offences. The net effect of the 'success' rates of the different types of application meant that in 1983, for example, defendants received legal aid in over 70% of trials for indictable offences in magistrates courts and in 95% of trials at the Crown Court. The amount paid under the scheme has risen quite spectacularly, even when corrected for inflation, from £6 million in 1969 to £121 million in 1983 – with contributions ordered from the defendant amounting to only £0.15 million (1969) and £1.32 million (1983). The reader interested in further discussion of legal aid and legal representation should consult Ashworth (1984) Chapter 6.

Time Awaiting Trial

We concluded above that the main reasons that appear to influence defendants'

TABLE 3.5   Applications for legal aid in proceedings at magistrates' courts and the Crown Court, 1969–83

	Magistrates' court proceedings				Crown Court proceedings	
	Trials of adults for:		Proceedings relating to committal for trial	All criminal proceedings in juvenile courts	Trials at the Crown Court	Appearance for sentence, after conviction at magistrates' courts
	Indictable offences	Non-indictable offences				
1969. No. of applications ('000s).	51	17	30	5	38	10
% of all persons proceeded against	(24)	(1)	(70)	(4)	(94)	(88)
1973. No. of applications ('000s)	104	30	42	17	51	12
% of all persons proceeded against	(45)	(2)	(71)	(13)	(94)	(97)
1978. No. of applications ('000s)	189	45	60	34	72	13
% of all persons proceeded against	(64)	(3)	(71)	(24)	(97)	(98)
1983. No. of applications ('000s)	281	60	53	44	87	9
% of all persons proceeded against	(80)	(3)	(56)	(42)	(95)	(97)

SOURCE: *Criminal Statistics, England and Wales.*

choice of venue are, for those opting for magistrates courts the avoidance of a long period awaiting trial, and for those electing to be tried by a jury, the belief that they would get a better hearing and a better chance of acquittal. These assumptions can now be looked at a little more closely.

The time factor is of crucial importance at every stage of the criminal process: for the victim, when the crime is being committed and responded to; for the police, in the early identification of offenders; for suspects, in the speed of determination of their fate; for witnesses called to give evidence; and for administrators and lawyers involved in court proceedings. All the decision stages considered so far have direct and often startling implications for the time that the whole process is likely to take – cases proceeded against by summons take on average very much longer to come to court than is the case when the offender is arrested and charged; defendants kept in custody by the police and the court before trial will know the final outcome very much sooner than defendants granted bail at some stage before trial, although they may not rejoice in the advantage they gain from pre-trial custody; finally, people who opt for summary trial will not have to endure the suspense of what could be a long wait for trial at the Crown Court.

In their study of four separate police force divisions in the North of England, Gemmill and Morgan-Giles compared not only the time spent by suspects 'in police hands' (!?), but also the time which elapsed between charge or warning for summons and first court appearance (or discontinuation of the case). In Bootle, the average time before an appearance in court following charge and bail was only 16 days, compared to 116 days following warning for summons. The difference in the other divisions studied was not as marked as that of Bootle, but even so the time to first court appearance for summons cases was three times as long as for those who had been charged and bailed (11–12 weeks compared with 3–4 weeks). These figures include both adults and juveniles, since in practice little difference was found in the times taken to deal with the two groups (Gemmill and Morgan-Giles 1980, p. 24).

Frankenburg and Tarling (1983) carried out a study for the Home Office of the time taken to deal with juvenile offenders in six courts, selected from Inner and Outer London, and the provinces. The sample was drawn from cases appearing during the period April–June 1980, and totalled 685 juvenile cases; just over two-thirds faced indictable or triable-either-way charges, and two-thirds of all the defendants admitted the charges brought against them. The average time taken to deal with all cases, from the time of the alleged offence to court sentence, was 14 weeks. It varied from 10 weeks (Croydon) to 17 weeks (Northampton). The average 'pre-court' time (i.e. before a defendant's first court appearance) was 9 weeks, and the average time for court proceedings was thus 5 weeks. Pre-court time varied from 7 weeks (Westminster and Croydon) to 13 weeks (Northampton and Reading); it can be divided into three stages:

(i) from offence to arrest or report for summons – averaging 1.4 weeks;
(ii) from arrest or report to charge or summons – averaged 4 weeks (ranging from 1.5 weeks in Waltham Forest to 7.5 weeks in Reading);
(iii) from charge or summons to first court appearance – average of 3 weeks (Frankenburg and Tarling 1983, Table 2 p. 6).

Once a case reached the juvenile court, the average time to final disposal was just under 5 weeks, with uncontested cases taking an average of 2 weeks (with little variation between the courts), but contested cases taking ten weeks, varying from 4 weeks in Reading to 15 weeks in Tower Hamlets (Frankenburg and Tarling 1983, p. 10).

Detailed evidence of the extent of waiting times at different stages in the criminal process has to be sought from special research studies like those quoted above. The only regular, if somewhat inaccessible, official sources that provide some information about the delays affecting certain categories of defendant, are the annual statistics from the Prison Department (which give details of the average length of time spent in custody by untried and unsentenced prisoners), and the statistics relating to proceedings at the Crown Court, which have been published since 1975 in *Judicial Statistics*, and for 1972–4 in *Statistics on Judicial Administration* from the Lord Chancellor's Department.

Prison Department statistics for 1983 show that the estimated average time spent in custody by all categories of untried male prisoners doubled from 23 days in 1970 to 47 days in 1983; for females, the increase was from 19 days (1970) to 31 days (1983). 10% of prisoners awaiting trial on 30 June 1983 had been in custody for more than 6 months since their first remand in custody, which was much longer than the corresponding figure for previous years (Home Office 1984c, pp. 36–37).

The rather uneven information from the Lord Chancellor's Department about time awaiting trial at the Crown Court shows that in 1972 (when the new court system was first established) the average time a person had to wait for trial was just over 11 weeks, with a wide variation between, at one end, 6 weeks on the Midlands and Oxford Circuit and, at the other extreme, almost 23 weeks in London. By 1980 the average waiting time had risen to over 17 weeks, although by 1983 it had been reduced again to just over 14 weeks. Some 25 years earlier, in 1958, the Government set up an Interdepartmental Committee on the Business of the Criminal Courts (the Streatfeild Committee) to see whether, amongst other things, improvements could be made to ensure that 'cases are brought before the courts and disposed of expeditiously'. So there was concern even then about unnecessary delays before trial, although the average time involved was only *five weeks*, with four-fifths of all cases dealt with in less than eight weeks – twice the proportion that are now dealt with in the same time (see Home Office 1961; Gibson 1960).

As in virtually all comparisons between bail and custody cases, those committed for trial on bail have to wait longer than those committed in custody: in 1972, the average time was 12.1 weeks for those on bail compared to 8.3 weeks for those in custody; by 1983, the difference was 15.4 weeks (on bail) and 9.7 weeks (in custody). From 1975 onwards, *Judicial Statistics* provide information showing the proportions of those waiting (a) less than 8 weeks (b) less than 20 weeks, according to whether they were on bail or in custody, and whether they had pleaded guilty to all charges or not guilty to at least one charge. Table 3.6 shows the trends for selected years between 1975 and 1983. In each comparison there is a significant difference between the waiting times, according to plea and whether committed for trial on bail or in custody. The overall trend shows a clear deterioration of the situation until 1980, but with signs of a slight

TABLE 3.6   Committals for trial to Crown Court: waiting times according to
whether on bail or in custody, and according to plea, 1975–83

| | Percentage waiting less than: | | | | Percentage waiting less than: | | | |
| | 8 weeks | | 20 weeks | | 8 weeks | | 20 weeks | |
Year	Bail	Custody	Bail	Custody	Guilty plea	Not guilty plea	Guilty plea	Not guilty plea
1975	52	71	88	95	68	37	94	82
1978	35	58	70	90	52	19	84	56
1980	32	54	63	87	49	18	79	50
1983	37	60	75	91	54	19	88	62

SOURCE: *Judicial Statistics*, Annual Reports 1975–83.

upward trend (i.e. reducing the time awaiting the trial) in the last three years. Nevertheless, in 1983, almost 10% of those committed for trial in custody had to wait for
more than 20 weeks, as had 25% of those on bail, and almost 40% overall of those who
pleaded not guilty. Furthermore, these average figures conceal considerable variation
in waiting times in the different circuits throughout England and Wales. Thus, for
defendants in custody the national average waiting time in 1983 was 9.7 weeks, but in
London was 16.2 weeks, compared to less than 8 weeks in the Western, North-
Eastern and Midlands and Oxford circuits; the waiting time for those on bail (average
15.4 weeks) ranged from 26.4 weeks in London to 9.4 weeks on the Midlands and
Oxford Circuit. For defendants who pleaded guilty, the national average was 11.1
weeks, varying from 20.8 weeks in London to 8.1 weeks in the Midlands and Oxford
Circuit; for those who pleaded not guilty (average 20 weeks), the waiting time varied
from just over 12 weeks in the Western and Midlands and Oxford Circuit to 27 weeks
in London (Lord Chancellor's Department 1984, Table 5.11 p. 65). The time that
any defendant must expect to have to wait for trial at the Crown Court is considerable,
making it readily understandable that this is a significant factor in the choice of venue;
those 'lucky' enough to be granted bail will have to wait longer than those in custody,
and those who elect to plead not guilty are also 'choosing' to increase their waiting
time by up to 100% more than those who plead guilty. What then of their chances of
being acquitted?

Pleas and Acquittal Rates

Acquittal rates are of obvious significance to all those concerned in the criminal
process. The controversy that has surrounded Home Office attempts in recent years
to provide better information for public debate is testimony to the fact that they are a
perfect paradigm of the problems surrounding the use and abuse of official statistics,

raising all the fundamental issues of definition, purpose, interpretation and manipulation that have been so astringently summarized by Baldwin and McConville, who felt that statistics of acquittal rates can be politically so dangerous that they ought to carry a Government Health Warning!

> Rates of acquittal cannot be regarded as neutral statistics, the meaning of which will be self-evident to any fair-minded observer. They are rather statistics with powerful socio-political overtones that have in the past generated extraordinary controversy and dispute. They are regarded by some observers as representing a measure of the quality of justice itself, if not a test of the impartiality and fairness of juries as against the magistracy. (Baldwin and McConville 1978, p. 196)

At the outset it should be stressed that an acquittal rate is correctly expressed only as a proportion of all those cases where there is a plea of not guilty. It is possible to present acquittal rates in relation to the total number of persons proceeded against, and such statistics would be meaningful for certain purposes, but are not to be presented here since they are not meaningful for most of the policy purposes for which they might be used. The analysis by McClintock and Avison (1968) may be used as an example. This showed a gradual increase in the proportion of offenders found guilty from 85% in the early 1900s to 94% in the 1960s. This is of little direct relevance to the current debate about the acquittal rate – as the authors were the first to point out:

> These figures . . . do not give the number of cases in which a person was convicted on his own plea of guilty, nor do they give the proportion of defendants that plead not guilty before a judge and jury and who are subsequently acquitted. In other words, the statistics cannot be taken as an indication of the problems relating to the workload of the courts nor, in particular, of the effectiveness of the present jury system. What they do show is that by the various means available in the administration of criminal justice the proportion of persons convicted has increased rather than decreased during the present century. (McClintock and Avison 1968, p. 152)

Although *Criminal Statistics* have for a very long time provided information of this sort, only recently did they begin to provide information linking acquittals to choice of plea, in an attempt to grapple with the inherent complexity of acquittal rates. Between 1976 and 1978 the annual volumes of *Criminal Statistics* included tables that purported to show the comparative acquittal rates of persons aged 17 and over pleading not guilty to indictable offences at magistrates' courts and at the Crown Court. On this evidence, magistrates' courts appeared consistently to acquit a slightly higher proportion of defendants in most offence groups than did the Crown Court. In the 1976 volume a separate chapter of the Commentary (Chapter 4) was devoted to a detailed explanation of the complexity of the exercise and the methods chosen for presenting the new data. It was explained how acquittal rates could be calculated *either* by dividing the number of *persons* acquitted (however the term acquitted is defined) by the total number of *persons* charged, *or* by dividing the number of *charges* resulting in acquittal by the total number of *charges*; furthermore, whether persons or charges are used as the denominator, different acquittal rates will be obtained when different definitions of 'acquittal' and 'total' are used. Is that quite clear?! (Home Office 1977, para 4.7). The operational definition of 'acquittal' chosen for these official statistics was based on what is known as the 'principal offence' basis – i.e. the number of *persons* found not guilty on all charges, after full evidence is heard, as a percentage of those who pleaded not guilty to all charges (see Vennard 1981, p. 21). As this definition treats as convicted any defendant who is convicted on some charges but acquitted on others, it tends to give a lower rate than a definition based on charges. Vennard also pointed out that it would tend to underestimate the number of acquittals in the Crown Court, where a higher proportion of defendants face multiple charges than is the case in magistrates' courts (Vennard 1981, p. 21). Apart from the case of the 'principal offence' definition, which has also been criticized by others (see Baldwin and McConville 1978), evidence from subsequent Home Office research studies has revealed discrepancies between official figures and those calculated by researchers so wide as to shed serious doubt on the validity of the official statistics:

> It was therefore inferred that the unexpectedly high percentage of acquittals recorded in the official statistics was likely to be the result of error in the statistical returns on which the rates were compiled . . . Error in the recording of plea may come about when a contested charge resulting in conviction is misrecorded as a plea of guilty in the process of transcribing the information from the court register into statistical returns. The net result would be to inflate artificially the rate of acquittal . . . The second type of possible error in recording arises from failure to distinguish cases resulting in acquittal after full evidence has been heard from cases in which the prosecution does not proceed with charges brought against defendants. Acquittals recorded in the *Criminal Statistics* are confined to cases in the former category. (Vennard 1981, p. 22).

The conclusions reached by Vennard suggest that, contrary to the impression created by the published statistics for 1976–8, magistrates' courts do *not* acquit as many of those who plead not guilty to indictable offences as does the Crown Court. Indeed, recent estimates of the average acquittal rate in magistrates' courts suggest that it is nearer to 25% than the figure of around 50% indicated in those volumes of *Criminal Statistics* (see Softley 1976; Vennard 1980, 1981; Butler 1983). Until further research results have been published on this contentious issue it is most unsafe to make any comparative claims about the relative likelihood of acquittal in contested cases by magistrates as opposed to the jury. The *Criminal Statistics* for 1979 included no information on acquittal rates 'pending investigation into the possible fault in the reporting of this information' (Home Office 1980, para 4.16). It is, however, possible to examine some evidence on the acquittal rate at the Crown Court from official statistics over the last ten years. The proportion of all defendants pleading not guilty in the Crown Court between 1972 and 1983 remained fairly steady at 37–40%, although the figure for the North Eastern circuit was consistently lower than average at 20–30%, and that for London was always higher than average at 53–60%. The proportion of defendants pleading not guilty to at least one count in the Crown Court, who were acquitted on all contested counts, has gradually risen from 42% (1973) to 50% (1983). Before examining the variation in acquittal rates in the different Crown

Court circuits, a further and often neglected feature of the interpretation of these statistics must be mentioned.

In the popular mind, an acquittal at the Crown Court means that a jury of 'twelve good persons and true' has decided that the defendant is not guilty. In fact, almost half of all Crown Court acquittals are not the direct outcome of full deliberation by a jury but are either *ordered by the judge*, when the prosecution offers no evidence against the defendants, or are *directed by the judge*, who, after hearing part of the case, reaches the view that there is insufficient evidence to put the case to the jury. Information now published annually in *Judicial Statistics* shows, for example, that in 1983 over a quarter of all acquittals were ordered by the judge, a fifth were directed, and only 53% were the direct result of jury verdicts (see also McCabe and Purves 1972; McConville and Baldwin 1981; and the discussion in Ashworth 1984 Chapters 12–13). Accordingly, an alternative way of presenting acquittal rates would be to say that in recent years about a fifth of all defendants pleading not guilty are acquitted by order or direction of the judge, and 25–30% a year are acquitted by a jury. The annual proportion of defendants (excluding those acquitted by order or direction of the judge) acquitted by a jury in all contested cases during the period 1976–1983 was almost exactly one third, except in 1980 when it rose slightly to 36% (see Butler 1983; McConville and Baldwin 1981). Analysis of the variation in the acquittal rates of different circuits must take into account possible variations between these different categories of acquittal.

Butler's (1983) survey of regional variations 1976–81, showed that the average acquittal rate by order or direction of the judge varied from around 17% in the South-East Circuit to around 27% in the Northern and North Eastern Circuits; when combined with a slightly higher than average rate for *jury* acquittals, this generated an overall acquittal rate for the Northern circuit of almost 60%. Even when the judge-ordered/directed cases are excluded from the analysis, the jury acquittal rate of the Northern circuit was still above average at around 40%, compared to the 30–35% rate of most of the other circuits in England and Wales (Butler 1983, Tables 5 and 6 p. 17). Yet again, therefore, do the statistics of the criminal justice process raise awkward questions concerning the nature of justice that can apparently vary so much according to geography and the vagaries of the agents and administrators of justice, both lay and professional.

4

Sentencing Trends and Statistics of Imprisonment

The sentencing of those found guilty by the courts, whether as a result of a guilty plea or following trial and conviction by magistrates or a jury represents the culmination of a process that may have begun many weeks or months previously, and for those who are sentenced to anything other than a discharge, a binding-over or a suspended sentence, marks the beginning of another stage in facing the consequences of their offending. In this chapter, we will discuss some of the trends in sentencing since 1963 and the availability of information on these trends. We will touch upon the issue of sentencing disparity, and speculate upon the general trends in social control which may underpin the more specific trends in sentencing. We will go on to examine in more detail the statistics on the most severe sentence available to the court, that of imprisonment.

Sentencing Trends Since 1963

Detailed statistics are available about many aspects of sentencing, and in the first part of this chapter it will only be possible to present a broad overview of recent trends. We shall continue to focus almost exclusively upon indictable offences and offenders. After a preliminary look at general trends, we shall examine sentencing patterns according to age group and gender, while reserving particular analysis of the sentencing of juvenile offenders to Chapter 5, where it will form part of a comparison of juvenile justice throughout the United Kingdom. Finally, we shall identify some of the salient characteristics of the use of a selection of sentences, specifically fines, probation, suspended sentences, community service orders and imprisonment. Other important topics in the analysis of sentencing, such as variations according to type of offence, and differences between sentences imposed by lower and higher courts, will be introduced at relevant points in the discussion.

Table 4.1 illustrates the major trends in the sentencing of indictable offenders

TABLE 4.1   Offenders sentenced for indictable offences (all courts), 1963–83

Year	Total	Discharge	Prob.	Supervision	Fine	C.S.O.	Att. Centre	Det. Centre	A.S./ Care Order	Borstal	Youth Custody	Imprisonment Susp.	Imprisonment Immed.	Other
1963														
%	100	16.7	19.7	*	40.3	*	2.0	1.3	2.0	1.7	*	*	13.6	2.6
no. (in '000s)	(211.2)	(35.3)	(41.6)		(85.2)		(4.2)	(2.7)	(4.3)	(3.6)			(28.7)	(5.6)
1968														
%	100	14.0	14.6	*	44.3	*	2.0	2.5	2.0	1.9	*	8.7	8.7	1.4
no. (in '000s)	(290.6)	(40.8)	(42.3)		(128.6)		(5.9)	(7.2)	(5.7)	(5.4)		(25.3)	(25.3)	(4.1)
1973														
%	100	12.8	7.0	4.8	51.3	*	2.0	2.3	2.0	2.0	*	6.2	7.9	1.8
no. (in '000s)	(338.6)	(43.2)	(23.8)	(16.2)	(173.6)		(6.7)	(7.7)	(6.8)	(6.8)		(20.8)	(26.7)	(6.2)
1978														
%	100	12.0	5.2	3.6	50.6	2.9	2.4	2.7	1.3	2.0	*	7.3	9.1	1.0
no. (in '000s)	(416.7)	(49.9)	(21.7)	(15.0)	(210.7)	(12.0)	(10.0)	(11.1)	(5.2)	(8.4)		(30.3)	(37.9)	(4.4)
1983														
%	100	12.7	7.4	2.8	43.1	6.8	3.2	2.5	0.5	0.7	2.5	7.3**	9.4	1.2
no. (in '000s)	(461.8)	(58.7)	(34.0)	(12.8)	(199.3)	(31.4)	(14.6)	(11.5)	(2.1)	(3.4)	(11.5)	(33.7)	(43.4)	(5.5)

NOTE   **inc. 0.8% partly suspended

SOURCE: annual volumes of *Criminal Statistics, England and Wales.*

between 1963 and 1983. The total number of offenders sentenced at all courts increased during this period by almost 120%, from 211 000 (1963) to 462 000 (1983). (The number of non-indictable offenders sentenced during the same period increased by just 30% from 1 107 429 (1963) to 1 444 200 (1983), of whom just under three-quarters were convicted of motoring offences. Over 95% of non-indictable offenders were fined). There were overall *decreases* in the proportionate use of the following sentences:

Absolute and Conditional Discharges: decreased from being imposed on 1 in 6 of convicted offenders in 1963 to about 1 in 8 from the early 1970s onwards; this may well have been related to the increase in cautioning following the 1969 Children and Young Persons Act (see above, Chapter 2).

Probation (and Supervision) Orders: supervision orders replaced probation orders for juveniles in 1971. The combined use of these sentences dropped from one-fifth of all cases (1963) to one-tenth in 1983, after an even lower trough in 1978.

Care (and Approved School) Orders: the proportionate use of these orders remained steady for the first half of the 1963–83 period, with an increase in absolute numbers from 4000 to almost 7000, but in the following decade their use dropped dramatically to just over 2000, representing a decline in proportionate use from 2% to 0.5%.

Fines   This sentence has always been the most frequently used sentence, reaching a peak of over 51% in 1973 for indictable offenders. In the last five years the use of the fine has declined to 43% in 1983.

Mental Health Sentences: Part V of the Mental Health Act 1959 (now amended by the Mental Health Act, 1983) covered orders for committal to hospital after criminal proceedings. Figure 4.1 represents trends between 1961 and 1982 in orders made by type of mental disorder. It will be noted that the graph would, if all types of disorder were combined, seem to represent a steady and simple decline in the use of such orders over time. In fact the decline is almost wholly restricted to those assessed as 'subnormal'. It reflects a general change in the admission practices of mental handicap hospitals since 1961 (Robertson, 1984), civil admissions having declined alongside criminal admissions. Another significant trend over the period has been the increasing use of Special Hospitals (Broadmoor, Rampton etc) and the corresponding decrease in the use of local hospitals for Section 65 (hospital order with restriction) patients. There was a 50–50 split in type of hospital admitting s. 65 patients immediately after the 1959 Act, but now local hospitals only take 30% of such patients. The reason is expressed by Robertson (1984) as follows 'Restriction orders have never proved popular with local hospital consultants who, as a consequence of these orders, have been unable to discharge a patient quickly on the basis of an improvement in mental state' (p. 25). A final substantial decline can be referred to: that is in transfers *to* hospital *from* prison under Mental Health Act s.72 during sentence. This has declined from around 160 in 1963 to around 40 in 1975, rising since to stand now around 80. Although small in

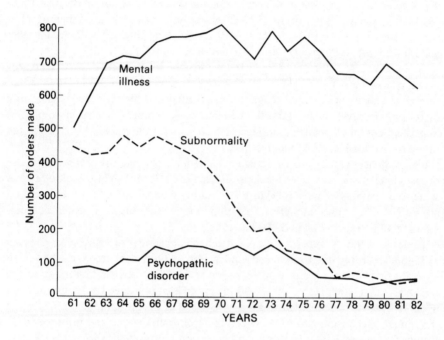

FIGURE 4.1 *Mental Health Act (1959) Orders (s. 60 + s. 65)* 1961–82, by type of disorder*

* Now replaced by Mental Health Act 1983, ss. 37 and 41, respectively.

SOURCE: Robertson 1984.

absolute terms, this trend may have significant effects upon prison function and prisoner morale.

Immediate Imprisonment, Youth Custody and 'Alternatives to Custody': the use of active prison sentences for indictable offenders dropped from 1 in 7 in 1963 to around 1 in 13 in 1973, but has risen marginally since then to 1 in 11 in 1983. Trends in the use of this sentence will be outlined briefly in this section, while the treatment of imprisonment in the latter part of the chapter will incorporate some discussion of the difficulties of interpretation of the statistics so glibly retailed here. For the moment, in this superficial tour of sentencing trends, a number of other disposals will be subsumed under, or linked with, the active custody category.

There were increases in the use of Attendance Centres and Detention Centres for young offenders during this period, and several new sentences derived from custody have become available to the courts. *Suspended sentences* were imposed upon nearly 9% of offenders in the year of their introduction (1968); their use dropped to 6% in 1973, after changes in law in the 1972 Criminal Justice Act restricted their use, but subsequently increased to 7% in the late 1970s and early 1980s. The figure for 1983 includes almost 4000 *partly suspended sentences*, and shows a slight decrease in relation to the year before, due largely to the introduction of youth custody sentences which cannot be suspended. *Community service orders* reached 3% by 1978, when they were available virtually throughout the country, and their use has risen steadily to its present level of around 7%. *Youth custody* replaced Borstal training and imprisonment for all young adults (aged 17–20 years) at the end of May 1983, so the figure represents just seven months' use.

If all sentences are divided into custodial and non-custodial, the proportionate use of custodial sentences dropped from just under 1 in 5 (19%) of all indictable offenders sentenced in 1963 to 1 in 7 (14%) in 1973, but has gradually crept up again to 1 in 6 (16%) by 1983. In absolute terms, this represents 72 000 custodial sentences, compared to 48 000 in 1973 and 39 000 in 1963.

Tables 4.2 and 4.3 present a more detailed breakdown of sentencing patterns 1973–83, according to age group and gender. Both of the general trends can be seen to have affected both age groups and each gender similarly. Interpreting trends in the use of custodial sentences for the 17–20 age group is complicated by the introduction of youth custody in 1983, which directly replaced Borstal training but also affected the numbers of young adults sentenced to Detention Centres and imprisonment. Comparing the use of youth custody and detention centres in the second half of 1983 with the use of Borstals, detention centres and imprisonment for 17–20 year-olds in the second half of 1982, the Home Office calculated that there was an increase in the overall use of custody in 1983, continuing the steady rise in custodial sentences for young offenders throughout the five years 1979–83 (Home Office 1984b, Table 7a p. 127). A Home Office Statistical Bulletin (2/85), published in February 1985, analysed the effects of the 1982 Criminal Justice Act upon the sentencing of young offenders, for the full year ending in June 1984 thus:

> Receptions of *males aged 17–20* under an immediate custodial sentence numbered about 410 a week in the year ending June 1984 compared with around 390 a week in 1981 and 400 a week in 1982. The increase after mid-1983 was not out of line with what might have been expected from the slow upward trend in recent years for this age group Receptions of *females aged 17–20* under an immediate custodial sentence rose to about 15 a week in the year ending June 1984 compared with 13 receptions a week in 1981 and 1982 of Borstal trainees and young prisoners combined. (Home Office Statistical Bulletin 2/85 paras 9–10)

Following changes in the minimum and maximum lengths of Detention Centre orders, and lower minima of 4 months (males) and 3 weeks (females) for Youth Custody orders when compared with the former Borstal minimum of 6 months (for

TABLE 4.2   Males and females, aged 17–20 years, sentenced for indictable offences, 1973–83

Year		Total	Abs./Cond. Discharge	Probation	Fine	C.S.O.	Attendance Centre	Detention Centre	Borstal	Youth Custody	Imprisonment Susp.	Imprisonment Immed.	Other
MALES													
1973	%	100	8	11	59	*	–[1]	6	7	*	3	3	3
	no. (in '000s)	(76.3)	(5.9)	(8.1)	(45.2)		(0.2)	(4.7)	(5.2)		(2.3)	(2.7)	(2.3)
1978	%	100	6	7	55	7	–[1]	6	7	*	5	6	2
	no. (in '000s)	(91.7)	(5.9)	(6.2)	(50.3)	(6.1)	(0.4)	(5.7)	(6.3)		(4.2)	(5.3)	(1.4)
1983	%	100	8	9	45	13	2	6	2	8	2	3	1
	no. (in '000s)	(115.6)	(9.7)	(10.8)	(51.8)	(14.9)	(2.4)	(6.7)	(2.8)	(9.6)	(2.1)	(3.3)	(1.4)
FEMALES													
1973	%	100	19	24	51	*	*	*	2	*	2	1	2
	no. (in '000s)	(8.4)	(1.6)	(2.0)	(4.3)				(0.2)		(0.2)	(0.1)	(0.2)
1978	%	100	17	18	54	2	*	*	2	*	4	2	1
	no. (in '000s)	(12.6)	(2.2)	(2.3)	(6.7)	(0.3)			(0.2)		(0.5)	(0.2)	(0.1)
1983	%	100	21	21	46	4	–[1]	*	1	3	2	1	3
	no. (in '000s)	(14.8)	(3.2)	(3.1)	(6.8)	(0.6)	–[2]		(0.1)	(0.4)	(0.2)	(0.2)	(0.1)

NOTE [1] Less than ½ per cent
[2] Less than 50.

SOURCE: based on Tables 7.9 and 7.10, *Criminal Statistics, England and Wales 1983*.

TABLE 4.3 Males and females, aged 21 years and over, sentenced for indictable offences, 1973–83

Year	TOTAL	Abs./Cond. Discharge	Probation	Fine	C.S.O.	Imprisonment Susp.	Imprisonment Immed.	Other
MALES								
1973 %	100	9	7	55	*	12	16	2
no.	(145.1)	(12.7)	(9.5)	(79.9)		(16.9)	(23.1)	(3.1)
(in '000s)								
1978 %	100	7	4	54	3	13	17	1
no.	(179.9)	(13.4)	(8.1)	(97.2)	(5.2)	(22.9)	(30.8)	(2.3)
(in '000s)								
1983 %	100	9	6	47	7	13[i]	18	1
no.	(216.2)	(18.4)	(13.3)	(100.8)	(14.3)	(28.1)	(38.0)	(3.1)
(in '000s)								
FEMALES								
1973 %	100	20	15	56	*	5	3	1
no.	(29.6)	(5.9)	(4.4)	(16.6)		(1.4)	(0.8)	(0.4)
(in '000s)								
1978 %	100	19	12	57	1	6	3	1
no.	(42.6)	(7.9)	(5.1)	(24.5)	(0.4)	(2.7)	(1.6)	(0.3)
(in '000s)								
1983 %	100	21	17	46	2	8[ii]	4	1
no.	(40.5)	(8.6)	(6.8)	(18.6)	(1.0)	(3.2)	(1.8)	(0.5)
(in '000s)								

NOTE   [i] includes 2% partly suspended
         [ii] includes 1% partly suspended

SOURCE: based on Tables 7.11 and 7.12 *Criminal Statistics England & Wales, 1983.*

both genders), there was a major switch by sentencers from Detention Centre to Youth Custody orders for males, with the average sentence for the former dropping to 11 weeks (as compared with 15 weeks before the changes); the average length of a youth custody sentence was just under 12 months, with about 40% of offenders sentenced to 6 months or less. For females sentenced to youth custody, the average sentence length was about 6 months, with more than half of those aged 17–20 sentenced to 4 months or less (Home Office Statistical Bulletin 2/85, paras 15, 17).

A number of interesting differences between the sentencing of males and females emerge from the data in Tables 4.2 and 4.3. Between 1973 and 1983 there was a larger increase in the number of females aged 17–20 sentenced than of males, 76% compared to 52%. In contrast, for those aged 21 and over the increase for males was slightly greater than for females (49% compared to 37%). In both age groups females are given absolute or conditional discharges proportionately twice as frequently as males (and it was seen in Chapter 2 that females of all ages are cautioned by the police more frequently than males). Probation orders are used twice as often for females aged 17–20 as for males of the same age, and three times as much as for women over 21. Community service orders are used three times as frequently for males as for females, and twice as frequently for 17–20 year olds of both genders as for older people. The proportionate use of all types of custodial sentences for males is some five times greater than for females. This is true for both age groups. Another gender difference is in availability of sanction. There are no Detention Centres for females.

The types of offence committed by females are somewhat different from those committed by males, and as sentencing obviously reflects offending this might explain the differences. In 1983, almost three-quarters of females' notifiable offences were theft or handling (compared to 45% for males); a further 9% were for fraud or forgery (compared to 5% for males). In the other direction, 18% of males were sentenced for burglary (compared to 4% for females) and 14% of males were sentenced for violent or sexual offences, compared to 6% for females (Home Office 1984b, Table 7.2 pp. 148–9). However a detailed comparison of the sentences imposed by offence group shows that some gender difference remains. Official statistics do not yield information on the previous convictions of males and females sentenced, and there is also the possibility that although the offence *categories* are the same, offence *seriousness* is not. Until we have routine or general information of these factors, we must be content with the research of Farrington and Morris (1983), which did take such factors into account, but was restricted to the decisions of magistrates in one town, Cambridge. Farrington and Morris concluded: 'In our study of magistrates' decisions, the sex of the defendant did not have any direct influence on the severity of the sentence . . . Women appeared to receive more lenient sentences . . . only because they had committed less serious offences and were less likely to have been convicted previously' (p. 245).

In order to bring together some of the findings and implications of this description of recent trends in the sentencing of adult offenders in England and Wales, a few salient features of currently available sentences will be examined.

Fines

More than 4 out of every 10 indictable offenders, and 19 out of 20 non-indictable, are fined by the courts. In the 1970s, half of all those convicted of indictable offences were fined. The slight decline in the popularity of the fine during the last 4–5 years may be attributed partly to the continued growth in the popularity of non-custodial penalties such as community service orders and suspended sentences of imprisonment, and may be a response to the increasing number of unemployed defendants appearing before the court, for whom a fine may be regarded as inappropriate (see Softley 1978, Moxon 1983). A related phenomenon has been the increase in committals to prison for fine default. As Richard Sparks (1973) pointed out, in one of the earliest studies of imprisonment for fine default, it is not possible to calculate precise committal rates for indictable and non-indictable offences, because of the different recording practices of different Home Office Departments. However, he estimated that between 1950 and 1968 the committal rate for males (aged 21 and over) convicted of indictable offences rose from 3.5% to over 6% of all those fined (Sparks 1973, pp. 93–4). Estimates of the overall rate of imprisonment for default of those fined for indictable *and* non-indictable offences during the 1970s indicated a proportion of 1% or less (Softley 1973; NACRO 1981). The most recent Prison Department statistics show that the annual number of males received into prison in default of payment of a fine increased from 0.7% of those fined in 1974 to 1.8% in 1983, for those aged 17–20, and from 0.8% to 1.4% of those aged 21 and above (Home Office 1984c, p. 97). For those convicted of indictable offences, the average committal rate appears to be around 5%, with variation from 2–3% of males fined for sexual offences to more than 13% of males fined for burglary, and over 20% of females fined for theft, handling and fraud (Home Office 1984c, Table 7.2 pp. 100–101; see also NACRO 1981).

Probation

From the early 1960s, and throughout most of the 1970s, there was a steady decline in the use of the probation order (and in the combined use of probation and supervision orders when these replaced probation for juveniles in 1971). There is no single explanation of this decline, although at different times the probation order can be seen to have lost clients to suspended sentences and community service orders. In the late 1960s and early 1970s it also seems that some offenders who would previously have been put on probation were being fined instead. It is hard wholly to account for the decline of the probation order. It is even harder to account for its resurgence in the years following the nadir of 1978, when fewer than 9% of those convicted of indictable offences were given probation or supervision orders; other non-custodial sentences have also increased during the same recent period, although, as noted earlier, fines are being used less frequently. It may well be that the speculation we made earlier, that probation supervision is seen by magistrates as more appropriate for many of the unemployed than a fine would be, is well-founded.

Since 1977, annual *Probation Statistics* have been published, providing more detail of the work of the probation service than was previously available. One important feature of the recent development of the service has been the introduction of the 6 month order in 1978, and a greater use of shorter orders in general. The proportion of 3 year probation orders decreased from 25% in 1972 to 4% in 1983, whereas the proportion of 1-year orders trebled from 11% (1972) to 33% (1983); by 1983, 5% of all orders were for less than 1 year (Home Office 1984d, Table 2.9, p. 32). 90% of those given probation each year have been convicted of indictable offences; half have been sentenced for theft or handling stolen goods; one in six for burglary; and some 2–3% for sex offences – although the use of probation for those convicted of sexual offences is higher than for most offence types, with 12–13% of them being given probation (compared with an average rate of 7%).

During the decade 1968–78, the decade of probation's decline, there were some major changes in the gender of those who got probation. The decline was sharper for males than females, the gender ratio changing from 77% male 23% female (1968) to 67% male 33% female (1978). The increase since 1978 has been accompanied by a slight reversal of this trend, so that in 1983 the ratio was 71%–29%.

Suspended sentences

When suspended sentences were introduced in 1968, following the Criminal Justice Act 1967, it was hoped by the Government that they would substantially, and permanently, reduce the number of persons given custodial sentences. But it was clear from the beginning that by no means all of the 25 000 offenders given suspended sentences in 1968 would have been given sentences of immediate imprisonment, if no provision for suspension had been introduced; instead, it is likely that many would have been fined or put on probation. Official estimates suggested that no more than half of those given suspended sentences would have been sentenced to imprisonment had the new power not existed (Bottoms 1981; see also Sparks 1971). Part of the reason for this 'malfunction', or failure of the courts to use the new measure in the way it was intended, was probably because, from the start, there were competing (or, in one sense, complementary) views about the aims of suspended sentences, so that alongside the official 'avoiding imprisonment' theory was a 'special deterrent' theory, that encouraged courts to use suspended sentences in place of *non-custodial* measures (see Bottoms 1981). Tony Bottoms' analysis of the operation of suspended sentences in their first decade showed that magistrates' courts appeared to use them rather more in the officially approved way than did the Crown Court. He also found clear evidence that 'magistrates' courts began to impose longer sentences in those cases where they suspended the sentence than they did in those cases in which they actually imposed imprisonment' (Bottoms 1981, p. 6). This is particularly significant in the light of the following facts. Three in ten of all offenders given suspended sentences are reconvicted of a new offence before the period of suspension has expired. Judicial instructions specify that under these circumstances the suspended sentence is usually activated (i.e. you go directly to jail). They further specify that any prison sentence in respect of the new offence be served consecutive to, and not concurrent with, the activated suspended sentence. In consequence, many of those reconvicted after a suspended sentence eventually go to prison for longer than they would if the original sentence had not been suspended. When it is also remembered that no more than half of those given suspended sentences would previously have been given a custodial sentence, it is clear that any contribution made by the suspended sentence to the reduction of the prison population can only be marginal. More importantly, the operation is unfair.

Community Service Orders

Although community service orders (CSOs) were introduced later and more gradually than suspended sentences (first in six 'experimental' areas, and later progressively throughout the country), their consistent growth in recent years marks an important development in penal policy. Their origins and implementation, like those of the suspended sentence, were surrounded by underlying theoretical ambiguities. As a result, most estimates have suggested that only 45–50% of those given community service orders received them as an alternative to custody (Pease *et al.* 1977; Pease 1981; Pease 1985a). The rate at which offenders are taken back to court for breaching the conditions of their CSO is almost half that of suspended sentences (which is only breached by a further offence), comprising about 17% of those given orders. Less than 40% of those breached are sentenced to immediate custody. These figures are comparable to those for the breach of probation orders, which occurs in around 16% of cases and results in the imprisonment of 40–45% of those who breach orders.

The 1982 Criminal Justice Act extended Community Service to 16 year-olds; in 1983 some 600 16 year-olds were given a CSO. It has always been a sentence disproportionately imposed on 17–20 year-olds, who constituted half of those given orders in 1983, a further third coming from the age group 21–30. Perhaps more surprisingly, and certainly more controversially, it is predominantly a sentence given to male offenders. In 1983 only 5% of those given CSOs were female (compared with 29% of those placed on probation), and there has been a slight decline in the proportion of females from the 7% of 1979. A quarter of those starting a CSO have been convicted of burglary, and less than half of theft or handling stolen goods. The previously recorded criminality of those sentenced to community service has increased in recent years. In 1983, only 11% were first offenders, compared with 22% in 1979; as many as 40% had served a previous custodial sentence, compared to 25% in 1979 (Home Office 1984d, p. 183).

Imprisonment: length of sentences
Despite widespread concern about prison overcrowding, there has been a slow but steady increase in the proportion of indictable offenders sentenced to custody since the mid 1970s. The recent introduction of youth custody in place of Borstal and imprisonment for young adults appears to have done nothing to stem the tide of prison receptions. The *rate of imprisonment* is, of course, only one of three related factors which importantly determine the size of the prison population. The other main factors are the *length of sentences* imposed and the operation of remission and other forms of executive discretion to release, such as parole, which combine to determine the prison population. A more detailed examination of this issue, and of the use of imprisonment, will be undertaken later in this chapter.

A special Home Office analysis of changes in the length of imprisonment 1968–78 showed that the proportion of sentences of up to and including six months dropped from 50% in 1968 to 46% in 1972–3, but then increased gradually to 55% by 1978; the proportion sentenced to over 4 years' imprisonment remained at around 3% throughout the period (Home Office 1979b, p. 45). *Criminal Statistics* for 1978 presented a similar analysis of trends during the same period for those sentenced to immediate imprisonment for all types of offence, which confirmed that there had been a decrease in shorter sentences between 1968 and 1973, followed by an increase – but the proportion of males sentenced to six months or less in 1978 was the same as the proportion in 1968, 60% (Home Office 1979a, Table 6.2). It is also of interest to note that the proportion of males and females given shorter sentences *by the Crown Court* in 1978 was much higher than it had been in 1968, whereas the proportion given shorter sentences by magistrates' courts was lower.

In the period 1979–83 the average length of sentence of imprisonment imposed on males aged 21 + for all types of offence and at all courts, dropped from 11.7 to 10.9 months (having dropped to 10.3 months in 1981–2). Most of the decrease occurred between 1980 and 1981, ostensibly associated with various judicial initiatives to reduce the length of prison sentences – including the perhaps undeservedly publicized cases of Upton and Bibi. Undeserved because the fall in average sentence length did not occur primarily in the types of case to which those judgements were directed. The changes were summarized as follows:

> After the first quarter of 1980, there were marked falls in the average length of sentence both at the Crown Court and at magistrates' courts, which seem to have been associated with these initiatives. There were further slight falls in 1981–2, which extended until the first half of 1983. For 1983 as a whole, the average sentence lengths for both types of court were the same as in 1982, but the overall average for all courts increased in 1983 because the proportion sentenced at the Crown Court rather than at magistrates' courts was higher in 1983 (59%) than in 1979–82 (54–55%). (Home Office 1984b, para 7.27)

In fact, at the same time as there was a drop in the average length of sentence at the Crown Court, there was a slight but significant increase in the proportionate use of imprisonment by the Crown Court from 49% of those sentenced in 1980 to 52% (1982–3). Sentence length and proportion imprisoned will vary negatively (imprisoning more people for short periods reduces average sentence length), so we should not be surprised by this. The net effect of the changes are set out thus: 'these factors have combined to produce an estimated eventual rise in the adult prison population of about 3000, almost entirely due to changes in sentencing at the Crown Court' (Home Office 1984b, para 7.32).

Sentencing Disparity and Sentencing Principle

No discussion of sentencing would be complete without some reference to the subject of sentencing disparity. An entire book could be written – many have been – on this single controversial yet fundamental topic. We have attempted to extend the range of points conventionally discussed in terms of disparity in the earlier chapters of this book. We have confirmed at least to our own satisfaction that disparity is evident at points in the process earlier than the pronouncement of sentence. Disparity is probably a ubiquitous feature of law enforcement and the administration of criminal justice. Accordingly no attempt will be made to add anything new to the continuing debate about disparities at the sentencing stage. Official statistical information is provided in one of the annual volumes of supplementary tables, showing details of sentencing practice at magistrates' courts and the Crown Court, according to police force area, and by Crown Court centre. Inspection of any of these statistics would reveal apparent and widespread discrepancies, with wide differences in the proportionate use of all available sentences. Any such 'surface reading' of the statistics can never be the end of the argument, 'proving' that disparities and injustice occur. They must instead be the *starting point* of the hard-grind research task of investigation of whether the many differences between the offences and offenders dealt with by courts in different parts of the country satisfactorily explain sentencing practices. While this is a sensible way of proceeding, when disparity is demonstrated, the response by sentencers 'Of course, we've changed things since you did the research. It's alright now.' should be ignored.

Much relevant research of the kind required has been done (see reviews in Hood and Sparks 1970; Bottomley 1973; Tarling 1979; see also Hood 1962, 1971). In this country, research to date has concentrated almost exclusively upon sentencing in magistrates' courts, with the judicial authorities denying the need and refusing the facilities for criminological research into sentencing in the Crown Court (Ashworth *et al.* 1984). When, or if, such research is allowed to take place, it will almost certainly reach conclusions consonant with those of research on magistrates' courts, and typified by the comments at the end of a recent Home Office study:

> . . . differences between courts in their use of the various disposals available cannot be accounted for wholly in terms of differences in intake and other external factors and . . . courts do have very different ways of dealing with similar types of offender. A reduction in these discrepancies is obviously a desirable aim and would result in a fairer and more just system of sentencing. (Tarling 1979, p. 44)

Having identified problems of disparity, it is perhaps worthwhile to determine whether the *overall* pattern of sentencing and sentencing change suggests anything about the styles of social control through the application of penal sanctions. Cohen (1979, 1985) argues that the degree of state control of individual behaviour has increased through greater penetration into informal networks of society. This view is encapsulated as a theory of dispersal of discipline. Bottoms (1983) has questioned this position, on the basis that those sanctions which are truly disciplinary have not been the ones whose use has increased in the recent past. He asserts that the major developments have been increases in those types of punishment (like fines, compensation orders and CSOs) which do not have a 'specific penal administrative apparatus designed to mould offenders into obedient subjects' (p. 176). In other words, penal control is becoming less disciplinary, not more so. Our reason for mentioning this debate is that the qualitative understanding of changing ideologies of social control can be addressed through statistics of punishment, yet Tony Bottoms was able, in 1983, to entitle his chapter '*Neglected* Features of Contemporary Penal Systems' (emphasis added). In other words, although it is possible to address ideological questions through readily available statistics, people haven't bothered. Developments like the rise of community service, and its mode of use for the unemployed, are ripe for analysis in terms of wider social theory.

Statistics of Imprisonment

In this section, statistics will be examined which deal with the sentence of imprisonment, its imposition, execution, reduction and circumstances. It takes off from the less detailed material in the earlier part of the chapter. The centrality of imprisonment to the British penal systems is the justification for this closer look.

There are many official statistics which deal with imprisonment, as befits the most severe sentence available in the English penal system. Many of these statistics are not beset by the same problems as were encountered with data in the earlier parts of the book. They are beset by different problems! For instance, there is not much room for argument that the number of people in prison now is significantly greater than it was in 1963, whereas there is doubt that the number of domestic burglaries has substantially increased between 1970 and 1982. However, whether the increase in prison population represents an increase or decrease in the severity of the agents of criminal justice is more open to doubt. Also open to doubt is the significance of the messages that come from statistics on prison discipline or prison medical treatment. However even the selective survey of official information on imprisonment which the reader will find in this section does pose important policy questions and offers insights into the effects of current policies.

Prisons and freedom: opposites in fact?

In the United Kingdom, the most severe penalty that can be imposed on an offender is imprisonment. The obvious question one would wish answered is how the use of imprisonment has changed over time. This is an extraordinarily difficult question to answer. It depends on what one counts as imprisonment and it depends on what one means by use. Prisons are not the only places where liberty is restricted. Most notably, Special Hospitals like Broadmoor and Rampton are places where people are sent by courts but which do not count in the statistics as prisons. Young people restricted by the local authority under care orders made by juvenile courts are not deemed to have been imprisoned. People in police cells are not recorded in prison statistics. People who are not prosecuted when they become voluntary patients in psychiatric hospitals are not counted as imprisoned. Offenders on whom hospital orders are made may be compulsorily detained in an appropriate hospital in lieu of punishment. Unless it is coupled with a restriction order, the hospital order enables a hospital to detain the patient only for a year in the first instance, albeit renewably. It may be thought that these mental health options (the general statutory framework is now to be found in the Mental Health Act 1959 (Amendment) Act 1983) are reasonable exceptions and do not seriously damage analysis of prison use (although see Waller and Chan 1974). However the liberality of use of ways of restricting people's freedom by means other than imprisonment clearly determines how many people remain to be imprisoned, and there are some major difficulties. For example, if the condition of an offender is determined to be mental impairment or psychopathy, the available treatment must be held to be such as to be likely to alleviate or to prevent a deterioration of his condition. This is perhaps a contributory reason for the trends in disposals of the mentally impaired under Mental Health legislation, which was described earlier in this chapter. Those whom treatment will not help take their chances in prison. If either treatment techniques or psychiatrists' self-confidence improves, all other things being equal there will be a reduction in the prison population by virtue of the conversion of prisoners into patients.

The looseness of the link between imprisonment and restriction of liberty means that even if the number of people in institutions designated prisons goes down, the total number of people without liberty may be going up. This may be true in the narrow sense set out above. It may also be true in a wider sense, namely that the number of things all of us can do and places we can go decreases. Prison is near one end of a continuum from total restriction to total liberty. South Africa provides a convenient example of an intermediate positon in which you need permission to live and work in particular places, and some places are completely forbidden to some people. Fences, regulations and lack of money restrict options for almost all of us, and in this wider sense the amount of imprisonment may be largely irrelevant to the amount of freedom generally.

Having recognized its limitations, we will nonetheless be dealing in this chapter with imprisonment in its narrowest sense, which involves the institutions run by the Home Office Prison Department in England and Wales. This does not mean that our problems of scope are over. The absolute numbers of people sent to prison or held in prison are the relevant statistics for a number of practical purposes. However, if one wants to express the number so as to discern changes in practice, does one use prison statistics in relation to the general population, or in relation to convictions for more serious (notifiable) offences? If the former, no allowance is made for changes in criminal activity in the population as a whole; if the latter, no account is taken of changes in police clear-up rate or prosecution policy. For example, the recent introduction and expansion of cautioning practice removes people from the statistics of those convicted. Statistics on those convicted or cautioned are swollen to the extent that the caution is used for at least some of those who would otherwise not have been officially processed at all (see Farrington and Bennett 1981, and the discussion in Chapter 5).

Prison receptions and prison population

A major choice to be made when examining statistics on imprisonment is that between statistics on prison receptions and statistics on prison populations. These two kinds of statistic are significantly different and generate significantly different conclusions when used in research or analysis. Table 4.4 shows the percentage of receptions and population by type of prisoner in 1983. Its purpose is simply to demonstrate that one gets an entirely different impression of the use of imprisonment by concentration on one rather than the other type of statistic. Because researchers and others so often fail to recognize these differences, it is important to labour the distinction somewhat.

Figures in the body of volumes of Prison Statistics tend to refer to either the number of people received into prison, 'receptions', or the number of people locked up on a specified date, 'population'. Table 4.4 contrasts statistics of the two kinds. What is the precise relationship between these two measures? The variable which links receptions and population is average length of detention. In the remainder of this chapter, analysis and illustration is restricted to prisoners under sentence of imprisonment, omitting civil prisoners, fine defaulters and those on remand. This means that average length of detention will be referred to as average length of sentence. This restriction to the number of prisoners under sentence is for ease of exposition only. The same principles apply, *mutatis mutandis*, for all groups of prisoner. Another simplifying assumption is that of constant sentencing policy over

TABLE 4.4   Prison receptions* and population, 1983

	Receptions (%)	Average Population (%)
Untried Criminal Prisoners	29	14
Convicted Unsentenced Prisoners awaiting Sentence or Enquiry	12	4
Prisoners Under Sentence	57	82
Non-criminal Prisoners	2	0
Total	100	100

NOTE   * The calculation of percentage receptions ignores the double counting involved as a result of, for example, a prisoner first being received as convicted but unsentenced and then again on sentence. Since the purpose of this Table is to demonstrate the different impressions conveyed by reception and population statistics, and since other conventions would have led to even more stark contrasts, this form of presentation is preferred.

SOURCE: derived from *Prison Statistics England and Wales 1983*.

periods of a few years. Again this assumption is for the sake of clarity. It does not make much difference to the figures to be presented, but the extra precision could be obtained by making adjustments. For present purposes, it isn't worth it.

The basic relationship between receptions under sentence and sentenced prison population is that population equals receptions multiplied by sentence length. Of course this relationship could equally well be stated as receptions equalling population divided by sentence length or sentence length equalling receptions divided by population. This sort of simple arithmetic makes it clear why statistics on receptions and population look so different. The prison population contains a higher proportion of long-sentence prisoners than does a cohort of receptions. This is a fact of fundamental importance in understanding prison statistics, and indeed statistics from other types of institution. The proportion of geriatric patients admitted to hospital is much lower than the proportion of geriatric patients in hospital at any time, because of the average long stay of such patients.

Returning to a discussion of prisons specifically, we should note that countries may vary in number of prison receptions, and may also vary in average sentence length. Many of the possible combinations are to be found somewhere. This point is illustrated by figure 4.2, which is taken from the Council of Europe's *Prison Information Bulletin* of June 1984. Along the bottom of the Figure is to be found the number of committals (receptions) to prison per 100 000 population, and down the side the prison population on a particular date. It will be noted that although the Netherlands and the Federal Republic of Germany have similar rates of reception, they have contrasting prison populations, with the German rate being about three times the Dutch rate. Contrasting Spain and Denmark, it will be seen that their prison populations are similar, but their rates of reception are very different. The message of this section, that population and reception statistics yield quite different and often contrasting images of prison use, is thus reinforced.

The data of Figure 4.2 demonstrate clearly the divergences between reception and population statistics. The Council of Europe data serve that purpose beautifully. However because of their lack of correspondence with some earlier data on the same topic (see e.g. Fitzmaurice and Pease 1982), judgement is reserved on whether they represent fair international comparisons. At the time of writing, one of us (KP) is scheduled to visit the Council of Europe in Strasbourg to clarify the issue.

But has the use of custody changed?

Enough has now been written to persuade the reader that discerning trends in custodial sentencing is by no means a simple matter. However the point in the chapter has now been reached at which we must stop bewailing the difficulties. We have chosen to express prison receptions and population in proportion to the number of convictions for indictable offences. This is because the people available to be sent to prison are those convicted of more serious offences, and the number of indictable offences provides a rough and ready index of such crime. It is rough and ready because not all imprisonable offences are indictable, juveniles convicted for indictable crime cannot be sent to prison, and it is clear that decreased use of police discretion will increase the number of indictable offences leading to conviction, and this will distort the trends. The analysis of trends is thus very approximate. One justification for doing the exercise is that, particularly if the trends for population and receptions differ, some insight into what may be happening may be gained. Figure 4.3 shows a steady decline in the number of prison receptions per finding of guilt, and an increase and subsequent decrease in the population per conviction for an indictable offence. This means that the average length of detention increased until about 1960, so much so that population increased despite a reduction in receptions. Since that time until recently the two trends have run roughly in parallel, suggesting that sentence length has stabilized, an impression generally confirmed in discussions of sentence length changes in annual volumes of criminal statistics. The increase in receptions during the last few years accompanied by a continuing decline in average sentence length is consistent with an increased use of short custodial sentences (since increasing receptions of trivial offenders for short terms of imprisonment will tend to reduce average sentence length, just as increasing admissions of the not-very-ill into hospital will reduce average length of patient stay). These, though, are merely preliminary thoughts. Following the hares released is well beyond the scope of this book. For the trends up to 1954, however, we have an authoritative study by the Statistical Adviser to the Prison Commission. He analysed changes in prison use between 1938 and 1954, and concluded that:

(i) The largest factor in the increase of prison population is the increased number of persons convicted of indictable offences; particularly of breaking and entering offences but with offences against the person also of importance.

(ii) The next largest factor is the increased average length of sentence at higher courts.

(iii) There is a slight tendency for higher courts to use imprisonment more . . . (Home Office, 1956, p. 46)

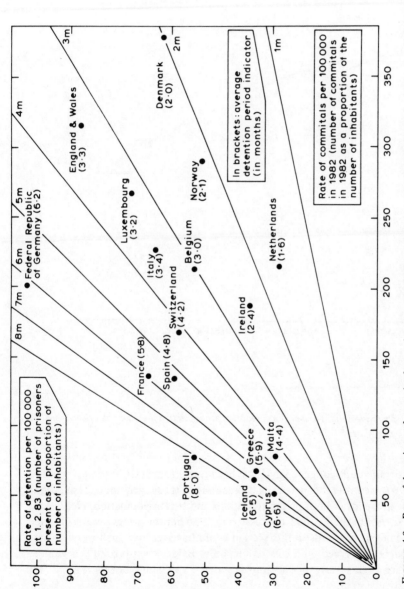

FIGURE 4.2 Rate of detention and committals to prison per 100 000 population, in Council of Europe member states, 1982–3

SOURCE: Council of Europe *Prison Information Bulletin*, No. 3 June, 1984, p. 24.

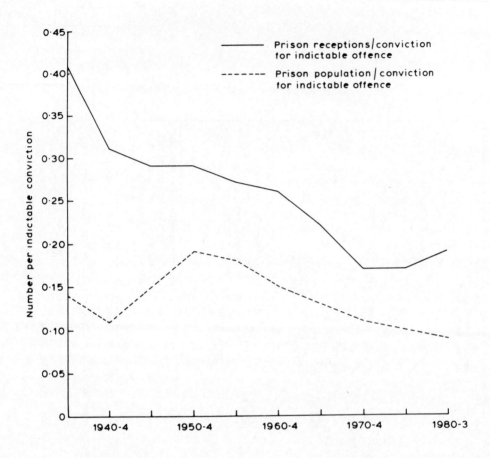

FIGURE 4.3　Prison receptions and prison population per conviction for indictable offence, England and Wales 1935–83

No equally detailed subsequent analysis has been carried out and is no doubt overdue. Baldock (1980) identifies the increasing prosecution of those aged under 21 as a significant factor in trends of both prison receptions and prison population. Neither the Statistical Adviser to the Prison Commission in 1956 nor the present writers in their superficial analysis of trends in this section could have reached such a conclusion, since they were concerned with convictions only. Baldock's approach is a salutory reminder that events early on do impact upon happenings downstream in the criminal justice system.

Early release and prison population trends

Figure 4.3 demonstrated a significant change of trends since the 1960s. It is tempting to implicate executive action in reducing sentence length in this shift. It was during this period that the Reports of the Prison Commissioners assumed an increasingly frantic tone about the problems of overcrowding in prisons, and was the period when action was taken to reduce this. Most important in the longer term was the introduction of parole, but changes in the rules governing remission for good conduct, and the counting of pre-sentence custody towards the time served after sentence were also important steps towards the regulation of sentence length by executive means. This is not the place to attempt a history of these changes in any detail. However this trend has been a significant one. The question which seems the right one to pose is 'How different would the sentenced prison population be if the sentence of the court was the sentence served?' Table 4.5 shows how this can be calculated for adult male prisoners received into prison to serve determinate sentences (i.e. excluding lifers) in 1983. Column 1 shows the sentence length band in months. Column 2 shows the number of receptions in that sentence band in that year. Column 3 shows what would be the average effective sentence length if the various executive devices like parole and remission did not exist, and column 4 shows the average effective sentence length for that group. Column 5 shows what the prison population would be if the sentence lengths in column 3 actually applied, and column 6 shows what the prison population actually was in this sentence band. (The reader will no doubt recognize that certain approximations are involved in these calculations: for example roughly constant sentencing practice is assumed, and no account is taken of events like deaths in prison. For column 3, all sentences are assumed to lie at the mid-point of the sentence band. Sentences of over ten years are assumed to be of average length twelve years (see Pease 1980)).

Contrasting columns 5 and 6, it is evident that the prison population is rather less than half what it would be if it were not for the various forms of executive intervention. In this way, it can be concluded that the Home Office is about as important as the judiciary and the magistracy in determining how much imprisonment is suffered!

The image we get, of a Department of State making spectacular reductions in effective sentence length and hence in prison population, is very much at odds with the rhetoric of the separation of powers between executive and judiciary. Furthermore, the relevant research shows not only an overlap in the determination of sentence length, but even an overlap in the criteria by which sentence length is adjusted. For both court and Parole Board, it seems, the information that is most crucial includes seriousness of initial offence and prior criminal record (see Nuttall *et al.* 1977). This correspondence should trouble those who see the separation of powers as a necessary safeguard against injustice. It reveals parole as in large measure a form of re-sentencing without appeal.

This may be illustrated by data from the 1984 Report of the Parole Board (Home Office, 1985d). Figure 4.4 shows the proportion of prisoners recommended for release after a first review in 1984. (The number of prisoners recommended for release is only trivially different from the number released, the difference being the

TABLE 4.5   The effects of executive release on 1983 prison population

1 Sentence bands	2 Number of Receptions in 1983	3 Effective sentence length in months, no executive modification of sentence	4 Effective sentence length in months to yield 1983 prison population	5 Prison Population, No executive modification of Sentence	6 Prison Population in 1983
Up to 3 months	11339	1.5	1.3	1417	1266
Over 3 months and up to 6 months	8873	4.5	3.3	3327	2474
Over 6 months and under 18 months	9655	12.0	6.4	9655	5164
18 months	2257	18.0	11.5	3386	2168
Over 18 months and up to 4 years	6019	33.0	15.7	16552	7888
Over 4 years and up to 10 years	1243	84.0	31.7	8701	3283*
Over 10 years	93	144.0	54.3	1116	421*
Total	39479	–	–	44154	22664

* In recent issues of prison statistics, population in these two bands has not been distinguished. The total falling in the two cells is correct for 1983. The proportions falling in the two cells are estimated from an earlier year (1977).

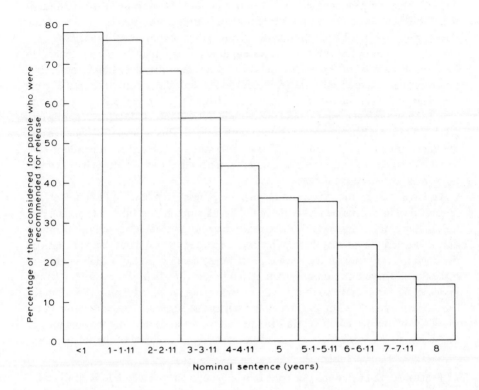

FIGURE 4.4   Parole release recommendations by sentence length, 1984

SOURCE: Derived from *Report of the Parole Board 1984*.

cases the Home Secretary vetoes). It is evident that the longer the sentence, the less your chances of being released. The same pattern is also in evidence for those receiving second or subsequent reviews. This pattern must emerge either because the offence and sentence itself is influential in the parole decision, or because experience has shown that people with longer sentences are reconvicted more. Table 4.7 below shows precisely the opposite to be the case. In short, the official published statistics of the Parole Board show that the Board operates in a way which is officially denied, as a resentencing body.

Were judges to resent the intrusion of the Parole Board into their proper domain, they would be able to strike back. Simply increasing the length of the sentences they impose would offset sentence reduction by parole and remission. It has been suggested (by, for example, Marshall 1974) that this has in fact happened. The evidence shows that it has not happened. Walker (1981a) shows there to have been no general increase in sentence length imposed to nullify executive sentence reduction. Walker's crucial Table is reproduced as Table 4.6. In fact, it could be argued that an aspect of this Table not mentioned by Walker reinforces his argument. Readers will note that the 2–3 year sentence band was increasingly used during the critical 1966–72 period. However the complex rules of parole eligibility mean that people sentenced to between 18 months and 3 years had the *same* parole eligibility date. This is incredible, but true. People sentenced within this band on the same day would have been eligible for release on parole on the same day, irrespective of the nominal sentence imposed. The 2–3 year sentence band should therefore literally empty if judges took parole into account. It in fact becomes more popular with judges. This is powerful evidence that the huge influence of the Home Office in determining time served in prison is real, and not the result of judges passing longer sentences in the expectation that they will be reduced by executive means.

We have seen in the preceding pages how general trends in imprisonment and release from imprisonment have moved. The statistics are useful in suggesting that the judiciary and magistracy have decreased their proportionate use of imprisonment during the period under study, but that the prison population is now held in check by the massive use of executive release procedures, notably parole, which operate to make the effective duration of sentences fall to less than half of the nominal length imposed. The statistics also show that judges have not retaliated against the increased use of executive release by passing longer sentences. In these ways and many others the fairly full published prison statistics provide a partial insight into the operation of the system. These insights are limited by the sheer complexity of the relationships

TABLE 4.6   Sentence-lengths over 18 months of men received into English and Welsh prisons

Lengths of Sentence	Cumulative percentages (i.e. each percentage includes the one(s) above)						
	1966	1967	1968	1969	1970	1971	1972[1]
Over 18 months but							
not over 2 years	35.4	37.3	36.5	38.2	40.1	36.2	36.3
under 3 years	46.7	47.1	48.9	53.3	55.4	50.1	49.9
not over 3 years	71.7	72.3	72.3	75.1	73.6	73.1	73.4
not over 4 years	83.3	83.8	84.6	86.8	85.3	85.3	85.2
not over 5 years	90.7	91.2	91.8	92.8	91.9	92.1	92.6
not over 7 years	95.7	96.1	96.4	96.6	96.6	96.4	96.6
not over 10 years	97.5	97.8	97.9	98.0	98.1	97.9	98.1
Total receptions[2] (= 100%)	5283	4970	5524	6663	8295	7493	7766

NOTE   [1]   It is not possible to analyse subsequent years receptions in this way, because in 1973 the Prison Department's relevant table combined some of the higher bands, *e.g.* grouping together all sentences over 18 months and up to four years.
[2]   Life sentences have been included in the small percentage which exceeded 10 years.

SOURCE: reproduced with permission from Walker (1981a), p. 830; based on Table C.5 of Prison Department Annual Reports.

involved. To some extent they are also limited by the ever-changing presentation of the statistics. One of the most infuriating problems that those using the statistics encounter is that there never seems to be a long enough run of years without some aspect of the tables being changed in ways which make them no longer comparable with earlier statistics. This accounts for most of what looks at first sight like some eccentric choices of time-span in this chapter. Finally, some important features of sentencing practice are not evident from the published statistics at all, or at least without supplementary data. Two of these will be dealt with here. They are the use of preferred numbers in sentencing to imprisonment, and the search for a reduction in prison population by the increased use of non-custodial sentences.

Preferred numbers

What is lacking from aggregate statistics on sentences of custody is any indication of how long individual sentences of imprisonment are. The only clues to be gleaned from this chapter so far is that in Table 4.5 there were 2257 receptions for sentences of eighteen months *alone*. In Figure 4.4 there were enough people given sentences of precisely five years to justify a separate column in that Figure. This is just the visible tip of an iceberg of conventional lengths which has been consistent for at least a century. The distribution of sentence lengths imposed has been very uneven, with particular lengths being used often, and others not at all. On 4th February 1884 Sir Edmund du Cane (remembered now, if at all, for the road named after him, on which stands Wormwood Scrubs prison) wrote to the Permanent Under-Secretary of State at the Home Office in a condition of obvious outrage 'I beg leave to request that you will call the attention of the Secretary of State to certain points connected with the terms of the sentences awarded by the various criminal courts, as I venture to think that . . . a considerable amount of unnecessary suffering might be saved without any diminution of the efficiency of the law; and that a very appreciable economy in the cost of our penal establishments might be effected.' Sir Edmund took part of the problem to be that of the tendency of judges to pass prison terms equivalent to periods of transportation conventionally used. He concluded – 'It is impossible (not) to feel that some more exact measurement is possible than is exhibited in the above figures, and, if it is possible, that the present arbitrary practice is incapable of justification.' Eleven years later Sir Francis Galton noted the same pattern, with short sentences clustering around the three, six, nine and twelve month marks, with longer sentences rounded to whole years, with even longer gaps between the conventional very long sentences imposed. Nearly a century later, Pease and Sampson (1977) noted the same pattern, reproduced here as Figure 4.5 So what? Ashworth (1983) describes the recognition of preferred numbers thus: 'This is a vital step towards understanding the way in which sentencing practice produces a given prison population, and it suggests that in medium or long prison sentences there is less regard to each month, let alone each week, of incarceration.' The crudity of scaling sentence against offence is something which does indeed lie at the centre of the pivotal decision in criminal justice, the sentence.

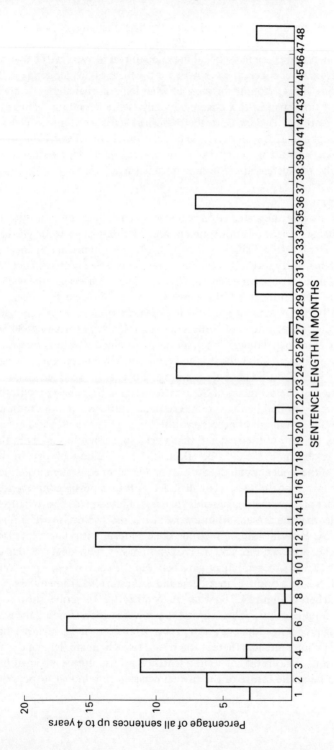

FIGURE 4.5   *Frequency of prison sentence by length*

SOURCE: first appeared in Pease and Sampson (1977).

Trying to reduce the prison population

Besides the executive release procedures which halve the prison population, there have been other attempts to reduce the number of people in prison by reducing the number of people sent there. That is to say, substituting non-custodial for custodial sentences has been tried in an attempt to reduce the prison population. 'Alternatives to custody' for adults introduced since 1960 have included suspended sentences of imprisonment, partly suspended sentences of imprisonment, supervised suspended sentences, probation orders with enforcable conditions, and community service orders. None of these sentence types has been used exclusively as an alternative to custody. This important point was dealt with earlier in the chapter. The best estimate of their use in place of active custody has approximated to 50% virtually whenever and wherever studied (Pease 1985a). Whether this partial success is worthwhile is open to doubt, given the confusion and active trickery which often attend the imposition of serious non-custodial penalties (see for example Vass 1984). However, the purpose of this section is not to pontificate on the value of alternatives to custody, but to use prison statistics to demonstrate that the substitution of non-custodial for custodial sentences is likely to provide a very low-geared means of reducing the prison population. The reader is invited to look back again to Table 4.5. Column 2 of that Table shows the number of receptions into prison (excluding fine and other defaulters) in 1983, by sentence imposed. Column 6 shows the prison population (with the same exclusions) by sentence imposed. It is evident that the sentence bands up to and including six months account for 51% of receptions but only 17% of population. It is the people given the shortest sentences who are the most obvious candidates for diversion from custody. However, to attempt to reduce the sentenced prison population by a mere 17%, over half the custodial decisions of the courts would have to be substituted by non-custodial decisions. As if this were not enough, it is also the case that the shorter the sentence, the higher the proportion of the people who are reconvicted, and the sooner after release they are reconvicted, as inspection of any volume of Prison Statistics will bear witness. One of the virtues of imprisonment is that people are unlikely to be reconvicted during a prison sentence. Replacing custodial with non-custodial sentences is bound to increase the speed of further conviction among that group which already includes the most frequent visitors to the dock. This means that the 51% of custodial decisions which would have to be changed to reduce the sentenced population by 17% is in fact a substantial underestimate. The real extent of change of sentencing practice which would be necessary to achieve that modest reduction is much greater. Obviously the general point about how difficult it is to achieve substantial reductions in prison populations by the use of non-custodial alternatives also applies to any particular group of short-term prisoners. Fine default is a convenient case in point. In 1983 there were 23 241 receptions of fine defaulters into prison, but the prison population of fine defaulters was only 900! To achieve significant reductions of the prison population by diverting the most obvious groups, like fine defaulters, is truly a daunting proposition. This is in no way to suggest that less serious offenders should not be diverted from prison. If they are, though, it should be on the basis of judgements that their offence is too trivial to deserve being locked up for. Nor are we denying that diversion from custody might achieve some relief for that part of the prison system under greatest pressure, namely local prisons. It is simply that one of the clear lessons of published prison statistics is the difficulty of making substantial inroads into the prison *population* by action to divert short-term prisoners.

Reconviction statistics

Annual prison statistics contain extensive information on reconvictions after a custodial sentence. Table 4.7 contains such information in some detail for adult male prisoners. It is instructive to note how completely overtones of success have been removed from presentations of such statistics as time has gone on. Between the wars, there was no reluctance to interpret reconviction rates as indicating relative success. Table 4.8 allows comparisons of male and female prisoners' rate of reconviction since 1975. It shows a majority of male prisoners and a substantial minority of female prisoners being reconvicted within two years of release. However the picture should not really be looked at in such an undifferentiated way.

At various points in this book we have referred to the idea of a criminal career, as a shorthand for the way in which people move through various encounters with the criminal justice system, and how and when they exit from it. Looking at criminal justice in this way offers an overview of events not otherwise possible. Information about the career is as yet largely unavailable, and it is probably true to say that only in North America has extensive research on this way of looking at criminality been attempted. However even the fragmentary information available in England and Wales may be worth having. Chapter 7 will suggest that, among juveniles, the best prediction a sentencer can make following a first conviction is that no second conviction will occur within two years of the first. If there is a second conviction, it is more likely to be for a different type of crime than for the same type of crime. This sort of information encourages a mental set of direct relevance to the sentencing task.

TABLE 4.7　Adult male prisoners: two-year follow-up of those discharged in 1980

Length of Sentence from which discharged	*Number Discharged*	*Percentage not Reconvicted*[*]	*Percentage Reconvicted but not Reimprisoned under sentence*	*Percentage Reconvicted and Reimprisoned under sentence*
Over 3 months up to and including 18 months	18151	47	24	29
Over 18 months up to and including 4 years	5992	52	22	26
Over 4 years	1279	71	12	17

[*] All reconvictions included are for standard list offences.

SOURCE:　derived from *Prison Statistics England and Wales 1983*.

TABLE 4.8   Persons reconvicted[1] within two years of discharge: by year of discharge and sex

Year of discharge	Males reconvicted		Females reconvicted	
	Number	*Per cent*	*Number*	*Per cent*
1973	20,800	54	360	33
1974	21,300	57	380	39
1975	24,600	60	500	41
1976	25,600	58	600	43
1977	26,600	59	580	40
1978	26,500	58	590	40
1979	27,200	58	640	42
1980	29,400	60	700	41

[1]   Estimates based on samples of discharges excluding those discharged from prison sentences of 3 months or less.

SOURCE: *Prison Statistics England and Wales 1983*, Table 8(a).

What can be said about the subsequent criminal careers of those discharged from prison in the most recent year on which information is available (1980)? Table 4.7 set out the relevant information in a simplified form. When looking at Table 4.7 it should be remembered that courts in England and Wales have a tendency to punish persistence. That is to say, an increased number of convictions will by itself increase sentence severity. Even so, it will be noted that almost half of those reconvicted were not recommitted to prison. How is this point relevant? There is an obvious danger in assuming that those released from custody who are reconvicted are reconvicted of an offence as serious as the last one. The statistics show that this assumption is clearly not tenable. In nearly half of the reconvictions after release from prison, the court, despite the offender's record, did not consider the offence to merit a further custodial sentence. This was true even where the previous prison sentence had been a long one. This message from prison statistics is an important one for a court to hold in mind when sentencing, and under the present system of parole also an important one for the Parole Board to think about when making release decisions.

Although data for adult females is not available in precisely the same form as for males, it is evident in Table 4.9 that reconvictions are less common for adult female ex-prisoners (41% within two years). The picture is less sanguine for young prisoners of either gender than for their adult counterparts, being gloomiest for the graduates of the now-defunct Borstals (defunct at least in name, although youth custody centres have taken over the buildings, and there is no sensible reason for hope of improvement in reconviction record). 71% of Borstal trainees were reconvicted within two years.

Data on other aspects of prison functioning

Various aspects of institutional life are covered in annual prison statistics and reports on the work of the Home Office prison department. Three will be briefly mentioned

TABLE 4.9 Percentages of offenders discharged in 1980 reconvicted[1] within two years: by type of custody and sex

Type of custody on discharge	Males		Females
		Percentage	
Adult prisoners	51		39
Young offenders:			
Detention centres	68		*
Borstal training – aged 15–16	81		46
– aged 17–20	69		41
Young prisoners	69		54
Total (young offenders)	69		46
All offenders	60		41

[1] Estimates based on samples of discharges excluding those discharged from prison sentences of 3 months or less.

SOURCE: *Prison Statistics England and Wales 1983*, Table 8(b).

as having particular significance. These are overcrowding, discipline and administration of psychotropic and hypnotic drugs.

On overcrowding, the statistics make it clear how specific the problem is to male local prisons. The average number of inmates in such prisons in 1983 was 44% greater than stated accommodation. Closed prisons for women were 21% and remand centres for male offenders 30% overoccupied, on average. In contrast, open training prisons for men and detention centres were underoccupied. The prison system as a whole was 12% overoccupied on an average day in 1983. It would be possible but unhelpful to plot the relationship between 'certified normal accommodation' and average population during the period of central concern to this book. Such an analysis would show the same basic pattern throughout the period, with local prisons for men being always the type of institution with the greatest excess of population over accommodation, with the size of that excess growing. The reason for scepticism about the usefulness of the approach lies in concern about the stability of the accommodation measure, which seems to change in ways not obviously related to building programmes and seems also to involve some complex discretionary judgements. In any event, it is instructive to note that the Prison Department also now uses the measure of 'maximum operational capacity' to denote the population at which some aspect of a prison's infrastructure (like the sewers) cease to cope with the demands placed on them.

Statistics on prison offences and discipline convince one what orderly places prisons must be! For both males and females in 1983 there were 1.6 punishments per head of average population. While double the figure of twenty years earlier, this still means that a prisoner is punished for an offence only once every 7½ months. Since each offence attracts 1.6 punishments, this actually means one offence per prisoner per year, a rate which no doubt many junior schools might envy. Furthermore, the vast majority of offences are those of the most vaguely-worded offences 'disobedience or insubordination' (28%) and the catch-all 'offences against order and discipline'

(27%). The more serious offences of assault against an officer or fellow-prisoner and actual or attempted 'gross personal violence', all combined, do not amount to more than 4% of offences. This, it will be recalled, is a figure which includes attempts. The triviality of the bulk of prison offences is reflected in the punishments awarded. Less than a third of punishments involved any forfeiture of remission.

Since 1979, the Prison Department's reports have included information about medicines dispensed. What has been remarkable about this information has been the extremely high levels of dosage of mood or arousal-changing drugs in women's prisons. This was lower in 1983 than in the preceding years because:

> the statistics for 1983 are the first to benefit from the instruction to prison pharmacists to deduct from their returns doses which had been dispensed but had not been used. The statistics . . . relate to doses administered, not (as in previous years) the number dispensed. (Home Office, 1984f, para 252)

Nonetheless, while for the system as a whole an average of 28 doses of psychotropic or hypnotic drugs were administered, in women's prisons the average inmate receives a staggering 195 doses per year. The prison reports deliberately disguise individual doctors: 'those establishments in which medical services are largely provided by a single doctor have been grouped with others as it is not considered appropriate to publish information about an individual doctor's prescribing practice' (Home Office, 1984f, footnote 3, Table 7). There remain wide differences between institutions, even where there are no obvious characteristics of the prison which might account for the differences.

Differences in drug prescription habits among prison doctors are easier to describe than to explain. Like many of the statistics produced by the prison department, they perform the useful function of demonstrating that there is something to explain. Whether anyone cares enough to follow up such differences is another matter. Sometimes the explanation of differences between establishments might lie in an unexpected quarter. For instance, one table in the annual prison statistics sets out 'means of restraint applied to violent or refractory inmates'. One of these means is segregation in a 'protected room'. For this fact to be recorded as such, the room used has to have been designated as a protected room. However some recent reports of the Prison Inspectorate have made it clear that some prison staff have been using rooms in this way other than those designated. To quote from the 1983 report of the Prison Inspectorate on Ashford Remand Centre:

> The hospital also contained a protected room and other rooms which were used as 'stripped rooms' occasionally. We were concerned that these rooms had not been certified in accordance with Prison Rule 23 . . . We were not satisfied that staff clearly understood the use of the 'stripped room'. In the absence of any requirement for this kind of room we felt that it was in the interests of both staff and inmates that they should either be designated as special cells or be converted to protected rooms. We recommend accordingly. (para 3.17)

The extent to which differences between establishments in recorded methods of restraint are an artefact of differences like this is not known.

Endnote

This chapter has had to select its facts from among those available to a greater extent than has been the case elsewhere in this book. In one sense this is a tribute to the Home Office in its proper readiness to provide information, information which is by no means used to its fullest possible extent. It is right that the need to provide information should be felt, since prison represents the greatest control which the state takes over an unwilling citizen. Another reason for accountability about prisons is their cost, currently around £600 million annually, having tripled in less than a decade. Current statistics on the imposition and exaction of the sentence of imprisonment are substantial. They provide a firm basis for the imaginative user to engage in informed debate on major policy issues. It is hoped that one of the aims of the book may be fulfilled in sensitizing readers to such possibilities.

5

Juvenile Justice in the United Kingdom

The last two decades have contained much debate about the treatment of juvenile offenders. In England and Wales we have moved from the optimism and radicalism of the early 1960s, through the dissatisfactions and disarray of the 1970s, into what some would regard as the tough realism, and others as the reactionary pessimism of the 1980s. This last flies under the banner of 'law and order' and is fuelled by the export of British football disturbances into the stadia of Europe.

In earlier chapters of this book some features of the official picture of juvenile offending in this country have been noted. The proportion of known offenders who are under the age of 17 has been steadily declining over the last 20 years. Nonetheless the peak age of offending remains within the mid-teens, as far as any judgements of this kind can be based on the ages of known offenders. The rate of known offending among *boys* aged 10–13 has hardly increased at all. The big increase in police cautioning that occurred during this period seemed to suggest that much juvenile offending, especially by those aged under 14, was of a relatively trivial kind, committed by those not previously known to the police.

Before examining the practice of juvenile justice throughout the United Kingdom, it must be emphasized that the sort of data being used here should not be regarded as yielding a definitive picture. This is true of both extent and type of offending 'out there' in the community. The official data may well exaggerate the contribution of juveniles, perhaps particularly those from poor families, to the perceived 'crime problem'. Less plausibly, but tenably, it may understate the extent of their responsibility for crime. The findings of surveys of self-reported delinquency do not conclusively aid us here, beyond the fact, now accepted as a truism, that most children and young people, like most adults, commit criminal offences for which they are never caught, and of which no official record of any kind exists. Given the limits of the information at our disposal, and the scope of this book, we must remain content to examine what has been happening in recent years to those young offenders who have been caught, and to see how far differences in official policy objectives are reflected in the practice of juvenile justice.

The remarkable fact is that the three jurisdictions within the United Kingdom operate with quite different structures and philosophies of juvenile justice. The differences within the jurisdictions are much more marked for juveniles than for adults. There were many instances during the remainder of the book where we were tempted to point up differences between the jurisdictions and consider their implications. For instance differences in changes in clear-up rates are worthy of comment, as is the fact that while Great Britain operates a parole system, Northern Ireland has conditional release, given to virtually all prisoners at the nominal 'half-time' of their sentence. It proved possible, albeit with difficulty, to forgo comparative essays for the adult sytem. We cannot forgo a comparative essay when dealing with juveniles. As one review body opined:

> Current arrangements for dealing with juvenile offenders in the United Kingdom . . .
> are the result of an accommodation of different ideologies. Neither Scotland nor
> England and Wales nor Northern Ireland adheres rigidly to solely welfare or criminal
> justice principles. (Black Report 1979, para 5.13)

Or, as another commentator on the Northern Ireland scene put it, when answering his own question on the role of deterrence in the official ideology of the juvenile justice system in each country: 'in the Scottish system "none"; in the English system "some"; and in Northern Ireland "quite a lot" ' (Gormally 1978, p. 147).

Recent experience in the three jurisdictions will be compared, particularly for the period 1968–83, as far as available data permit. The three primary, and related, questions to be addressed are:

(i) What trends are apparent in the rate of known offending among juveniles, in comparison with that of adults?
(ii) How far are juvenile offenders being diverted from formal court hearings, and does this take place at the cost of 'widening the net' of juveniles of whom official notice is being taken?
(iii) To what extent does each jurisdiction resort to custodial measures in responding to juvenile crime?

Trends in Juvenile Offending

Most public statements about the extent of juvenile delinquency in a country are based upon the number of juveniles found guilty in court, in comparison with the number of their elders suffering the same fate. Such statistics, taken by themselves, are of very little value in any serious discussion of trends. There are two problems here. The first is that burgled homes, for instance, do not usually contain information about the age of the burglar! Whenever *nothing* is known about an offender, obviously his/her age is not known. Thus, the relative amounts of juvenile delinquency and adult criminality are unknown. The second problem is that there are substantial efforts made to keep juvenile offenders out of court. Insofar as these efforts are successful, the conclusions drawn from court data will be misleading. There is no real answer to the first problem, short of large-scale and trustworthy self-report studies. As to the second, it is essential for those who wish to use court statistics on juveniles to say something about juveniles in criminal justice more generally to think again. Court statistics must be linked to information on the use of alternative measures for juvenile offenders, such as police cautioning, and it is also essential to be aware of changes in the police clear-up rate, which determines the number of juveniles available for processing through the system.

It might seem at first sight that it should be possible to make basic comparisons in these terms within the United Kingdom. However, differences in the alternative methods available for dealing with juvenile offenders make this difficult. This is compounded by inadequacy of, and incompatibility between, published statistics on juvenile offenders amounting to perversity. However, perhaps the recognition of the limits of currently available information is the beginning of criminological wisdom!

The annual *Criminal Statistics* for England and Wales do include quite detailed information about known juvenile offenders, defined as all those found guilty of or cautioned for, notifiable offences. The inclusion of those cautioned by the police transforms the official picture, particularly following the rapid rise in the cautioning of juveniles at the beginning of the 1970s (see Chapter 2). Table 5.1 shows the broad pattern of known offenders for the period 1968–83, during which the grand total almost exactly doubled. During the same period the number of offences recorded by the police increased by over 150%, and the official clear-up rate dropped from 42 to 37%. Table 5.1 shows that the number of offending juveniles increased by about the same amount as the number of offenders aged 21 and over. The greatest rate of increase occurred among those aged 17–20. Although adults and juveniles display the same change comparing the beginning and end of the period, the trends were in fact different. Juvenile offenders increased markedly in number between 1968 and 1973 and declined between 1978 and 1983, whereas the number of adults increased steadily throughout the period. Part of the explanation for the more erratic change among juveniles might lie in the use made of cautioning during the period. If cautioning were used much more towards 1973 for children who would earlier have had no action taken against them, and if this use of cautioning declined after, then the pattern identified would be the expected one. The reader is referred to the discussion of net-widening below.

When demographic changes are taken into account, the rate of offending per 100 000 population of 10–13 year-old boys in 1983 was almost the same as it had been in 1968, but for those aged 21 and over the rate increased by almost two-thirds. Thus, although it remains true that known juvenile offenders are processed out of proportion to their numbers in the population, comprising about 30% of all known offenders, there are signs of what may be a real decline in offending among younger juveniles in England and Wales (see Pratt 1985). Certainly, demographic changes make it likely that there should be *less* juvenile offending in absolute terms in the next decade than during the last.

TABLE 5.1   Known offenders, England and Wales, 1968–83

(i) *Number of offenders, (in '000s), by age group*

Year	10–16	17–20	21 and over	TOTAL
1968	90.2	59.9	142.2	292.2
1973	156.5	88.8	183.0	428.2
1978	177.1*	108.0*	233.9*	519.0*
1983	167.9*	135.5*	271.1*	574.5*
% change 1968–83	+86	+126	+91	+97

(ii) *Males, rate per 100 000 population, by age group*

Year	10–13	14–16	17–20	21 and over
1968	2809	5060	4503	820
1973	3411	7072	5810	944
1978	3442	7858	6685	1122
	3187*	7382*	6245*	1157*
1983	2926*	7532*	6944*	1349*
% change 1968–83	+4	+49	+54	+65

NOTE   *   Based on indictable offences as redefined by the Criminal Law Act 1977, and on the new counting procedures.

SOURCE: *Criminal Statistics, England and Wales*, relevant vols. 1968–83.

The picture of known juvenile offending in Scotland is very difficult to discover and describe in ways directly comparable to England and Wales. There are complicating technicalities, such as the fact that the Scottish classification into 'crimes' and 'offences' is different from the English means of distinguishing the more serious offences from the rest. The relevant age range in Scotland is now 8 to 15, not 10 to 16 as it is South of the Border. Apart from problems like these, the main difficulties were created by the implementation of Part 3 of the Social Work (Scotland) Act 1968. This introduced a totally new system of children's hearings and reporters, to which the vast majority of juvenile offenders are referred by the police and the procurators fiscal, instead of being prosecuted directly in the courts. *Criminal Statistics, Scotland* provides details of the small number of juveniles convicted each year in the courts. It also has a chapter on initial reports on children, with information about police action taken when children are believed to have offended. This has to be considered alongside information on all referrals to reporters and children's hearings, available in a series of statistical bulletins, *Children's Hearings Statistics,* produced by the Social Work Services Group of the Scottish Education Department, and first published in 1976 as a delayed successor to the publication *Scottish Social Work Statistics* which appeared from 1971 to 1974. What then can be gleaned from these various sources?

In 1968 almost 12 000 juveniles (at that time, juveniles included those aged between 8 and 16 years) were found guilty of *crimes* in all Scottish courts, comprising exactly one-third of all persons against whom charges were proved or admitted. In the same year, an identical number of juveniles were found guilty of the less serious *offences*. Throughout the 1960s just under a quarter of all juveniles known to have committed crimes or offences were given police warnings (including juvenile liaison referrals); as more warnings are given to less serious offenders, it is likely that 10–15% of juveniles known to have committed *crimes* were given police warnings, and should be added to the number found guilty in the courts (see also Arnott and Duncan 1970).

In 1982, almost 23 000 juveniles (now defined as 8–15 year-olds) were recorded by the police on suspicion of having committed crimes (plus a further 8000 for offences; see Scottish Home and Health Department 1984). Although many of these police cases are not subsequently referred to the reporter or procurator fiscal, the number is very close to that of children referred from all sources to the reporter on 'offence grounds' (which, to confuse matters, means on suspicion of having committed offences *or crimes!*) This number was 22 747 (Social Work Services Group 1984). In the same year, 60 000 persons of all ages were found guilty of crimes in the Scottish courts. This suggests that in Scotland between 1968 and 1982, known juvenile offending increased by about 90% (close to the 86% in England and Wales) at a time when adult offending increased by about 150% (compared with 101% in England and Wales). The recorded crime rate in Scotland increased by some 186% over the same period, and the clear-up rate decreased from 38 to 30%.

Since the introduction of standardized data collection methods in 1977 comparisons can be made with more confidence. There has been a steady decline in the annual number of juveniles proceeded against by the police or by referral to the reporter: the number of initial police reports on children dropped from 25 327 in 1977 to 22 876 in 1982; similarly, the number of offence referrals to the reporter dropped from 23 340 to 22 747. However, when the drop in the number of children in the age group (8 to 15) is taken into account, the rate of initial police reports on children remained at 35 per 1000 population throughout this period. This includes children given police warnings (similar to English cautioning), who comprised about 1 in 6 of the total in 1982, and over 1 in 5 in 1978. An examination of children's hearings statistics reveals that 'no action' is taken by the reporter in 4 out of 10 offence referrals; a similar proportion of all referrals to children's hearings results in withdrawal or no formal action (see below). Clearly by no means all such cases signify 'not guilty' verdict equivalence, but this massive degree of case attrition in the Scottish juvenile process provides a salutary reminder of the dangers of drawing hasty conclusions about the extent and nature of juvenile delinquency in any country.

Whereas for Scotland a certain degree of confusion is introduced by the large amount of diverse statistical information about children's offending, the situation in Northern Ireland suffers from the opposite problem; a dearth of regular and reliable statistics about juvenile crime. Until 1971, summary tables of the criminal statistics of Northern Ireland were published in the annual *Reports on the Administration of the Home Office Services*; similar tables appear in the Northern Ireland *Annual Abstract of Statistics*, and, since 1975, in *Social and Economic Trends in Northern Ireland*. Statistics of recorded crime are also published annually in the report of the Chief

Constable of the Royal Ulster Constabulary. None of these publications contains any detailed analysis or interpretation of trends in juvenile offending. The main source for the Northern Ireland data used in this chapter is the very timely *Commentary on Northern Ireland Crime Statistics 1969–1982* (Northern Ireland Office 1984).

The procedure for dealing with juveniles accused of crime follows a fairly traditional judicial model, similar to that in England and Wales prior to the implementation of the 1969 Children and Young Persons Act. In 1968, 1298 juveniles were found guilty of indictable offences, representing 28% of all persons convicted of such offences. By 1973, only 702 juveniles were found guilty (20% of the total) but by 1983 the number of juveniles had risen to 1009, representing just 12% of all persons convicted of indictable offences. Thus, between 1968 and 1983 there was a drop of 23% in the number of juveniles convicted in the courts of Northern Ireland, whilst the number of adults convicted rose by 122%. During the same period the number of recorded crimes increased by more than 200%, and the clear-up rate plummeted from 58% to below 20% in 1982.

Since 1977, there has been a significant increase in the use of cautioning in Northern Ireland, for juveniles and for adults. Expressed as a proportion of those found guilty or cautioned, juveniles cautioned for all types of offence rose from 17% in 1977 to 57% in 1981 and 49% in 1982 (Northern Ireland Office 1984, para 4.8). In absolute terms, there was more than a fourfold increase during the six-year period in the number of juveniles cautioned, but a *10% drop* in the number prosecuted. As these cautioning statistics relate to all offences, it is not possible to calculate exactly how many juveniles cautioned for indictable offences should be added to those found guilty in the courts, but even with an estimated addition the total number of known juvenile offenders in 1983 would be only some 10–20% higher than in 1968. This confirms that, in all three jurisdictions in the United Kingdom during the last decade and a half, known juvenile offending appears to have been rising (if at all) at a much lower rate than was the case for adults, and at a time of falling clear-up rates.

Alternatives to Prosecution: Diversion or Net-Widening?

The major changes in juvenile justice procedures and policies embodied in the legislation of the late 1960s, in both Scotland and England and Wales, had in common an emphasis on the desirability of diverting children and young people from formal court prosecution wherever possible, and substituting some less formal and less interventionist approach. In England and Wales, although a crucial section of the 1969 Children and Young Persons Act was never implemented (it would have phased out the prosecution of all those under the age of 14), nevertheless significant developments took place around the time the Act was passed. These dramatically increased the numbers of juveniles cautioned by the police. In Chapter 2 (see Table 2.4 p. 51), it was seen that between 1968 and 1973 the proportion of juveniles cautioned virtually doubled, with an absolute increase from 25 000 to 77 000 cautions. Although the rate of increase in cautioning subsequently slowed down, by 1983 three-quarters of boys aged 10 to 13 dealt with were cautioned by the police, as were 90% of girls of the same age. Furthermore, recent initiatives from the Home Office bespeak official support for a further extension and standization of cautioning practices, for juveniles and adults alike (Home Office 1984a; Home Office Circular 14/1985).

In the circumstances, it might seem rather unfair to question the diversionary achievements of the last 15 years. Yet this is what some commentators have done, by invoking the issue of what has generally become known as 'net-widening'. It is claimed by such critics that increases in the number of juveniles cautioned by the police may not only reflect a diversion from court prosecution. It may also, it is argued, be replacing previous decisions by the police to take No Further Action (NFA) in some cases, thus drawing some young offenders into the criminal justice 'net' who would otherwise not find themselves there. A double significance is attached to this process; in the first place, it renders unsound any statistical comparisons between known offenders before and after the change; in the second place, it could have potentially very significant effects upon the future criminal careers of those juveniles who reoffend after a caution, and who are unlikely on that subsequent occasion to escape more formal criminal justice processing.

The likelihood of a 'net-widening' effect seems high. Moreover, the existence of such an effect receives confirmation in the experience of many of those involved with the juvenile justice system at work. It is difficult to measure the precise extent to which it might be happening, but for any open-minded observer the evidence that some net-widening takes place now verges on the overwhelming. Perhaps the best-known empirical study which sought to address this issue (but not the first, for which see Ditchfield, 1976, pp. 11–12) was carried out by Farrington and Bennett (1981) who monitored changes following the introduction of the juvenile bureau scheme in the London Metropolitan Police District at the beginning of 1969. The most crucial part of the analysis was the plotting of arrests, findings of guilt and official processing (i.e. findings of guilt plus cautions) between 1968 and 1970. By 1970 every division in the force was operating the juvenile liaison/cautioning scheme. The central prediction to be made on the basis of diversion is that the total number of people being dealt with remains the same, since those subtracted from the original sentence or process are simply moved to the new alternative, no new cases entering the system. The net-widening prediction is that new cases enter the system, with those who had been sentenced/processed still being dealt with in the same way. So at the centre of the net-widening prediction is an increase in the number of people entering the system and no reduction in the number of people being sentenced as before. To anticipate their conclusion somewhat, Farrington and Bennett showed precisely this picture among offenders over 13, and some net-widening for those aged 10–13.

After making certain allowances for changes attributable due to the introduction of the Theft Act in 1969, they concluded:

> . . . the increases in arrests between 1968 and 1970 were 85% for 10–13 year-olds, 44% for 14–16 year-olds, and 24% for 17–20 year-olds. These figures suggest very strongly that, after the introduction of the cautioning schemes, there was a widening of the net of arrested juveniles, especially in the youngest (10–13) age group. It is implausible to suggest that there was anything approaching such a marked increase in juvenile

offending, or any other marked change unconnected with the introduction of the cautioning scheme, during this short period. The same conclusion follows for the figures on official processing. The findings on findings of guilt suggest that 10–13 year-olds were diverted, but not 14–16 year-olds. These conclusions differ in emphasis from those of Ditchfield (1976) in showing a very marked net-widening effect of cautions and a diversion effect only for the 10–13 year-olds (who were most affected by net-widening). How far these results can be generalised to the whole of England is not known. (Farrington and Bennett 1981, pp. 128–9)

Despite the importance of this study in drawing attention to the net-widening potential of schemes intended to be primarily diversionary, its generalizability may be limited, as Farrington and Bennett acknowledge in the quotation above. The practices and experiences in the MPD may well not be entirely typical of concurrent activities in provincial police forces (its cautioning practices have always been different from most of the rest of the country). Further, it may not even be generalizable to practices in the MPD when police officers have become used to the new arrangements. Reworking the data of Farrington and Bennet reveals a number of relevant points. Table 5.2 confirms the dramatic increase in cautioning for juveniles, especially in the younger age group who are to some extent clearly diverted from official court proceedings. The figures in Table 5.2 also show that much larger proportions of those arrested in 1970 and 1972 had 'no further action' taken against them, compared with 1966 and 1968. So it is arguable that pressure was even then being exerted on the arresting officers not to bring in many of the people they did, which pressure would in due course decrease the number of arrests made of juveniles. Consistent with this sort of speculation, a preliminary analysis by Norman Tutt (1984) of MPD data for 1976–9 has shown that 'the massive increase in arrests decribed by the previous researchers did not persist into the latter half of the decade' (Tutt 1984, p. 304). What happened was that police arrests of 10–16 year-olds reached a peak in 1977 and dropped back over the next two years 'although the proportion cautioned remained surprisingly constant: in 1976 some 32% were cautioned; in 1977, 1978 and 1979 some 34% were cautioned' (p. 365) at a time when the national average for England and Wales increased to over 50%.

What emerges from this debate, and will become even more important as cautioning schemes proliferate alongside the establishment of the new Crown Prosecution service, is that a proper assessment of the effects of cautioning must pay heed to 'no further action' decisions and their implications. Hints at what might be revealed are to be found in the study of the operation of the 1969 Children and Young Persons Act, in Bristol and Wiltshire, by Priestley, Fears and Fuller (1977). A significant group of NFA decisions in both areas were made on children under the age of criminal responsibility, but the use of NFA for 10–16 year-olds varied considerably between the two areas – 'Bristol police made NFA decisions in 25% of the juvenile offence cases they processed, more than twice the rate found in Wiltshire, where only 10% of the age group was dealt with in this way' (Priestley *et al.* 1977, p. 60). In Bristol, the under-twelves and the over-fifteens were cautioned in a high proportion of cases, with the latter group including 20 NFA decisions on older children who

TABLE 5.2 Arrests, findings of guilt and official processing, London Metropolitan Police District, 1966–72

Age Group	1966	1968	1970	1972
10–13 years:				
(a) Arrests	3848	4527	8918	9959
(b) Findings of Guilt	3317	3645	2551	2479
(c) Official Processing	3367	3742	6586	6810
(% of (c) cautioned)	(1.5)	(2.6)	(61.3)	(63.6)
Arrested, but no further action, (a) – (c)	481	785	2332	3149
(% no further action)	(13)	(17)	(26)	(32)
14–16 years:				
(a) Arrests	6446	7243	13617	16369
(b) Findings of Guilt	5566	6254	7067	7755
(c) Official Processing	5675	6376	10839	11859
(% of (c) cautioned)	(1.9)	(1.9)	(34.8)	(34.6)
Arrested, but no further action, (a) – (c)	771	867	2778	4510
(% no further action)	(12)	(12)	(20)	(28)
17–20 years				
(a) Arrests	10377	10809	16430	17402
(b) Findings of Guilt	9177	9868	13618	14013
(c) Official Processing	9286	9985	13779	14179
(% of (c) cautioned)	(1.2)	(1.2)	(1.2)	(1.2)
Arrested, but no further action, (a) – (c)	1091	824	2651	3223
(% no further action)	(11)	(8)	(16)	(19)

SOURCE: Adapted from Farrington and Bennett (1981), Table 2.

were already in the care of local authorities; in such instances the interpretation of NFA is surely to be found in police consideration of what is being done to/for the juvenile concerned. It is much less plausibly seen as a simple 'no action' dismissal of the case. On Merseyside, in the late 1970s, Howard Parker and his team found a much lower NFA rate of 3% in the Metropolitan area, and in their view this confirmed that cautioning was being increasingly used so that it had a 'net-widening' or a 'push-in' effect:

> Because the sifting is in the hands of front-line policemen operating, quite appropriately, in organisational terms, traditional policing goals there is a 'natural' 'push-in' tendency . . . Only 3% of all juvenile cases that formally enter the system are dealt with by NFAs, and as this proportion actually includes those children under the age of

criminal responsibility the NFA category is almost non-existent in terms of diversion. NFA figures are not available in the published Criminal Statistics (perhaps a significant fact in itself, in explaining why the police prefer to 'push in' and thus be seen to be clearing up crime). (Parker *et al.* 1981, p. 37)

The trouble is that precisely the same data could be used to demonstrate the *absence* of net-widening. A low figure for NFA could mean either:

i) Police officers are using discretion so that very few cases which do not merit any action are getting to the stage of *recording* as NFA. They are being diversionary already.

ii) Police officers are arresting everything young and moving, and senior officers cannot bring themselves to forgo any of the cases they get. This is a slightly more colourful version of the Parker *et al.* account.

Despite the inherent ambiguities, a provisional conclusion seems warranted. Juvenile cautioning in England and Wales is not entirely diverting young people from criminal process of a more severe kind. It does to some extent widen the criminal justice net, ensnaring some of those who might have previously escaped with a stern word. The precise extent to which net-widening occurs is difficult to measure. The extent to which it does occur is likely to vary according to the pressures on and inclinations of police officers to take no action rather than to caution. The NFA decision is an interesting index of one possible source of pressure on the arresting officer. Guidelines are needed: further research is needed: not necessarily in that order!

Of the jurisdictions in the United Kingdom, Scotland has undertaken the most radical restructuring of its juvenile justice system, following the report of the Kilbrandon Committee (1964) and the subsequent implementation of the Social Work (Scotland) Act 1968. Juveniles accused of the most serious offences, such as murder, arson and rape, or those who have offended jointly with an adult, are still tried in the traditional courts of law. In 1973, children under the age of 16 constituted only 1% of all those against whom a charge was proved in Scottish courts; by 1983 this proportion had dropped to less than one third of one per cent. All other children suspected of committing crimes or offences are either given official police warnings or referred to the reporter for action, including possible disposal by children's hearings, which are made up of specially selected lay persons and have no connection with the criminal justice system (for a useful comparative discussion of the Scottish system see McCabe and Treitel 1984).

Criminal Statistics (Scotland) 1980–1982 (Scottish Home and Health Department 1984) presents information on police action in the case of initial reports on children during the period 1977–82. From this it can be seen that, for crimes and offences combined, police warnings dropped slightly from a fifth to a sixth of all cases, whereas police referrals to the procurator fiscal increased from 1 in 4 to almost 1 in 3 of all cases (see Table 5.3). During the 1960s, the police issued warnings to about a quarter of all the children under the age of 16 with whom they had formal dealings; by 1972 this had increased to one third, but since then there has been a steady decline in the

TABLE 5.3   Initial reports on children, action by police, Scotland, 1977–82

Scotland		*Number of reports*					
Police action		*1977*	*1978*	*1979*	*1980*	*1981*	*1982*
Total reports		*33378*	*31757*	*32542*	*33087*	*33578*	*30859*
Given police warnings (inc. juvenile liaison)		6251	6956	6530	5661	5020	4821
	(%)	(19)	(21)	(20)	(17)	(15)	(16)
Referred to reporter		19546	16876	16276	16741	18147	16540
	(%)	(59)	(53)	(50)	(51)	(54)	(54)
Referred to procurator fiscal		7581	8285	9736	10685	10411	9498
	(%)	(23)	(26)	(30)	(32)	(31)	(31)

SOURCE: adapted from *Criminal Statistics (Scotland) 1980–1982*, Table 5.1.

extent to which the police use their discretion to give formal warnings, to the extent that warnings are now used proportionately less than they were before reorganization. More detailed information is available for some years, showing that police decisions on children involved in *crimes* followed the same trends, with a decrease in police warnings and an increase in references to the procurator fiscal, although almost 6 out of every 10 crime cases are referred to the reporter. Police warnings are generally given only for minor offences, so that, for example, in 1982 35% of offenders in shop-lifting cases were warned; the reporter received a high proportion of sexual crimes (68%), housebreaking (64%) and fire-raising and other criminal damage (62%); younger children were less likely to be referred to the procurator fiscal than were older children, irrespective of the nature of the offence (Scottish Home and Health Department 1984 para 5.12).

Following the implementation of the new Act in Scotland, in the early 1970s there was an immediate and wholesale diversion of juveniles from the criminal courts. Whereas in the period 1968–70, 77% of juveniles known to the police for crimes or offences were prosecuted, by 1972–3 this proportion was only 9%. This was not accompanied by any significant increase in the juvenile arrest rate, which suggests that net-widening was not a major problem. Apart from retaining their power to issue warnings and refer cases to juvenile liaison schemes, the police now have relatively little control over what happens to delinquent children in Scotland. To assess the full effects of the changes, it is necessary to examine the statistics relating to the work of reporters and children's hearings (see Table 5.4).

Each year for the last ten for which statistics are available (1973–82), the number of referrals to reporters (on all grounds) has been between 25 000 and 30 000. Referrals on 'offence grounds' dropped from above 26 000 in 1973 (88% of all referrals) to fewer than 23 000 in 1982 (79% of the total), reflecting the drop in the number of children coming to the notice of the police for delinquent behaviour. (There is an

TABLE 5.4 Referrals to reporter, and initial action: Scotland, 1973–82

	1973		1978		1982	
(i) *Source of referrals*	no.	(%)	no.	(%)	no.	(%)
Police	24156	(82)	17029	(64)	17219	(59)
Procurators Fiscal	2349	(8)	4883	(19)	6474	(22)
Social Work Depts.	476	(2)	1068	(4)	1715	(6)
Educational & Other	2403	(8)	3460	(13)	3818	(13)
Total referrals	29384	(100)	26440	(100)	29226	(100)
(ii) *Grounds for referrals*	(%)		(%)		(%)	
Offence	88		81		79	
Non-attendance at school	7		11		9	
Other	5		8		12	
(iii) *Initial action, in offence referrals*	(%)		(%)		(%)	
Referred to hearing	48		48		44	
Police/Juvenile Liaison	7		7		8	
Referred to Social Work Department	4		4		4	
Other action	1		–		–	
No action	40		41		44	

SOURCE: *Scottish Social Work Statistics 1973; Children's Hearings Statistics*, 1978, and 1982.

average of 1.5 offences for each 'offence referral', so the total number of offences involved in 1982 was over 35 000.) The proportion of referrals which came from the police dropped from 82% to 59%, while at the same time there was an increase in the proportion coming from the procurators fiscal (from 8% in 1973 to 22% in 1982), the Social Work Departments and from schools and other sources. The proportion of *offence* referrals coming from the police decreased from 78% to 72% in the last five years, coinciding with the increase in the proportion referred by the procurators fiscal.

An examination of the initial action taken by the reporter in offence referrals shows that less than one half are referred to a children's hearing; 7–8% are referred to the police for a warning or juvenile liaison, and in more than 4 out of every 10 cases 'no formal action' is recorded. Statistics are now collected on the reasons for reporters taking no further action, which show that of the 10 000 offence referrals in 1982 which resulted in this decision, 59% were because compulsory measures of care were considered unnecessary, 29% because the child was already under a supervision requirement, and 11% because there was insufficient evidence.

What happens to the cases referred to children's hearings will be considered in the next section, but on the evidence at this stage of the discussion it does seem that the Scottish system has achieved a substantial measure of diversion from formal proceedings, with apparently little if any widening of the net of social control over Scottish children. As the procedure is particularly complicated and may be unfamiliar to many readers, Figure 5.1 presents, in diagrammatic form, a summary of children's hearings decisions in 1982.

The system of juvenile justice in Northern Ireland is much more straightforward.

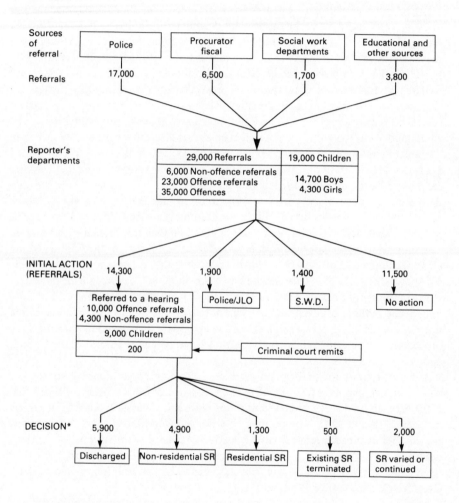

FIGURE 5.1   Representation of childrens hearings statistics, 1982

SOURCE: Scottish Education Department, Social Work Services Group *Children's Hearings Statistics, 1982*, part of Figure 1.

There has been no major legislative change or restructuring comparable to that which took place elsewhere in the United Kingdom in the 1960s and 1970s. The Children and Young Persons (Northern Ireland) Act 1968 has been described as 'not much more than a reenactment of earlier legislation, introducing into the Province the welfare principles and most of the measures of the Children and Young Persons Act 1933 which applied to England and Wales' (McCabe and Treitel 1984, p. 46). The Children and Young Persons Review Group, whose report offers hope for the future reform of juvenile justice in Northern Ireland, agreed that 'the Act contained no hint of the more radical ideas of the mid-60s for dealing with children and young people', stating that 'so far Northern Ireland has held more closely to the traditional tenets of the criminal law but the welfare of the child is not neglected' (Black Report 1979, para 5.12, 5.13). Provision was made in the Act for cooperation between police and welfare authorities in deciding whether to prosecute, and the setting up of the Review Group gave a new impetus to the possible diversion of juveniles. Its Report advocated substantial extension of police cautioning, to first *and second* minor offenders who admit guilt – 'only cases which pose a real or serious threat to society should go before the juvenile court' (Black Report 1979, para 6.5). As a result, the late 1970s witnessed a substantial increase in the proportion of all juveniles who were cautioned, the figure reaching 50% or more in 1981 and 1982 (see Table 5.5). It saw too a steadily decreasing number of juveniles found guilty in the courts, and an *increasing* proportion receiving absolute or conditional discharges – from 25% in 1968 to 36% in 1983. Here too there has been the suggestion that the dramatic increase in cautioning during the last 6 or 7 years probably had an inflationary or net-widening effect (Jardine 1983 discussed in Northern Ireland Office 1984, pp. 24–26). Table 5.5 shows that, if 1977 is taken as the base year, there was an increase of more than 400% in the use of juvenile cautions over the following years, accompanied by a *20% drop* in the number of juveniles prosecuted, representing an overall increase in the number of officially processed delinquents of about 50% 'while about 600 *fewer* were prosecuted, over 2000 *more* were cautioned'. (Northern Ireland Office 1984, para 4.8)

As a postscript to the net-widening debate – although unquestionably not the last word – we can quote the findings of an analysis by the Northern Ireland Office's Statistics Branch of the use of cautioning for adult and juvenile indictable offenders between 1978 and 1980. The number of recorded crimes increased by one quarter, the number of prosecutions remained relatively stable, but the number of cautions doubled – 'It would appear, therefore, that during this period at least the police seemed to have used cautions as an alternative as well as an addition to prosecution'. (Northern Ireland Office 1984, para 4.9)

As a footnote to all our discussions of cautioning, we must remind the reader of a question which is crucial for considerations of justice and which has not been addressed here. No comparative information is available about it, but it must be mentioned. The analogy of a net for the scope of social control is apposite (see Cohen, 1985). Bigger nets catch more fish. The mesh is also important. Small fish slip through nets. The finer the mesh, the smaller the fish has to be to escape. Justice requires uniform mesh size. That is to say, justice is served if acts which are only tri-

TABLE 5.5   Juveniles cautioned, Northern Ireland, 1977–82

	1977	1978	1979	1980	1981	1982
Official Cautions	549	1124	1725	2397	2908	2440
(%)	(17)	(32)	(39)	(48)	(57)	(49)
Prosecutions	2794	2433	2646	2580	2176	2513
(%)	(83)	(68)	(61)	(52)	(43)	(51)
TOTAL	3343	3557	4371	4977	5084	4953

SOURCE: *A Commentary on Northern Ireland Crime Statistics, 1969–1982*, Table B, p. 24.

vially offensive escape punishment. If the factors determining escape from punishment are to do with social background rather than offence, there is cause for disquiet. The content of some police force cautioning forms, particularly that used by the Royal Ulster Constabulary, suggests that social background will lead to a caution, rather than triviality of offence. An analysis of West Yorkshire statistics by Fisher and Mawby (1982) shows that the factors associated with caution or prosecution decisions are a mixture of the social and the offence based (see Figure 5.2). In some cases even *parental* remorse can make the difference. Insofar as cautioning decisions both widen the net of social control and bias those caught in it, on grounds of social background, its value must be seriously questioned.

The Use of Custody

The final question to be posed in this chapter concerns the extent to which the different official strategies of juvenile justice in the United Kingdom are reflected in the use of custody for those under the age of 16. A simplistic guess might be that the use of custody should be highest in Northern Ireland and lowest in Scotland, with England and Wales mid-way between them, perhaps closer to Scottish usage in view of the explicit non-custodial/decarceration objectives of the 1969 Children and Young Persons Act.

Guesses can be simplistic, but in this case analysis must be tentative. The problem of the denominator raised so often in these pages is posed again. There is no obviously right base from which to calculate relative disposal rates – should it be only those formally prosecuted, or should it include all officially known offenders, even at the risk of including victims of net-widening? Should custodial receptions be used, thus taking no account of lengths of custody? (We did).

During the period being studied, the custodial sentences for juvenile offenders in Northern Ireland included remand home, training school, Borstal Training (until 1980) and youth imprisonment. From 1968 to 1978, around 250–350 juveniles a year received custodial sentences, representing 10–15% of those found guilty of indictable and non-indictable offences in all courts. More detailed figures for 1978–82 show that in the Lower Courts the use of custodial sentences for indictable juvenile offenders

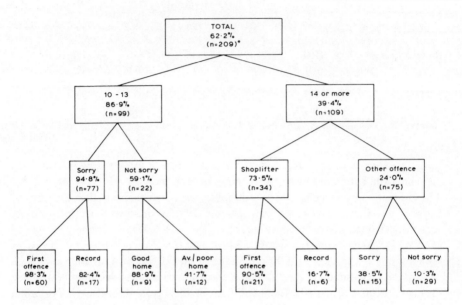

*In each case 'n' in box refers to total who were cautioned or prosecuted

FIGURE 5.2   *For those for whom outcome known, percentage in different categories who were cautioned rather than prosecuted*

*   In each case 'n' in box refers to total who were either cautioned or prosecuted.

SOURCE: Fisher and Mawby (1982), Figure 1, p. 71.

was particularly low in 1978 and 1982 and higher (over 20%) in the period 1979–81. In the Crown Court, where an average of 110 juveniles were sentenced each year, the proportion of custodial sentences dropped steadily from 57% to 26% of all cases, with probation being used in over 40% of cases in 1982, compared to only 16% five years previously. Combining these figures shows that 24% of juvenile indictable offenders were given custodial sentences during the period 1979–81, but only 20% in 1978 and less than 18% in 1982. The rapid increase in cautioning, particularly in 1980–81, might be thought to contribute to the explanation of the high rate of custody in those years, but the cautioning rates in the low-custody years, 1978 and 1982 were the same as those of the higher rate years, 1979 and 1980. So the obvious interpretation of reduced custody stands.

In Scotland during the 1950s and early 1960s, when very few juveniles were dealt with outside the courts by police warnings or official cautions, over one third of all juveniles were given only nominal sentences (e.g. absolute discharge, admonition), and about 1 in 7 were given custodial sentences (Arnott and Duncan 1970). This same pattern of sentencing continued throughout the 1960s, with 35–40% being given admonitions or absolute discharges, 13–15% receiving custodial sentences, and around a quarter being put on probation. In the 1970s the new system came into operation but amazingly, of the small number of juveniles still prosecuted in the criminal courts (averaging less than 1000 a year in recent years, compared with the annual average of 12 000 in the 1960s) *the same proportion continued to receive a nominal sentence and only 10–15% were sentenced to custody!* But it is to the outcome of children's hearings that we must look for a comprehensive picture of the effects of the reorganization. Did the new 'welfare' approach result in a significant change in the degree of intervention and supervision (whether residential or community-based) of delinquent children?

We have already seen that the police continue to give official warnings to a significant minority of children who come to their notice for offences, and refer the rest to the reporter or procurator fiscal. In almost half of the offence referrals to the reporter, from the police and the fiscals, no further action is taken. A similar proportion of cases is referred to a children's hearing. Table 5.6 shows the disposal of reports referred to hearings on offence grounds. In four out of ten of all cases, where the ground is established, no supervision requirement is made and the case is discharged; in about one in seven of all cases a residential supervision requirement is made or continued, and in the remaining cases (constituting half the total in 1973 and a third in 1978 and 1982), a non-residential requirement is made.

The latest statistical bulletin summarized the position in 1982, as follows: (see also Figure 5.1 above)

> ... from a total of about 23 000 referrals representing approximately 35 000 offences and 15 000 children, 10 000 were further referred to a hearing where about 4000 referrals resulted in a supervision requirement being made (or varied). (Social Work Services Group 1984, para 9.3)

TABLE 5.6 Disposal of reports referred to children's hearing, (offence grounds established), Scotland, 1973–82

Disposal	1973		1978		1982	
	no.	(%)	no.	(%)	no.	(%)
Supervision requirement						
Non-residential	5495	(50)	3373	(32)	2770	(33)
Residential	1421	(13)	1522	(15)	1159	(14)
Supervision requirement continued	n.k.		1094	(11)	976	(12)
No Supervision requirement:	4133	(37)	4413	(42)	3374	(41)
TOTAL	11 049	(100)	10 402	(100)	8279	(100)

SOURCE: *Scottish Social Work Statistics, 1973; Children's Hearings Statistics, 1978, 1982.*

In other words, only 5% of offence referrals (already partly sifted by the police) resulted in a residential supervision requirement and only a further 12% in non-residential supervision. In 6 out of every 10 cases no further official action was taken. It seems impossible to deny the diversionary achievements of the Scottish welfare approach, with the added bonus that there is little evidence of net-widening.

Finally, in this chapter, we need to consider the effects of the 1969 Children and Young Persons Act upon the use of custody for juveniles in England and Wales. There is substantial agreement amongst those who have studied trends in juvenile justice during the decade or so following the implementation of the Act that many of its objectives and expectations were not fulfilled. The sentencing trends of the early 1970s have been described as 'merely exaggerations of trends which had been developing over the previous ten years' rather than effects of the 1969 Act (Thorpe *et al.* 1980, p. 10). Norman Tutt has claimed that the statistics of sentencing for 1968–78 'clearly illustrate that the decade of the welfare approach to juvenile delinquency, so vociferously proclaimed as a failure, in fact never occurred' (Tutt 1984, p. 249; see also Tutt 1980):

> For those children between 10 and 14 years of age coming before the juvenile court the introduction of the 1969 Act in 1971, far from leading to massive intervention by social workers, had no impact on the proportion receiving a care order or the equivalent but led to a *decline* in the proportion receiving supervision by a social worker and an increase receiving a fine or attendance centre order, a disposal which the Act believed would atrophy with the widespread introduction of intermediate treatment.
>
> The picture for those young people between 14 and 17 years is even more dramatic, the proportion made subject of a care order being halved along with a substantial reduction in the proportion receiving supervision orders. At the same time attendance centre and detention centre orders, both of which were to be abolished, expanded substantially after the introduction of the 1969 Act. (Tutt 1981, pp. 249–251)

One potential limitation of most recent studies of juvenile sentencing is that they have been based only on those *appearing in court*. In view of the large increase in cautioning from the late 1960s onwards, it seems important for many purposes to express the use of different measures as a proportion of all known offenders, whether found guilty or officially cautioned by the police. Such analysis might, in its turn, be considered a little suspect in view of the possible net-widening effects, but on balance it seems a sounder basis for comparative study than the more usual restriction to offenders found guilty in the courts. Table 5.7 shows the main trends in the disposal of juvenile indictable offenders from 1968 to 1983.

For 10–13 year-olds, the proportion receiving no formal action beyond either a police caution or court discharge increased from 56% (1968) to 86% (1983). As the proportion fined dropped from 12 to 4%, only 1 in 10 of this age group now receives a sentence involving any form of supervision, whether residential or community based. The number receiving an Approved School or Care Order has more than halved (dropping from 5% of the total to 1%) and whereas in 1968 almost one fifth of this age group was given probation orders, by 1983 the proportion given the equivalent supervision orders had fallen to 4%. There was a drop in the use of Attendance Centre

TABLE 5.7 Disposal of juveniles found guilty or cautioned, England and Wales, 1968–83

A. Males and Females, aged 10–13 years

	Total found guilty or cautioned	Caution or court discharge	Probation/ Supervision Order	Fine	Att. Centre	App. Sch./ or Care Order	Other
1968							
%	100	55.8	18.0	11.7	6.6	5.4	2.3
(no. in '000s)	(42.8)	(23.9)	(7.7)	(5.0)	(2.8)	(2.3)	(1.0)
1973							
%	100	76.4	8.5	7.4	3.6	3.8	0.3
(no. in '000s)	(66.1)	(50.5)	(5.6)	(4.9)	(2.4)	(2.5)	(0.2)
1978							
%	100	79.0	6.7	7.1	4.0	3.0	0.1
(no. in '000s)	(67.3)	(53.2)	(4.5)	(4.8)	(2.7)	(2.0)	(0.1)
1983							
%	100	85.9	4.4	4.0	4.4	1.2	–
(no. in '000s)	(56.9)	(48.9)	(2.5)	(2.3)	(2.5)	(0.7)	–

TABLE 5.7 contd

B. Males and Females, aged 14–16 years

	Total found guilty or cautioned	Caution or court discharge	Probation or Supervision Order	Fine	Att. Centre	D.C.	A/S. or Care Order	Borstal/ Youth Custody	Other
1968									
%	100	33.0	20.6	28.5	5.2	3.0	5.9	1.4	2.3
(no. in '000s)	(57.2)	(18.9)	(11.8)	(16.3)	(3.0)	(1.7)	(3.4)	(0.8)	(1.3)
1973									
%	100	48.7	11.6	25.2	4.4	3.3	4.6	1.6	0.6
(no. in '000s)	(90.4)	(44.0)	(10.5)	(22.8)	(4.0)	(3.0)	(4.2)	(1.4)	(0.5)
1978									
%	100	50.1	9.5	24.3	6.3	5.0	2.9	1.7	0.3
(no. in '000s)	(109.8)	(55.0)	(10.4)	(26.7)	(6.9)	(5.5)	(3.2)	(1.9)	(0.3)
1983									
%	100	57.9	9.2	15.9	8.8	4.3	1.3	1.8	0.9
(no. in '000s)	(111.0)	(64.3)	(10.2)	(17.6)	(9.8)	(4.8)	(1.4)	(2.0)	(1.0)

SOURCE: Derived from relevant vols. of *Criminal Statistics, England and Wales.*

orders between 1968 and 1973, but in the last ten years their use has steadily increased, so that as many now receive this sentence as receive supervision orders. Latest information confirms that all these trends continued in the year up to June 1984, following the implementation of the 1982 Criminal Justice Act: cautioning and discharges increased, there was a small increase in the use of Attendance Centres, and the proportions given fines, supervision orders and care orders continued to decrease (Home Office 1985c, para 3).

For 14 to 16 year olds, the proportion cautioned or given a court discharge increased from 33% in 1968 to 58% in 1983, and there was a drop in the proportion fined from 28 to 16%. Thus only one quarter of this age group received any form of supervisory sentence in 1983, compared with over a third in 1968. The proportion receiving probation or supervision orders more than halved from 21% in 1968 to 9% in 1983; but, as with the younger age group, the use of Attendance Centres has increased rapidly, doubling in the last ten years, after a slight drop between 1968 and 1973. The use of Approved School/Care Orders dropped steadily throughout the period, from 6% of all offenders in 1968 to just over 1% in 1983; but there was a big increase in the use of Detention Centres and Borstal Training/Youth Custody, with a virtual tripling of these sentences, representing an increase of from 4% (1968) to 6% (1983).

The rising trends in the use of Attendance Centres and Prison department establishments for the custody of offenders in this age group (accompanied by drastic reduction in Care Orders) are clearly contrary to the spirit of the 1969 Act. The decline in the use of community supervision also appears to go against the welfare premises of that Act. On the other side of the coin, particularly when police cautioning is taken into account, there appears to have been a significant increase in at least the commitment to official non-intervention during the period. England and Wales have a rate of use of custodial measures which is almost as low as that which obtains in Scotland, and a degree of use of supervision in the community which, for the younger age group, may even be lower than it is in Scotland, and for the older group only marginally higher. However, when the full effects of the 1982 Criminal Justice Act become evident, some of these trends may change. First indications are that the replacement of Borstal Training by Youth Custody, and the introduction of shorter minimum sentences for Detention Centres and Youth Custody, have done little to reduce the courts' reliance on custody; and the development of Intermediate Treatment schemes, and Community Service Orders for 16 year-olds, may encourage courts to become more interventionist (Home Office 1985a, 1985c).

Despite the often shaky basis for this preliminary comparative exercise – which must argue the need for much closer collaboration between the Government statistical services of each jurisdiction – we hope that the reader will feel the attempt was worth making, and perhaps its defects will urge colleagues to make more detailed and satisfactory comparative exercises along similar lines. Evidence from all parts of the United Kingdom suggests that the rate of offending among juveniles, especially the youngest ones, may be slowing down quite substantially, despite media impressions to the contrary. Furthermore, for a variety of reasons, ranging from the penal philosophical to the cynically pragmatic, the proportion of known juvenile offenders being diverted from prosecution in the criminal courts, whether by police cautioning, juvenile liaison schemes or decisions by hearings to take no further action, is on the increase, and outside Northern Ireland affects the large majority of juvenile offenders. At what cost in terms of net widening must remain an open question, and one to which we suspect the answer may be constantly changing. Finally, it seems that the legislative changes stemming from the years of debate and political ferment over juvenile justice in the 1960s have kept the rate of intervention, by custody and supervision, in the lives of young offenders, at a surprisingly low level. There will soon be a real test of the reformed juvenile justice systems of these countries. Can they prevent current levels of intervention rising in response to the growing 'law-and-order' lobby? Since levels of intervention and levels of crime are largely independent (see Chapter 7), it is not a statement of political colour to say that we hope they can.

6

Crime Statistics in Context

'It is a psychological commonplace that people strive to achieve a coherent interpretation of the events that surround them, and that the organisation of events by schemas of cause-effect relations serves to achieve this goal.' (Tversky and Kahneman 1982, p. 117). The same writers go on to show that 'when the same data have both causal and diagnostic significance, the former is generally given more weight than the latter' (p. 125). That is to say, it seems to come more easily to people to think of events as causes of future events than consequences of prior events. People invited to speculate on the significance of an increase in the use of solar energy are more liable to think of it as a *cause* of a reduction in pressure on other forms of energy than as a *consequence* of the scarcity of other forms of energy. There is no logical basis for this.

The bias in thought described above is of very great importance in understanding the criminal process. It is also of importance when one seeks to link statistics on crime with other variables. The variables chosen and the way comparisons are made are shot through with causal thought.

If an offender is young, drunkenness at the time of the offence is a factor used to mitigate the severity of sentence imposed (Thomas 1979). In this way, drunkenness is seen as a cause of the criminal act. 'Understanding' this, we are moved to reduce sentence accordingly. But the same set of facts could equally well be used in precisely the opposite way, as symptomatic of a deviant character. If he's the kind of person who lacks self-control and gets as drunk as that, the reasoning might go, he is also the kind of person who can't resist the temptation to commit crime. If drink is seen as a symptom of a weak personality rather than a cause of offending, it would be an aggravating factor in sentencing. Youth itself, like drunkenness of the young, is typically regarded as a mitigating factor in sentencing (Thomas 1979). Yet committing crimes as a child may readily be seen as the consequence of a flawed personality, and hence an aggravating factor. Age at first conviction is a good predictor of subsequent convictions (Home Office 1985b). The younger an offender at first conviction, the more likely he is to be reconvicted. We venture to suggest that the unquestioned use of youth as mitigation is less likely to be mawkish sentimentality than the simple cognitive bias towards causal thinking described here. Bring something into focus for the human mind and it responds by looking forward for its consequences rather than backwards for its causes. This is equally true for general social problems like crime as for the way in which individual offenders are sentenced. At the time of writing, heroin is being id :ntified as the cause of many social ills, including much crime. Yet heroin use may be seen equally well as causal of crime, or as the result of a dispositon to be deviant. It can be thought of as causing the start of a criminal career or reflecting the previous start of a criminal career. It may be helpful to illustrate the point by another example: a broken marriage may be thought of as a cause of sexual offending. Alternatively it may betoken a personality also prone to offend sexually. Given that it is equally plausible to regard drug use as causal of crime or as resulting from some earlier state, it is almost always depicted in the media (and in speeches in mitigation?) as a *cause* of crime. In the United States, the presumption of a causal link between drug use and crime played a significant part in the passage of the Harrison Act of 1914, the first major legislation regulating the distributon and use of opiates and cocaine (Auglin 1983). An item in the Manchester Evening News of October 8th 1984 illustrates the point. 'Councillor Basil Herwold, a solicitor, talked of the heartbreak of heroin addicts and solvent sufferers who get into trouble with the law.' Another article in the same newspaper later the same month tells the same causal story 'A number of youths stole goods which were . . . sold in pubs . . . some were motivated by the desire to get money for heroin'. It is surprising to learn later in the same story that, of the three youths sentenced, two 'did not take heroin'. The drug is thus identified as a criminogenic agent so powerful as to merit prominence in the report even when it was irrelevant to two of the three people convicted.

An obviously crucial piece of information when untangling the relationship between crime and drug use is when the two types of behaviour started. If criminal careers start *after* first drug use, it is more plausible to see drug use as causal than if criminal careers start before drug use. The result of such research as has been carried out is that criminal deviance generally *precedes* drug use (Gandossy *et al.* 1980), although it should be stressed that there is no British research known to the authors which bears on this issue. However, as far as it goes, the evidence strongly suggests that there should be no easy assumption of a causal link from drug use to crime. It offends against intuition to suggest that there is no link between the use of drugs and crime frequency and perhaps type of crime. If you badly want something you can't afford, intuition suggests that crime may result. Figure 6.1 also presents seductive evidence from Stockholm, illustrating the rates of theft from vehicles, breaking and entering, and rates of inoculation hepatitis. This disease used to offer a convenient proxy measure of use of those drugs injected rather than ingested, since it is typically contracted by the use of non-sterile hypodermic syringes. The relationship looks irresistible, but it could be argued that the rates of inoculation hepatitis should lag behind the other two curves, on the basis that hepatitis will follow a period of use sustained by crime. The precise coincidence of the curves may be more consistent with interpretation along the lines that both drug use and crime may be the product of some underlying change in Swedish society. In short, it offends against common sense that the

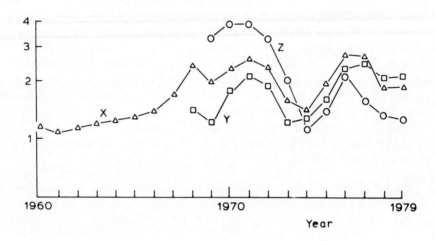

FIGURE 6.1   Relationship between some property offences and inoculation hepatitis

SOURCE: Lenke (1980), Graph D, p. 36.

desire for heroin or a new Volvo does not generate some crime. Nonetheless the easy assumption of direct cause is not consistent with the evidence and the causal pattern is far from clear and likely to be far from simple. The relationships between all social factors and crime are likely to be complex too. Yet our brains and our newspapers lead us into temptation to think of simple causes. Although textbooks warn that corre-lation does not imply cause, nonetheless it is *only* through seeing correlations that we start thinking about causes. To ask us to eschew thinking causally about these relationships is probably fruitless.

Unemployment and Crime

Drug use promises to be one of the liberal knee-jerk responses to questions of crime increase during the late 1980s. The social variable which performed that function during the late 1970s and early 1980s was unemployment. The relationship between unemployment and crime will be dealt with at some length because of this, and because it illustrates even more clearly the problems in identifying causal relationships between crime and variables in its social context. The purpose is not to show that unemployment is not associated with crime. There is a strong statistical association between the variables (see for example Hakim 1982). The problem is whether the association is directly causal, in which case action to reduce unemployment will *ipso facto* reduce crime, or whether it is indirect via poverty, availability of time, police entrapment etc., in which case higher levels of employment will only reduce crime insofar as the really important variables are also changed. The problem is one of identifying the truly causal variables. Social variables tend to go up and down together. It is thus extremely difficult (though not always impossible, see Heise 1975) to untangle the links, and extraordinarily hard for researchers to avoid the importation of value preferences into statistical method. The tone of this chapter is basically pessimistic about the use of routine statistics to do more than locate possibilities, to be tested by more detailed research.

Figure 6.2, reproduced from Tarling (1982), details the trend of crime and unemployment during the period 1950–80. He comments on this relationship as follows:

> The association between the two over the entire 30-year period was very strong. But within this period the evidence was not uniform; the association during the first half – 1950 to 1965 – was much weaker and not statistically significant. Because crime has generally been increasing, any other series that exhibits the same overall trend will be highly correlated with it. It would not be difficult to find a range of other measures, some obviously irrelevant, which mirror the crime figures equally as well and more consistently throughout the period. Indeed, the consumption of alcohol, the consumption of ice cream, the number of cars on the road and the Gross National Product are all highly correlated with rising crime over 1950–1980. (Tarling, 1982, p. 29)

As if that were not enough, the problem of the ecological fallacy presents itself. This fallacy would in this context be the argument that because unemployment and crime go up together, crime is being committed by the unemployed. To recognize this as a fallacy, one has only to take the hypothetical case of an increased use of public transport and a decreased incidence of road deaths. This should not lead us to the conclusion that it is the people who took to the buses who would have killed people while driving their cars! Likewise it should not be concluded that it is the unemployed who are to blame for the extra crime. Stevens and Willis (1979) analysed white, black and Asian arrest rates and various demographic factors, including rates of unemployment for the same three ethnic groups. Their results were too complex to report in full, but it is fair to take their analysis of assault as an example. Arrests of whites for assault covaried with white unemployment rate but not with Asian or black unemployment rates. However, Asian arrest rates for this offence did not covary with any of the unemployment rates and black arrest rates covaried with rates of unemployment for all three ethnic groups! There was thus no neat correspondence between arrest and unemployment rates within a particular ethnic group. The only United Kingdom evidence on a specific association between being unemployed and committing crime comes from Northern Ireland (Gormally *et al.* 1981) and the Northumbria Police

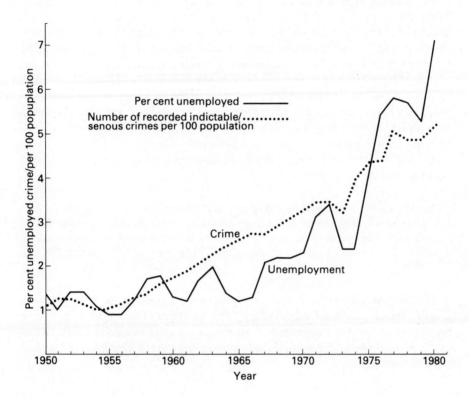

FIGURE 6.2   Unemployment rate and crime rate, in England and Wales, 1950–80

SOURCE: Tarling (1982), p. 30.

(1980). Both these studies separate the employed from the unemployed, and find that the latter group admit (Gormally *et al.*) or are apprehended for (Northumbria) more offences than the former. Even if we were to regard this evidence as conclusive, however, it would not mean that unemployment *per se* was criminogenic. For example it could be plausibly argued that levels of unemployment benefit would influence the relationship between unemployment and crime *if* unemployment were really a 'marker' for poverty. We know of no research looking for a relationship between employment, level of unemployment benefit and crime, but such research on aggregate data might complement the data on individuals which Tarling (1982) argues, with reason, is necessary now.

Other plausible ways in which unemployment might impact on crime are suggested by social control theory, where, as people invest time and energy in conventional activities, criminal behaviour is avoided as jeopardizing these investments (Hirschi 1969), and strain theory (Merton 1957) where crime involvement stems from the absence of alternative means of achieving success. It is difficult to distinguish these alternatives in ways which help to test their individual value (but see Johnson 1979). It is also timely to note that unemployment and police strength/capita are *negatively* associated (Carr–Hill and Stern 1979). It is worth remembering this when interpreting *positive* associations between recorded (by the police) crime and unemployment! It 'allowed' Carr–Hill and Stern to 'accept the null hypothesis that unemployment should be excluded from the equations for the recorded offence rate and the clear-up rate' (p. 247).

One adds a new order of complexity to the situation by considering the possibility of causal effects in both directions:

> For at least the variables of unemployment and criminal involvement, a reciprocal causal structure is more appropriate than a traditional unidirectional one. Crime does not appear to be a simple product of unemployment; rather, these two variables appear to influence one another mutually over time. (Thornberry and Christensen 1984, p. 409)

To see how that might plausibly occur, one has only to consider the likely effect of a criminal record (possessed until spent, by over one-third of men aged 28 or over in England and Wales) on employment prospects. In the extreme case, concerned about the 'quality' of potential employees, an employer may prefer a high technology/low employment option.

Other Social Factors

Drugs and unemployment have been selected as fashionable and 'obvious' causes of crime. An attempt has been made to show that, while undeniably fashionable, they are not obvious, on the basis of available data. Similar arguments could have been advanced for other variables like ethnicity, neighbourhood types, class and gender distribution and age. Not one of these variables can be simply and causally linked with rates of crime. In each case, they must be considered along with other variables before anything usable in policy emerges. To be realistic and thereby to risk being labelled as cynical, the police and penal system need a relatively steady and plentiful supply of crimes and criminals to justify their continued existence or expansion. This all-too-human need to be seen to be doing one's job is likely to smooth out major differences (and perhaps create others) in statistics of criminal justice. Some of the ways in which this might happen are implicit in Carr–Hill and Stern (1979). This perspective is also relevant to the demographic changes which will lead to a declining proportion of the population in the most crime-prone age groups (Gladstone 1979). This should yield reductions in rates of crime, but there is a strong current of criminological opinion which suggests that this will not happen, but that instead agents of criminal justice will draw more events and people into the criminal justice net, where they will be kept for longer (see Pratt 1985 as an example of this view). The justification for such a view is evident from the research reviewed later in this chapter which demonstrates how system needs override rates of misbehaviour outside.

Crime and Major Social Change

Another way of approaching the issue of the relationships between crime and other social measures is to start by acknowledging that variables do come in clumps, and to try to isolate the effects of the clump of variables rather than singling out particular variables for special attention. A justification for taking this line is that if variables 'as found in nature' do go together, there is no policy advantage in knowing the effects of a variable which will never be in a position to express itself in pure form. This sort of reasoning leads one to look at major social changes, or era differences, and to try to trace their overall impact on rates of recorded crime: four types of change will be superficially examined below. They are:

general elections;
party in Government;
generations; and
war.

In no case will results prove conclusive, but in all cases it is thought they are suggestive.

Elections

Despite a largely bipartisan approach to criminal justice issues during the post-war years, until recently there have been general differences in economic and social policy between the major parties which have persisted over time. The perception of these is probably most acute during and after general elections, the post-election state being characterized by knowing what you're in for given the policy of the party newly in power. For this reason, it was thought interesting to look at rises in recorded serious crime in an election year (compared with the pre-election year) and the post-election year (compared with the election year). Two alternative hypotheses were toyed with. The one we didn't favour was that post-election euphoria (the winning party's programme must have sounded good for them to win) would make recorded crime rate increases slow down after elections whichever party won. The hypothesis we put to the test was that the hope of alleviating poverty, the hope of narrowing income differentials and protecting vulnerable groups would lead to some restraint on the commission, reporting and recording of crimes. This hope would be more characteristic of new Labour administrations than of new Conservative administrations. Thus the prediction was that after Labour election victories crime would slow down its increase. This hypothesis yields similar predictions to the alternative one that agencies of criminal justice, notably the police, have more to gain from exaggerating crime problems by liberal recording of crime after a Conservative victory. It is also not easily distinguishable from the proposition that Conservatives win election victories after particularly steep rises in crime, with the exception that this latter position would mean that crimes rates increased more *during* Conservative victory years than Labour victory years. Table 6.1 presents the relevant data. It will be seen that for the four elections during the 1963–83 period it was possible to look at (the reader will recall that 1980 and 1979 statistics of crime are not precisely comparable and the 1984 statistics are not yet to hand) the pattern is as predicted. Further, the rate of crime in the year of the Conservative election victory was not higher than in the years of Labour victory. All three Labour victories are followed by a slowing in the increase of recorded crime, the Conservative victory being followed by a faster increase. Looking back further to all post-war elections, the pattern holds good for seven out of the nine elections with data available for analysis, the exceptions being the Conservative victory of 1951 and the Labour victory of 1950. Of course, the pattern could well represent the operation of mere chance. The reader is in a more privileged position than the writers, since s/he will be in a position to see whether the pattern continues with the publication of the 1984 statistics. Any increase in crime that year will represent a continuation of the pattern, since notifiable crime declined slightly in 1983 relative to 1982.

Political Party in Power

As we all know, the bright new dawn of fresh Governments turns into a depressed mid-term period. The analysis offered in the last section bears on the comparison of new Governments with their years of election in terms of crime change. A separate analysis can deal with changes in crime rate during a Government's term of office. Percentage changes in indictable crime between adjacent years were calculated at times when the same party held office throughout both years. Then Labour and Conservative administrations were compared. The period of the analysis was 1963–83. The average crime increase during Conservative administrations was 4.3% and during Labour administrations was 4.7%. For both parties, there was a wide range of

TABLE 6.1   Changes in indictable crime rates after General Elections between 1963 and 1983[1]

Year of Election	Party Winning	% Crime Increase, Election Year	% Crime Increase, First Post-Election Year
1964	Labour	10.5	6.2
1966	Labour	5.8	0.1
1970	Conservative	4.7	6.2
1974	Labour	18.4	1.4

[1]   The precise effects following the 1979 General Election cannot be identified because of changes in recording practice.

levels of increase. Thus, if the last section really did indicate that new Labour administrations brought with them lower levels of crime increase, it was because they were Labour *and* new, not just because they were Labour.

Despite its crudity, the results of this analysis should not be overlooked. Neither of the major parties can claim to have presided over shallower increases in rates of recorded crime than its rival in the period since 1963. To be fair, this may be because the levers which work rates of recorded crime are not closely linked with rates of misbehaviour in society. If this is what the politicians wish to contend, so be it. By the same token, they cannot claim credit for reducing misbehaviour when the recorded crime rate fortuitously falls during their term of office.

Generations

Both of the major changes whose effects we have striven to plot in the last few pages are external to people and operate through them. There may also be changes which represent real differences between whole generations of people reflected in the way in which they behave. The classic attempt to investigate this, indeed the only British attempt known to us, was completed before the period of focal concern to the book, but it remains of sufficient interest to be mentioned here. It was Leslie Wilkins' research monograph entitled 'Delinquent Generations'. In it, statistical analysis of crimes committed by different birth cohorts was undertaken. The basic idea was that some generations pass through experiences which change them in ways linked to their inclination to commit crimes. The results of Wilkins' analysis of children who were at some stage of infancy during the Second World War is presented as Table 6.2. Wilkins concluded

> The greatest crime-proneness is thus found to be associated with that birth group who passed through their fifth year during the war . . . Whether this means that distorted

TABLE 6.2 Average percentage by which the observed crime rate differs from that expected when the number of children passing through the war at different ages is maximized

Maxima passing through		England and Wales		Scotland
		Males	*Females*	*Males*
First year of life (0–1 year)]		−1.1	−0.3	−2.5
Second year]		+2.8	+3.0	+1.5
Third year]		+5.1	+5.0	+4.2
Fourth year]	during the 1939–45 war	+7.5	+7.7	+6.7
Fifth year]		+8.6	+8.7 (Peak)	+8.3 (Peak)
Sixth year]		+7.9	+7.3	+7.8
Seventh year]		+5.4	+4.4	+6.8
Eighth year]		+2.5	+1.7	+4.4
Ninth year]		−1.0	−1.2	+1.9

SOURCE: Wilkins (1960), Table p. 8.

social conditions have their major impact on children between the age of four and five is not proved, but this is a likely hypothesis. It is not clear how any hypothesis which relates the greatest impact of disturbed social conditions to a much earlier age could be consistent with these results. (Wilkins, 1960, p. 8)

It is extraordinarily difficult to separate age effects from era effects. To illustrate the point, let us take the generation of sixty-year-old people in England and Wales who are the only generation to have been twenty in 1945. Unhappily for our interpretation of their behaviour, they are also unique in having been thirty in 1955, forty in 1965 (the swinging sixties just passed them by, that could be why they are the way they are now) and so on. Their difference from other generations cannot be ascribed only to the time when the war ended and they were young. It is the aggregate of all their unique age/era experiences. In the same way, the troubled cohort which was five during the war was also unique in being ten in immediate post-war Britain. The generation may have reached its age of greatest criminality at a time when, for one reason or another, those committing offences had the greatest chance of appearing before the court. Wilkins' analysis was subject to criticism (see e.g. Rose 1968), and he himself now regards his analysis as inconclusive (personal communication). Even so, his analysis is not without its implications. If the same pattern as Wilkins identified was also evident in countries with widely different post-war histories, it increases the likelihood that being five years old and at war does change your life. In any event, Wilkins' position is not established rather than having been demonstrated to be wrong. In situations like this, those who frame public policy have to take into account the costs of behaving as though a particular position were right, and the costs of behaving as though it were wrong. The primary cost of behaving as though Wilkins is right is extra expenditure on child care. The primary cost of behaving as though Wilkins is wrong is that of dealing with a 'delinquent generation'. Only having thought about relative costs in this way is it clear where the burden of proof should prudently be placed. Thus the Wilkins approach cannot be dismissed as having no possible policy implications. At the very least, it was an imaginative and innovative piece of work. The research tradition which it represents has recently enjoyed something of a revival in the United States (see for instance Greenberg 1983).

A recent study of criminal careers includes prevalence estimates (Home Office 1985b) and some of its results are presented as Figure 6.3. The analysis was of the criminal convictions of people in three birth cohorts, from those born in 1953, 1958 and 1963. Figure 6.3 represents cumulative percentages of those who have been convicted of standard list offences. The surprisingly high prevalence of convictions among males will be commented on later. For the moment, we are concerned with possible generation differences. The possibility of such differences would be evident in differences in the *shape* of the three curves. Looking first at males, the later onset of first conviction of those born in 1958 and 1963, and the fact that they catch up the 1953 cohort later, looks like the effect of an increase in the use of cautioning for the younger cohorts rather than generational differences. For females, there are generational differences which are more difficult to explain:

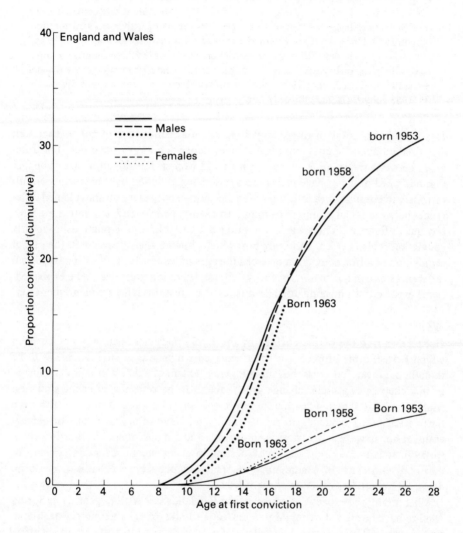

FIGURE 6.3 *Persons born in 1953, 1958 or 1963 who were convicted of 'standard list' offences by age at first conviction*

SOURCE: Home Office (1985b).

It appears that for females the cumulative conviction rates for those born in 1958 and 1963 were slightly higher than for those born in 1953: the cumulative conviction rate for females born in 1958 was over 5% by age 22, as compared with about $4\frac{1}{2}$% for those born in 1953. Up to age 17 the cumulative conviction rates for females born in 1958 and 1963 were very similar. Although the conviction curves for the three cohorts are close, especially in the early years, the figures suggest that a greater proportion of the females in the 1958 and 1963 cohorts were convicted of at least one offence than of the females in the 1953 cohort. (Home Office, 1985b, p. 3)

It is tempting to think of this change in terms of a reduced use of police discretion exercised in favour of girls, but there is no evidence one way or the other. The difference between the criminal careers of men and women remains immense. The fact that one third of males have picked up a criminal conviction by their twenty-eighth birthday, in contrast with only 6% of females, is one of the largest unexplained differences between social groups to be found. In a sense, people tend to ignore these most obvious differences. The same is true of the age variable, whose relationship to first conviction is also evident in Figure 6.3, which shows a sharp increase in the rate of acquisition of a first conviction between the ages of 14 and 16. Eschewing biological differences as a major reason for the difference, there is a great deal to be explained. Some of the pitfalls in using official statistics to address this issue are mentioned later.

War

Happily, during the period covered by this book, there has been only one event in which British armed forces have been engaged which was of such a scale as to be thought of as war. This was the Falklands engagement of 1982. War merits inclusion in this chapter as a social change great enough to be reflected in crime statistics. Mannheim (1965) reviews earlier literature on crime and war and suggests 'there is a fairly widespread tendency to regard the initial stage of a war as one of general enthusiasm, a wave of patriotic sentiments, and a consequent decline in crime' (p. 595). It is not entirely clear why decline in crime should be a consequence of patriotic sentiments in Mannheim's analysis, but plausible mechanisms could no doubt be hypothesized. More of them later.

What might one expect the impact of the Falklands war with Argentina in Spring 1982 to have been? Following Mannheim, one should expect a temporary decline in serious crime. The war with Argentina is of particular interest in that it did not affect the material standard of life in Great Britain in any significant way, (you can scarcely call the removal of Argentinian corned beef from supermarket shelves significant), so that changes in crime pattern could not plausibly be linked to changes in material quality of life. Further, the numbers of those engaged in the war were sufficiently small, and the duration of the war so brief, as to make any suggestion that crime change could result from demographic factors equally implausible.

It is convenient for present purposes that the war began without real warning on April 2nd 1982 and ended on June 14th, thus falling into a single quarter of 1982, the quarter being the unit of report of criminal statistics in Home Office statistical bulletins. One would expect any effect to persist at least into the third quarter of 1982, when the 'Falklands Factor', euphoria in victory, was at its height.

The method used was as follows: Table 3 of Home Office Statistical Bulletin 3/83 contains data on notifiable offences in each quarter of 1980, 1981 and 1982. Since hostilities were not forseen in the first quarter of 1982, there is no way that the Falklands issue could have affected crimes committed during that time. Therefore, for each type of offence, and for all offences combined, expected crime patterns for the rest of 1982 were calculated on the basis of the way 1980 and 1981 had progressed. For example, 5.9 thousand offences of robbery were recorded by the police in January–March 1982. By reference to the 1980 and 1981 data, robberies in January–March comprised 22.9% of robberies in the whole year, so on previous trends, at the end of March 1982 one could anticipate 25.8 thousand robberies in the whole of 1982 (i.e. $1/.229 \times$ the number of robberies in January–March 1982). Likewise, one can estimate the number of robberies which would occur in the second, third and fourth quarters of 1982, which turn out to be 6.3 thousand in April–June, 6.5 thousand in July–September, and 7.1 thousand in October–December. Turning then to the actual number of offences committed in 1982, one can compare this with the predicted number, the difference between the two being possibly associated with the war and its effects. Table 6.3 summarizes the data. It tabulates the differences between predicted and actual number of offences in each offence category in each quarter. The row indicating total offences is likely to be more reliable, being based on larger numbers less liable to chance variation. The columns do not add up to the total because of rounding errors and the omission of the 'other offences' category. An error in the Statistical Bulletin itself for the second quarter of 1982 adds a further problem. Nonetheless the scale of the differences tabulated is such as to make these difficulties unimportant.

TABLE 6.3   Discrepancies between expected and actual levels of notifiable crime by quarter, 1982
(Negative values indicate actual levels of crime lower than expected. Numbers are crimes/1000)

Offence	First Quarter[1]	Second Quarter	Third Quarter	Fourth Quarter
Violence vs person	0.0	−0.4	−0.1	+1.3
Sexual Offences	0.0	+0.1	+0.5	+0.8
Burglary	0.0	−13.1	−9.1	−0.5
Robbery	0.0	−0.8	−1.2	−1.0
Theft and Handling	0.0	−5.8	−20.2	−8.4
Fraud and Forgery	0.0	−0.2	−0.2	+0.5
Criminal Damage	0.0	−8.3	−8.3	+2.3
Total[2]	0.0	−28.9	−33.7	−7.2

[1]   By definition, this will always be 0.0. The column is included simply to clarify the trend over the year.
[2]   The total deviates from the sum of individual offences because of rounding errors and the omission of 'other offences'.

SOURCE: this analysis first appeared in Pease (1983).

At the foot of the second column of Table 6.3, it will be seen that there were 28.9 thousand offences fewer than expected during the second quarter of 1982. At the foot of the third column, it is evident that there were 33.7 thousand fewer than expected in the third quarter. During the fourth quarter, only 7.2 thousand offences fewer than expected were recorded. This pattern is consistent with an interpretation in terms of the war, namely that recorded crime declined during and immediately after the Falklands war, returning towards the predicted level by the end of 1982. The most notable changes for individual types of crime occur for burglary, criminal damage and robbery, the last being the largest effect in proportional terms, but probably the one least interpretable in terms of the war, since it showed the least marked return to predicted levels at the end of 1982.

Clearly, there are a variety of reasons why the picture was as it was:

1. Chance (by no means to be underestimated);
2. Fewer opportunities for crime (people were in their houses watching news broadcasts, and were thus unlikely to be burgled and were unavailable to be victims of street crime);
3. National solidarity leads victims to report less crime ('When compared with what our lads are suffering in the South Atlantic, my burglary is trivial');
4. National solidarity leads the police to record fewer of the crimes reported to them ('When compared with what our lads are suffering in the South Atlantic, your burglary is trivial');
5. National solidarity leads offenders to wish to commit less crime, or be less tempted to because they too are indoors watching the news broadcasts.

In any event, it may have been that the major social change which the war represented had an effect on crime levels. At the time of writing, thirty-eight people have just died in rioting at the Heysel soccer stadium, Brussels, before the European Cup Final. The effect of this upon British people seems to have been very considerable. Whether it will amount to a social context in which crimes against the person temporarily decline (or increase because of greater victim and police enthusiasm to 'crack down' on such offences), remains to be seen. The reader may wish to apply the method described in relation to the Falklands war to the quarterly returns published between the time of writing and the time of reading, to see how events turned out.

Other major events may change crime levels. David Phillips (Nigel Walker, personal communication) has discerned in the United States a three-week reduction in the murder rate after world title prize fights. This sort of effect has never, to our knowledge, been investigated in Great Britain. It should be.

Crime and Punishment

Earlier in the book we have drawn attention to some of the complexities in how events come to be recorded as crimes, and ambiguities in how to think about amounts of punishment, in particular amounts of imprisonment. On a purely descriptive level, how have numbers of notifiable crimes known and number of prison receptions under sentence covaried over time? Andrew Rutherford (1984) has pointed out how crime and punishment do not necessarily go together when considered cross-nationally. Within England and Wales, how have they gone together during the period 1963–79? (The reader will recall that the 1980–82 data are not precisely comparable with data for earlier years because of changes in recording practice). The crude index of punishments is prison receptions under sentence, being preferable to prison population, which incorporates the consequences of sentencing practice from earlier years (see Chapter 4). The crude index of crime is the number of indictable offences known to the police. In fact the association between these is quite close (r = + .78), as might be expected of two indices of growth in a growth industry. Laura Norder is growing like Topsy! What is interesting, and a point which also shows that correlations should not be interpreted without also looking at relative rates of growth of the variables, is that for every additional 1000 indictable offences, there has been a mere 12.5 more receptions into prison. So although recorded crime and (at least this index of) punishment go up together, they go up at vastly different rates. The practical implications of this are largely determined by why you think the relationship is as it is, and some of the complexities involved in making this judgement are evident from earlier chapters. The relationship does set the scene, however, for our conclusions in the final chapter, that what you do about crime and what you do with criminals are best approached as separate questions.

Social Factors and Punishment

To what extent is punishment responsive to social factors? This really resolves into two questions. What are the factors which determine the total amount of punishment inflicted? What are the factors which determine how punishment is distributed among people punished? These two questions will be addressed in sequence.

How much Punishment?

It is clear that executive release decisions operate to reduce total punishment exacted to a level well below the level imposed by the courts. This reduction may have given rise to the recently fashionable view that there is a roughly constant amount of punishment over time. The seminal paper, by Blumstein and Cohen (1973) advanced the view that levels of custodial population in a society remain fairly constant over time in proportion to national population. Blumstein, Cohen and Nagin (1976) developed this argument. These writers link their suggestion to the classic Durkheimian view that crime is a natural outgrowth of the processes generating social solidarity. In consequence, Blumstein *et al.* (1976) argue:

> the standards or thresholds that define punishable behaviour are adjusted in response to overall shifts in the behaviour of the members of a society so that a roughly constant proportion of the population is always undergoing punishment. Thus, if many more individuals engage in behaviour defined as punishable, the demarcation between criminal and non-criminal behaviour would be adjusted to redesignate at least part of the previously criminal behaviour as non-criminal, or the intensity or duration of punishment for those convicted would be reduced. (Blumstein *et al.* 1976, p. 317)

In support of the stability contention, Blumstein Cohen and Nagin present 'imprisonment rates' for the United States between 1930 and 1970, for Norway between 1880 and 1964 and for Canada between 1880 and 1959. The data for all three countries show a remarkable stability. If this stability is general, it can be regarded as revolutionizing the international study of prison populations, in that the most interesting question then becomes why prison populations in different countries stabilize at different levels. Because the implications of acceptance of the Blumstein position are so great, his stability hypothesis requires, and has been given, some critical scrutiny. This has been of two kinds – criticism of the data which Blumstein *et al.* used, and the presentation of data suggesting instability of prison populations over time. Waller and Chan (1974) argue that Blumstein and Cohen (1973) cut the prison population of the USA in half by using a definition of prison which omitted local jails. Of course the crucial point for the stability hypothesis is not that this is true, but whether the local jail population fluctuated more than the population which Blumstein and his colleagues examined. If it did not, the stability hypothesis stands. Waller and Chan do not present data on this point. However they do present data on four other countries between 1920 and 1973, which show clear and occasionally dramatic instabilities in three cases, including England and Wales. The Waller and Chan data are reproduced here as Figure 6.4. Greenberg (1980) also presents data on Polish prisons between 1923 and 1971 which show variations over time inconsistent with the stability hypothesis.

In summary of the stability hypothesis, there may yet be some mileage in a modified version, but the evidence now available shows it to have been wrong in its simple form. The use of carceral punishment varies substantially over time in relation to total national population. In any case, taking prison populations as a measure of the amount of punishment generally may be misguided (see Chapter 4, above).

The tripling of the England and Wales prison population in the fifteen years from 1940 gives particular pause for thought. It took place alongside an increase in the number of indictable offences of which people were convicted, but the interesting analysis in the 1955 Report of the Commissioners of Prisons makes it clear that another major factor, operating in addition to this increase, was an increase in the average length of sentence passed. One factor which might be relevant was the availability of new prison estate in the form of camps for the armed forces which were no longer required. Perhaps, as to be discussed later, available space drove sentencing practice. The data presented in Chapter 4 make it clear that in England and Wales variation in prison population during the period covered by this book would have been very much greater had sentences been served as imposed. Executive release decisions smooth out variations. It may be that the relative stability noted by Blumstein results from this sort of executive thermostat model of prison population.

The executive thermostat is particularly in evidence in statistics of Borstal training. The Borstal sentence was indeterminate between six months and two years, so Borstal staff could regulate time served within those limits. Figure 6.5 shows clearly that as the number of those admitted to Borstal increased, the length of time for which they stayed in Borstal decreased, so that the Borstal population stayed conveniently within what the Borstals could hold. The particular fear, at a time when the prison building

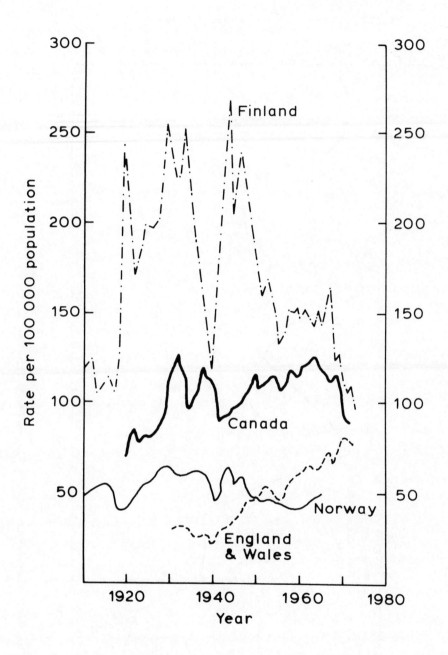

FIGURE 6.4   *Number of persons in prison per 100 000 population in Canada, England and Wales, Finland and Norway (1920 to 1973)*

SOURCE: Waller and Chan (1974).

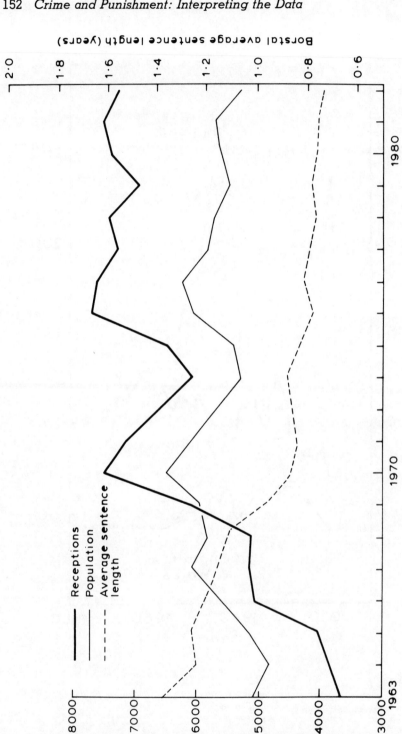

FIGURE 6.5   *Borstal receptions, population and effective sentence length, 1963–82*

programme is so extensive, is that new places will engender extra imprisonment. It is but a short step from reducing effective sentence length to keep custodial populations within bounds, to allowing the increase of effective sentence length to utilize new custodial capacity. There is clear evidence that this happened in the United States as regards custody, both penal and psychiatric (Krisberg and Schwartz 1983, Poulin 1980, Schwartz *et al.* 1984). Krisberg and Schwartz (1983) report that 'an exploratory attempt to explain the large variations in state rates of corrections admissions suggested that most of the variation in detention admissions can be explained by the number of detention beds per 100 000 youth population' (p. 333). This is a matter of urgent current interest at the time of writing, when in a written answer to Alf Dubs MP on April 4th 1985, Home Office Minister David Mellor revealed that the number of prisoners in England and Wales at the end of March 1985 was 46 215, an increase of 1221 on the same date the previous year. The increase is remarkable given that the prison population in March 1985 would have been some 2000 higher but for the relaxation in parole eligibility criteria in July 1984. The context of the increase is the major prison building programme which will provide an extra 10 600 prison places. In his speech at Blackpool on 11 October 1983, the Home Secretary announced that there was to be both an acceleration and an extension of the major prison building programme already in progress. He said

> Overcrowding in our prisons makes control and security far more difficult. But I am not in any way embarrassed to say that it is unacceptable in itself because it is inhumane . . .
> I am, therefore, glad to say that the measures I have outlined today will put us on course for ending prison overcrowding by the end of the decade. (Home Office, 1984e, p. 22)

If we are right in our interpretation of the data, prison capacity will 'drive' sentencing practice so that population will continue to outstrip capacity and the provision of extra capacity is self-defeating in its purpose to reduce overcrowding. Whether the amount of prison sentencing currently given is a correctly gauged response to current wickedness is a metaphysical question to which statistics cannot help to give an answer. But these are not the grounds on which the increased prison capacity is justified. In a book which should be required reading for those interested in the influence of policy choices on prison populations, Andrew Rutherford (1984) also identifies an increase in personnel as a characteristic of the 'expansionist *option*' (emphasis added), and notes a virtual tripling of prison officers during roughly the period of interest of this book, accompanying only (?) a 50% increase in prison population.

Who gets punished—and how much?

In Chapter 4 dramatic differences between countries in their use of imprisonment were identified. The question of why these differences should exist was not addressed. Wilkins (1984) makes the fascinating suggestion that there might be what one could regard as national differences in tolerance of differentials. This would imply, for example, that income *inequality* covaries with differences in the *length* of prison sentences. From a tentative forthcoming analysis (Wilkins *et al.* 1986) it does look as though the prediction is fulfilled. It may really be that our use of long prison sentences is predictable from the way we view differences generally.

Having treated the relationships between the distribution of sentences, can we say anything about the social circumstances of those convicted and changes in the ways in which they have been dealt with between 1963 and 1983. The brief answer is, from official statistics, not really. It is clear that in various ways enforcement practices of the criminal law are unequal in their dealings with members of different social classes (see Bottoms 1977, Lidstone *et al.* 1980, Downes 1983, Box 1983) but the question here is, once convicted, who is punished more. Official statistics give only the barest details (gender, age, and previous convictions) of those convicted. They give no details about those not convicted, and those convicted are almost certain to represent a changing proportion of those who could have been convicted. The only hints about changes come from one-off research exercises like that presented as Figure 6.3. To illustrate some of the difficulties we are likely to encounter, the case of gender offers itself. The women's movement generally has provided many insights into the ways in which women are disadvantaged. It has also generated, at least in the view of the male writers of this book, a tendency to construe as disadvantage areas where the evidence is not such as to be capable of sustaining that view. We will draw heavily on Nigel Walker's (1981b) commentary on this issue. He points out that Mawby (1977) and Smart (1977) both start with the fact that a higher proportion of women imprisoned have no previous convictions than is the case for men. They go on to conclude that 'when previous record is taken into consideration, females are more likely to be imprisoned than males' (Mawby 1977, p. 4) and women 'are five times as likely as men to be sent to prison for their first offence' (Smart p. 137). As Walker points out, the number of women who are imprisoned on first conviction as a proportion of all women imprisoned tells one nothing about the proportion of women who are imprisoned on first conviction. To say that 40% of people killed while making parachute jumps were making their first jump tells one nothing about the proportion of people making their first jump who get killed.

Writing of Smart (1979) Walker observes:

the author tries to play down the sharp rise in women's convictions for violence between 1965 and 1975, which is sharper than the male increase, by arguing
1. That expressing increases in percentages is misleading when numbers are very small. She points out that there was a 500% increase in women convicted of murder because only one woman was convicted of murder in 1965. True, but the fuss is not simply about murder, it is about manslaughter, grievous bodily harm and other serious and deliberate injuries. On her own showing, 857 females were found guilty of such offences in 1965 but 2785 in 1975. These are not small numbers, and the increase is 320% per cent., twice the percentage increase for males.
2. That anyway convictions for violent crimes by women are not a new phenomenon. But the very figures she cites herself show much smaller increases – and even one decrease – in earlier decades.
    The moral seems to be that if the statistics don't prove what you want, don't be too discouraged; see what you can do with them. (Walker, 1981b, p. 381)

Walker's fairly devastating critique does not show that there are no examples of punishment discrimination against women in the literature. Dominelli (1984) points out that a much lower proportion of women than men receive community service orders. Nonetheless, there are great difficulties in making sensible inferences from gender differences in official statistics. A recurrent implicit theme of the book has been what might be called the problem of the denominator, which gets worse as one advances through the criminal justice system. This is the problem that the total in relation to which criminal justice actions are expressed is highly selected from the total available to be in the table. Proportions of those convicted who are imprisoned depends upon the stability of the number convicted – but changes in recording and cautioning rates make the number convicted a changing proportion of those who could be convicted. Changes in the numbers and characteristics of those imprisoned change the denominator in paroling rates. Changes in reconviction rates reflect changes in intake criteria of the sentence to which they refer, and so on. No wonder, then, that even on the criteria of age and gender for which data are included in official statistics, there are few firm conclusions to be drawn. Perhaps the best that can be said firmly is that prior convictions make sentences more severe!

Social Data Not Given In Criminal Statistics

Apart from the basic social data on offenders available in official statistics, there is an absolute dearth of social information on offenders which might allow calculations of the extent to which social groups are over-represented among those convicted. Visiting prisons, youth custody and detention centres, one's eyes tell one that there are a lot of black prisoners, and that many of those in custody are small and thin, but one would be hard put to it to justify either of these assertions from official statistics. Indeed such research as has been done (McConville and Baldwin 1982, Crow and Cove 1984) gives very little reason to suppose that courts at least are discriminatory by race. The denominator problem should alert us to the possibility that discrimination might occur earlier in the process.

Much social information of potential usefulness is maintained by the Home Office. For example the Parole Index contains social and criminal history data on all males on whom a parole decision has been made since the scheme started operation in 1968. This information is not publicly available. Frankly, neither does it seem to inform Home Office publications other than the Annual Reports of the Parole Board. In any event, to demonstrate that a group is overrepresented in prison is only the first step in demonstrating that it is undue punitiveness which has made things as they are. (Nor should it be lost sight of that underrepresentation of certain groups in prison might reflect discriminatory practices). It is convenient to use the relationship between unemployment and punishment to illustrate matters.

Gladstone (1979) reproduced Canadian data on the relationship between prison admissions and unemployment rate and British data on youth unemployment and Borstal receptions (reproduced here as Figures 6.6 and 6.7). In the most thorough study of British origin to date on the topic, Box and Hale (1982) argue that unemployment is related to imprisonment independently of the rate of crime. They contend that 'after controlling for other relevant factors, an increase of 1000 in the number of

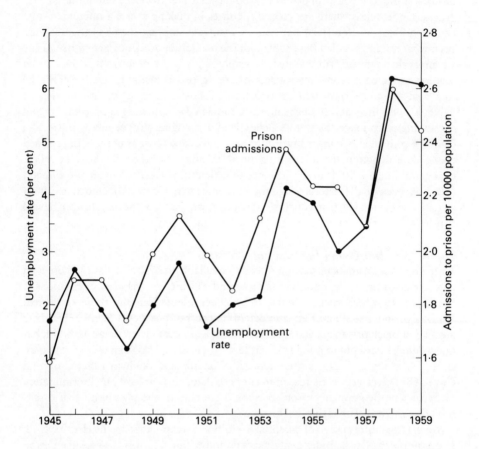

FIGURE 6.6 Prison admissions and unemployment rate in Canada, 1945–59

SOURCE: Gladstone (1979), Fig. 3, p. 40.

unemployed will lead, on the average, to ten more people receiving prison sentences'
(p. 28). The work of Box and Hale offers an excellent example of how the relationships between crime, punishment and unemployment can be reconceptualized
sensibly away from traditional criminology, which is:

> limited to one banality, which consequently becomes enshrined as orthodoxy. Reduced
> to its bare essentials, this orthodoxy states that as unemployment increases, the rate of

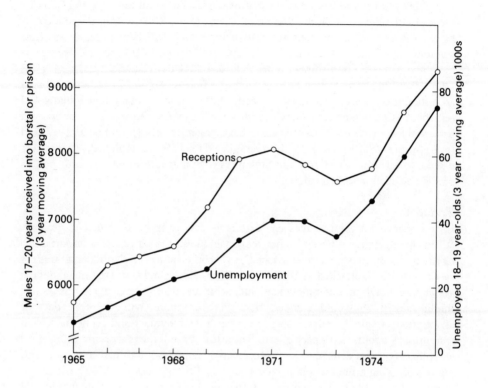

FIGURE 6.7 *Prison and borstal receptions and unemployment in late adolescence, 1965–76*

SOURCE: Gladstone (1979), Fig. 4, p. 41.

criminal behaviour increases, and this not only results in more people being sent to prison, but also leads to an extension of the period for which they are imprisoned. (Box and Hale, 1982, p. 20)

They offer the alternative explanation that increased use of imprisonment is 'not a direct response to any rise in crime, but is an ideologically motivated response to the perceived threat of crime posed by the swelling population of economically marginalised people'. (p. 22) However neither the Box and Hale study nor Gladstone's statistics show that it is the unemployed who are being locked up more (it's that old ecological fallacy again) and it may be that a generally depressed economic climate creates both unemployment and general punitiveness, general in the sense that it is not directed specifically at the unemployed. To try and disentangle the possibilities, Iain Crow and Frances Simon of the National Association for the Care and Resettlement of Offenders and the Prevention of Crime (NACRO) are engaged in a court-based study of unemployment and sentencing which will help to tease out these variables. Until research of that kind is reported, it is premature to link unemployment and increased punishment other than as a mere correlation.

One should perhaps not end this section on a note of pessimism and delay. There are established, fairly predictable, specific links between unemployed status and sentence passed. Community service orders are longer (not because the unemployed have committed more serious offences or have longer records) (Jardine *et al.* 1983) and fines are lower (Softley 1978) for the unemployed than for the employed, other factors taken into account. The Crow and Simon research may allow more general and less predictable differences to emerge!

Endnote

In this chapter, it would have been extremely easy to indulge political argument. When linking crime rates and other social variables, it is particularly important to clarify policy options, otherwise associations become mere rhetoric-fodder, as was the case in the articles attacked by Walker (see above). If Box and Hale are right about the association between unemployment and sentence severity, what are the policy implications? We would contend that there are none without other data or assumptions about the relationships between unemployment and crime itself, and assumptions about the impact of criminal justice on offenders (specific deterrence) and others (general deterrence). If Conservative administrations had coincided with periods of rising crime, would it have been a bad thing? It depends on the place of crime control in the policy pantheon. It may be that there are legitimate intellectual questions to answer (for example about the notion of a society's general tolerance of inequality manifesting itself in diverse places) but we should not delude ourselves that, without much complexity and many assumptions, data of the kind presented here, are likely to inform, or should inform, policy choices.

7

Evaluating Criminal Justice by Numbers

A pervasive theme in this book has been the way in which the 'facts' can so readily be misinterpreted or manipulated to serve particular professional or political interests. Despite appearances to the contrary, statistics of this kind are not neutral commentaries upon or accounts of social facts and official decision-making. This should come as no surprise.

Some would argue that crime statistics are biassed, partial and often misleading because of the perceived significance of crime and punishment for the social and moral fabric; in the face of real or imagined threats to personal safety and security, official statistics are naturally turned to for information and reassurance. More specifically, it is commonly expected that they should be able to indicate whether the crime problem is under control, and how effective the law enforcement and penal processes are in combatting it. We would go further, to argue that any form of information-gathering cannot be accurate in any absolute way, but only usable for a purpose or set of purposes. Certainly the way in which data are collected and organized depends on what you want to do with them. This is a difficult point to recognize until a novice researcher comes to analyse a first major data-gathering exercise.

Although what follows is implicit or explicit in much of what went earlier, we should end the book with some brief reflections on the role of official statistics in evaluating criminal justice policy and practice. It will be concluded that the regularly published criminal statistics provide few, if any, significant answers to many of the important traditional questions of evaluation. The fact that many of the available statistics *appear* to provide such answers means that extra caution is needed in their interpretation. On the other hand, criminal justice statistics are informative in a variety of ways, and should not be discarded as meaningless, as has sometimes been their fate. Let us then look at some typical questions to which it might quite sensibly be thought that criminal statistics would provide answers.

Hesitant Questions and Tentative Answers

Earlier chapters have addressed, directly or indirectly, many of the questions about the effectiveness of the criminal justice system to which answers are often sought from published statistics. The work of the police and the effectiveness of sentencing are two topics where such questions are often posed. As far as the police are concerned, the basic question is perhaps about how successful they are in clearing up the crimes which become known to them; for sentencing, the basic question has often been taken to concern the relative reconviction rates of those given different sentences. Both questions bring with them untested assumptions about objectives and methods.

In the discussion of the police clear-up rate (in Chapter 2) we emphasized the importance of recognizing that many crimes are automatically solved by the very fact of becoming known to the police, that in many crimes against the person the offender is immediately identifiable, and that in consequence much of the variation between the clear-up rate of different police forces is attributable to the crime mix of the area. Among the additional factors suggested by Burrows and Tarling (1982) which might explain variations in clear-up rates, are arrangements for investigating crime (e.g. the role of the uniformed branch and specialist squads), the ways in which crimes come to police notice, the incentives offered by the police hierarchy and CID case screening procedures (Burrows and Tarling 1982, p. 12). To these might be added police culture factors, like the desire to avoid the appellation 'snatcher', applied by officers in Chatterton's research (Chatterton 1976) to their colleagues who resolved problems by arrest rather than negotiation involving no crime record.

These conclusions not only have direct implications for the interpretation of variations between police forces. They also raise serious doubts about the extent to which any clear-up rate, whether local or national, should be used as a measure of police work outcomes. The basic invalidity of this statistic for the purpose of internal or external monitoring is fully recognized by the police, as indicated in this excerpt from Sinclair and Miller's survey:

> The danger is that the pressure to produce measures will result in considerable costs and statistics which distort police effort . . . Policemen interviewed all pointed to the ease with which statistics such as clear-up rates could be changed by legitimated changes in recording practice. They were afraid that the use of these statistics as measures of effectiveness would yield unreliable statistics. Some said that 'league tables' could result in undesirable practices . . . It was said that whereas most police measures are concerned with crime and its detection, most police activities are concerned with something else. (Sinclair and Miller 1984, p. 15)

A recent review of research into the relationship between police work and crime, by Clarke and Hough (1984), confirms that clear-up rates bear little relationship to the realities of detective work and are not an appropriate measure of police effectiveness. Most detective work is concerned with relatively routine burglary and theft, where the investigation is either straightforward (because the offender is caught red-handed or directly implicated from the start) or very unpromising (Clarke and Hough 1984,

p. 9). Available research suggests that 'increases in detective manpower and technological improvements yield only marginal gains in clear-up rates'. It seems much
more likely that trends in clear-up rates are directly affected by changes in the balance
between *prima facie* detectable and undetectable crimes amongst those recorded by
the police (Clarke and Hough 1984, pp. 11–12).

Widening the consideration of police effectiveness from clear-up rates to the
generally assumed crime preventive function of police patrol does not enable any
more optimism about the appropriateness of the statistics to the performance of police
work. After a thorough review of the research evidence, from Britain and overseas
(especially North America), on the effectiveness of both general and specialized police
patrols, of criminal investigation and community policing, Morris and Heal (1981)
concluded – 'At the risk of some over-simplification the message most obviously to be
drawn from this review is that it is beyond the ability of the police to have a direct
effect on a good deal of crime' (Morris and Heal 1981, p. 49). Similarly, Clarke and
Hough (1984) agree that there is little evidence that increasing the number or frequency of foot or car patrols actually reduces crime, although they do qualify the
otherwise very negative impression that might be created:

> The report does not argue that nothing can be done about crime – that 'nothing
> works' – nor that the police have little impact on crime . . . Rather that there is only
> limited scope for enhancing the impact which the police already have on crime. (Clarke
> and Hough 1984, p. 2)

The apparent failure of traditional measures of police effectiveness to reflect any
direct impact by the police on crime levels has led to a reassessment not only of the
adequacy of the measures themselves but of the appropriateness of a monolithic view
of the police function in simple crime control terms. Thus, among the legitimate and
desirable roles for the police in this broader conception of their crime-related task,
Morris and Heal emphasized police responsibility for alleviating the community's
fear of crime 'which in practice may be only loosely related to the actual level of crime
occurring, and is possibly more socially harmful,' and also their important role in
victim support, since for the victim 'the aftermath of the incident may well be more
distressing than the incident itself' (Morris and Heal 1981, p. 52). Likewise, Clarke
and Hough felt that there should be more explicit recognition of the important police
objectives of increasing the public's feeling of security and improving public satisfaction with the police response to reported crime victimization (Clarke and Hough
1984). Attempts should be made to produce a better and wider range of measures for
the various elements of the police role:

> The public must receive better information about police work and about the effective-
> ness of crime control efforts. There must be more informed discussion about the tasks
> which the police should and should not perform . . . developing adequate 'output
> measures' for the totality of police work – difficult though this may be – must therefore
> rank high on the research agenda. (Clarke and Hough 1984, pp. 20–21)

The material that has already come from the British Crime Survey on public perceptions of crime risk and the actual rates of crime victimization provides a good example of the way regular statistics could be used to produce a different 'consumer-oriented' angle upon overall police effectiveness and public satisfaction (Hough and Mahyew 1983, 1985; Maxfield 1984; Gottfredson 1984).

The discussion of sentencing at the beginning of Chapter 4 hardly touched upon the question of what happens to offenders *after* they have been sentenced. In fact, despite the vast amount of information set out in a detailed series of Tables about persons proceeded against at the higher and lower courts, which have always been a feature of official criminal statistics in England and Wales (or *Judicial Statistics*, as they were more aptly titled in the 19th century), there is much less information included about the extent of future reoffending. Compared with the period between the wars, there is now less information about reconviction rates, and more data about the front end of criminal justice, as penal pessimism and concern with criminal justice as an efficient, rather than an effective, system, have increased. The two main exceptions to the lack of reconviction statistics in current data concern breaches of various kinds of conditional and supervised sentences, and the reconviction rates after imprisonment described in Chapter 4 and published in the annual *Prison Statistics England and Wales*.

Information on the proportion of offenders proceeded against each year for breach of a court order is of some significance in its own right, because it shows how 'successful' sentencers are in selecting offenders who will abide by statutory conditions and/or how 'successful' probation officers appear to be in inducing clients to behave in accordance with expected norms of behaviour. It does however introduce a somewhat unfortunate comparative or competitive dimension *vis-à-vis* the breach rate of different measures, *as if* identical offenders are given each sentence, so that any difference in outcome can be attributed to the merits or deficiencies of the particular measure and the way in which it is administered, like medicine to a group of clones. This comparative obsession also ignores the 'negotiable' element inherent in most breach proceedings, as well as the different statutory criteria that can count as grounds for proceedings. Some measures impose a much wider range of conditions on those subjected to them. Community service orders and parole licences contain conditions well beyond the simple requirement not to reoffend. This is important because the institutionalized norms and individual practices of the exercise of discretion in initiating breach proceedings is so wide as to render wholly suspect any detailed comparisons purporting either to describe or evaluate what is really going on. The most that can be said of breach statistics is that they superficially monitor some aspects of the officially recognized misbehaviour of those on whom court orders are made or licences granted. Beyond that, speculation unfettered reigns.

A similar situation obtains with respect to the Prison Department's statistics of reconvictions of those who have served sentences of imprisonment (see Chapter 4). The central point that bears repetition here is that the value and proper use of statistics depend wholly on what *purpose(s)* the user has in mind. Most of those who are interested in reconviction rates want to be able to see whether one sentence is 'better' than another in this respect, or whether the 'success rate' of a particular type of sentence has changed over time. There is no way in which the information currently available in regularly published statistics can provide adequate answers to these questions. The dedicated enquirer must delve into special research studies or other 'one-off' Home Office analyses, and will only then begin to discern the complexities of the problem and the essential tentativeness of the conclusions. The basic research technique begins with the identification of those characteristics of offenders which are found to be associated with reconviction, irrespective of sentence. Among the factors that have been so identified (of those for which regular information is usually available in official records) are the gender of the offender, age at first conviction, number of previous criminal convictions and nature of current offence. The reconviction rates of those given each type of sentence are then calculated and compared with the reconviction rate that would have been expected after taking into account the characteristics of those given that particular type of sentence. Of course this only works if people similar in offence and record are given a range of different sentences, but there is enough sentencing disparity sloshing around the system for this not to be a problem. This done, one is in a position to compare *actual* and *expected* rates of conviction. Any such differences may then form the basis of provisional claims that some sentences are more successful than others in reducing reconviction. Evaluative research of this kind by the Home Office in the early 1960s led to a number of tentative conclusions that were given wide publicity in the official handbook for magistrates, *The Sentence of the Court*. Included among the conclusions were the following:

(i) fines were followed by the fewest reconvictions compared with the expected numbers for both first offenders and recidivists of almost all ages;
(ii) probation produced relatively better results when used for offenders with previous convictions;
(iii) Approved School results were also better for offenders with previous convictions;
(iv) Detention Centre results tended to be slightly inferior to Borstal results;
(v) Imprisonment results were better for offenders with previous convictions . . .
(Home Office 1964, para 161)

An acknowledged and quite serious weakness of this research was that the number and type of factors used to calculate the overall 'expected' reconviction rates were rather limited – 'the courts may have made allowance for factors not recorded in the documents available for research, and the possibility cannot be ignored that particular sentences may have been used more frequently for the "worse" or for the "better" offenders in any of the categories studied' (Home Office 1964, para 164).

A later study for the Home Office by Phillpotts and Lancucki (1979) examined the pattern of reconvictions for a sample of 5000 offenders sentenced for standard list offences during January 1971. 50% of the males and 22% of the females were reconvicted within a 6 year follow-up. Despite the important influence of age and number of previous convictions upon reoffending, the authors concluded that 'it was generally the case that males given custodial sentences had higher reconviction rates than males given suspended sentences or probation or supervision orders, and these in turn had higher reconviction rates than males given a fine or an absolute or conditional discharge' (Phillpotts and Lancucki 1979, p. 16). Although this research is as good as one could imagine with the data its authors had to hand, it is not entirely immune from the same kind of criticism as was levelled at the earlier Home Office study.

Continued doubts about research methods in this area, and an increased fashion for retribution as a penal purpose, has resulted in widespread scepticism in many quarters about the capacity of any sentence to change the future behaviour of an offender significantly more or less than any other sentence. Thus, the current edition of *The Sentence of the Court* (3rd edn. 1978), after summarizing the results of this eva- luative research, concludes that 'research studies have almost unanimously failed to show that any one type of sentencing measure is more likely to achieve reform than any other' (Home Office 1978a, para 291). We think such a conclusion is overstated, and that a much more open-minded approach is necessary. The 'nothing works' pessi- mism of the 1970s was premature. On matters methodological, at least one extremely good prediction instrument (see Nuttall *et al.* 1977) based on sixteen criminal history/social background variables is in current use in the administration of the parole scheme, and has wider applicability (Sapsford 1978). On substantive grounds, *both* Home Office studies of the reconviction of paroled prisoners (Nuttall *et al.* 1977, Home Office 1978) *suggest* that parole may reduce the likelihood of reconviction. This is not conclusive, since explanations other than the effect of supervision and threat of recall to prison are possible, which well-designed research should address. Walker (1985) reviews other evidence suggesting how, for some people at some stages of a criminal career, different sentences may have different effects. Most funda- mentally, we have been much too inclined to behave in evaluation as though all prisons, all probation officers and all community service tasks had the same impact on people. Greater differentiation among sanctions in the same nominal category is necessary. Our penal agnosticism, it should be recognized, is based on ethical as well as empirical grounds, since we fear a new barbarism if no purpose is seen for penal sanctions beyond simple retribution and incapacitation.

Research has continued into patterns of reconviction, albeit generally in ways which do not address the question of the effectiveness of sanctions in reducing recon- viction. There has been an interesting shift of focus towards a 'criminal career' per- spective. Although this perspective is unlikely to become incorporated as a regular feature of official statistics, which are largely *offence* oriented rather than *offender* oriented, there are signs of a developing interest within the Home Office that might result in regular supplementary criminal career data being produced, in a similar way to that in which British Crime Survey data are being published in parallel with data on officially recorded crime. It is certainly significant that the Home Office Statistical Department is now geared up to consider criminality in this way. Home Office Sta- tistical Bulletin 7/85 examined the criminal careers of those born in 1953, 1958 and 1963. It confirmed that the reconviction rate of those who were first convicted at an early age was generally higher than that of those first convicted later in life, but sug- gested that the conventional use of a 2-year follow-up period for purposes of recon- viction should be reconsidered in the light of evidence that reconviction rates *after 8 years* were often more than 50% higher than after 2 years (Home Office 1985b, para 19). To this our answer is – it all depends on what you want to use them for. If the *relative* risks of reconviction of different groups are the same at 2 years as at 8, there is only a restricted range of purposes for which 8-year rates are preferable.

Reconviction rates of juveniles were found to vary according to the type of sentence imposed, but many of these differences disappeared when the nature of the offence was taken into account. The below average reconviction rates of those fined or given conditional/absolute discharges were found to be attributable to a significant extent to type of offence, but the above average rates for those given supervision were not. Those convicted of burglary were generally more likely to be reconvicted, whatever the sentence, than those convicted of other types of offence, but with the usual caveat that 'those results also may reflect circumstances of the offender which were taken into account when the sentence was imposed but which are not reflected in the classifications used in this analysis' (Home Office 1985b, para 26).

A novel feature of this Home Office analysis was its examination of the relationship between the type of first conviction as a juvenile and the probability and type of any second conviction within two years. This information is of direct significance and importance to sentencers, as it enables them to answer such questions as: 'What chance is there of this juvenile offender being convicted of this type of offence within the next two years? What chance is there of his being reconvicted for a different type of offence within the next two years?' Table 7.1 is based on a reworking of some of the relevant data from the Bulletin and shows that for all types of offence the probability of there being *no* second conviction is greater than the chance of a second conviction within two years. Furthermore, for all offence types, where a further conviction does occur, it is more likely to be for a different type of offence than for an offence of the

TABLE 7.1 Males born in 1953, 1958 and 1963 and convicted of one or more standard list offence before the age of 16, by principal type of offence on first conviction, and reconviction outcome after two years

Principal Offence on First Conviction	*Percentage Reconvicted of Offence of Same Type*	*Percentage Reconvicted of Offence of Different Type*	*Percentage Not Reconvicted*
Violence against the person	2	28	69*
Burglary (inc. robbery)	19	25	57
Theft and handling stolen goods	16	20	64
Fraud and forgery	0	38	63
Criminal damage	3	24	73
Other Indictable	2	34	64
Summary offences (excluding motoring)	3	25	72
Motoring (mainly theft/unauthorised taking)	9	30	60
Total n	16 195	57 005	73 200

* Rows do not always sum to precisely 100 because of rounding.

SOURCE: first appeared in Pease (1985 b).

same type as the first. This is true even for offences such as burglary and motoring, commonly thought of as being committed by 'specialists' rather than 'generalists', and is of particular importance where the first conviction is for a serious offence (such as violence) where there is a strong likelihood that a court would tend to over-sentence on the assumption that the offender may be on the first rung of a criminal career ladder of similar offences in the future. It is understandable for sentencers to over-estimate the likelihood of the same type of offence recurring in a criminal career, so any statistics or research studies that provide evidence that runs counter to this 'common-sense' assumption deserve special publicity. The development of the kind of criminal career information contained in Statistical Bulletin 7/85 provides a valuable model for application to other decision stages in the process which also involve predictive assumptions. These may occur upstream in the process, as in bail/remand in custody decisions, or 'downstream', as in parole decisions (Pease 1985b).

Alternative Evaluations of Criminal Justice

The findings of research into the effectiveness of policing and sentencing have wide implications. They do far more than simply showing the inadequacy of statistics of clear-up rates and patterns of reconviction. When considered alongside the findings of criminological research into the apparent causes and correlates of crime, they offer a crucial insight. This is that criminal justice policy and practice has a strictly limited effect on rates of crime. Increasingly, it is coming to be recognized by those who work in or study the penal services that the impact of the criminal justice system upon crime is marginal. Further, this would continue to be true of any realistically attainable state of criminal justice policy under any tenable theory of criminal behaviour. The problem of what to do about crime and the problem of what to do with convicted criminals are for most practical purposes different problems with different answers. This is *not* inconsistent with the possibility of some penal sanctions having rehabilitative or other effects on the offender or potential offender. It simply results from the arithmetic of report, clear-up and conviction and the notion that inclination and environment presses towards or away from crime in ways which overwhelm the potential effects of penal sanctions.

   This conclusion could be seen as having a liberating effect upon those involved in the criminal justice process or concerned about how it ought to be evaluated. No longer need one feel guilty about the inability to interpret the technicalities of recon-viction rates and follow-up periods, or the convoluted mathematics of North American studies of the general deterrent effect of sentencing. If it were seen as comforting, the reader should pause. A criminal justice system stripped of utilitarian purpose might in fact end up a system bereft of humanity. And a recognition that the treatment of criminals is largely irrelevant to the amount of crime is different from an assertion that treating criminals in ways which would make the marginal differences should not be a penal purpose. We fear that some people must still try to understand deterrence mechanisms! Nonetheless, the policy separation of dealing with crime and dealing with criminals inescapably does make evaluation of criminal justice in other terms (like humanity, 'fairness' and cost), of more central importance.

The role of criminal statistics in the evaluation of these alternative objectives or criteria varies. Any assessment of the *humanity* of the criminal justice process must ultimately remain a matter of values, but the state of affairs disclosed by many descriptive statistics may have a considerable influence on any public debate about the humanity of the process. Examples of the kind of statistics which are likely to be very relevant in this debate include the general level of the use of custody as a penal sanction, and the degree of security imposed upon those imprisoned; the extent of overcrowding and cell-sharing in prisons; the use of discipline and prescribed drugs in prison; the sanctions for breaching the non-offence conditions of sentences or statutory licences (e.g. recall of parolees or life sentence prisoners); the length of time awaiting trial, and so on.

Similarly, the concept of '*fairness*' must inevitably rest on perceptions and principles. This has given rise to the wide-ranging philosophical, ethical and empirical controversy about what is entailed in a criminal justice system that claims to reflect a 'justice-model' approach. Once again, however, data from official sources can provide a helpful starting point for fundamental questions about fairness and consistency to be raised. In fact there is the probability that any debate about justice will be sterile which is not informed by information about extant inequalities and their determination as justified or unjustified. There are many examples of disparity and variation in the criminal justice process, which suggest *prima facie* evidence of unfairness. They invariably require more detailed research to test initial impressions. Among the most significant variations, of which many have been discussed in earlier chapters, are those related to the grant of bail by police and magistrates courts, the police decision to caution or prosecute, the grant of legal aid, entering guilty pleas, conviction, sentence and release from custody. While statistics of these decisions can rarely be conclusive proof of unfairness or injustice when taken alone, they can often suggest areas for further enquiry. Where this has been carried out, it is rare for the apparent inconsistencies to have been fully justified or 'explained away' by relevant background factors. Apparent inconsistencies, on investigation, have usually turned out to be real inconsistencies.

Information on the relevant *economic costs*, both direct and indirect, of different penal sanctions, can be found scattered around a number of Government publications, but rarely in a form that enables easy comparisons. A short-lived attempt was made by the Home Office to bring together some limited comparative data on the relative expenditure on the four areas of criminal justice for which it is responsible, in a valuable series of statistical publications that was discontinued after only two years – on economic grounds! (see Home Office 1979b). This analysis showed that throughout the period 1971/2 to 1977/8 the police accounted for about three-quarters of all Home Office expenditure on the criminal justice system; prisons accounted for about 15% of total expenditure; and the administration of justice for about 8%. Total expenditure on the probation service was much smaller than for any of the other three services (Home Office 1979b, pp. 73–77). A one-off direct comparison showing roughly similar proportions was undertaken in the Home Office's Working Paper on Criminal Justice (Home Office 1984e).

An excellent example of the much more specific type of analysis that can be done is provided by Stephen Shaw's survey *Paying the Penalty: An Analysis of the Cost of Penal Sanctions*, commissioned by NACRO (Shaw 1980). Among the fairly predictable conclusions that he was able fully to document were that, in almost all cases, non-custodial sanctions were very much cheaper than sentences of imprisonment; the income from fines virtually paid for the entire magistrates' courts system; and that the costs of housing inmates in different types of custodial institutions varied dramatically, largely related to their security classification. The need to consider both direct and indirect costs was argued persuasively, and the conclusions were very apt in the current state of penal and economic crisis:

> An attempt to analyse the penal system on the basis of costs is both feasible and generates interesting and useful results. A proper understanding of relative costs is essential if policy-makers and practitioners are to make rational decisions about the balance between the various penal alternatives . . . Cost may be only one factor, but at a time when expenditure on custodial sanctions is increasingly under the spotlight, it is a factor of growing significance. (Shaw 1980, pp. 74–5)

This analysis by Shaw shows the potential value of the economic approach. However, the only comparable (but very limited) financial information that appears in the regular statistical publications relating to the criminal justice system is the cost of keeping a man or woman in prison, and data from the Probation Service about the costs of various kinds of community supervision. Thus, the *Report on the Work of the Prison Department 1983* showed that the average weekly cost of keeping a person in prison in 1982–3 was £218 – but with a considerable variation between different types of establishment ranging from £200 per week in local prisons and remand centres for males, £308 per week in all establishments for females, to £433 for men in dispersal prisons. In stark contrast to these figures for the cost of custodial sentences, the estimated weekly cost of each person on probation was £11, for a juvenile receiving supervision under the Children and Young Persons Act 1969 the cost was just £9 per week, and for those sentenced to a Community Service Order it was £10 (Home Office 1984d, Table 12.3 p. 114). Even if economic factors are not the primary consideration in the choice of sentence or the development of a coherent penal policy, simple figures like those should offer plenty of food for thought, especially in a cost-conscious administration. That their interpretation is not easy is evident from factors like the following:

(i) One must distinguish marginal and capital costs – even if custody is used less, until prisons start being closed, costs will not significantly decline.
(ii) Crimes prevented by imprisonment may not be prevented by non-custodial sentences.

Have Crime Statistics a Future?

In view of the constant criticisms levelled against official statistics by politicians, practitioners, and, not least, academics, this question does need to be asked, if only for us to put on record our unequivocal belief in the importance of *more* routine statistical information, not less, and the wider (which also means cheaper) dissemination of what is published to the public, in whose name the criminal justice system exists and to which that system ought to be directly accountable. Putting the question another way, what would future debate on criminal justice policy and practice be like *without* routine statistics? In England and Wales we have an array of official statistical publications that, despite their limitations, provide an unrivalled basis on which to develop a more informed climate of public debate and political action. Although some would argue that we had to wait far too long for the first national crime victimization survey, there is no doubt that with its eventual arrival in 1982 the British Crime Survey has added a new dimension to our knowledge about crime, victimization, police recording practice and public attitudes towards and perceptions of crime.

Committed believers in the present and future value of official statistics do not, because of their commitment, have to surrender their critical faculties. We have stressed, perhaps *ad nauseam*, the very real and ever-present danger of too little knowledge in interpretation of much of the data concerned, but almost always it is the case that *no* knowledge would be worse, and that what we have can be put to use, if only, sometimes, in excluding possibilities or demanding closer attention to an issue. Social statistics never provide a simple mirror image of a state of the world 'out there'. Virtually all of the crime statistics surveyed in this book are *records of decisions*, made in very personal, private or professional contexts, whether by a victim deciding to report an incident to the police, by a police officer deciding what action to take, a jury or bench of magistrates deciding whether to convict, a judge or magistrates how to sentence, or a local parole review committee deciding whether to recommend a prisoner's early release. In order to begin to understand or properly to interpret any such statistics, their status as the products of personal interactions in their social and legal contexts must be fully appreciated. This is one of the primary reasons why comparative statistical studies, between jurisdictions or over extended periods of time, are bound to be such difficult exercises.

Another important feature to be aware of, in using any statistics, is the way in which they are perceived by those who have been responsible for their compilation. Statistics that are not regarded as in any way reflecting on the capacities, qualities and preferences of those whose actions they purport to describe are less liable to distortion; in contrast, those that are seen as 'productivity measures', 'success rates' and the like, require much more subtlety in their interpretation, if indeed they do not remain forever opaque.

Simple descriptive studies can sometimes have a powerful influence that their lack of technical or theoretical complexity may at first belie – consider, for instance, the important effect upon public attitudes towards capital punishment of basic information about the 'typical' murderer as someone caught up in a stressful domestic situation to which no other solution is seen but a tragic murder–suicide attempt, or the important message from research that most house burglaries involve only quite modest financial losses and no violence by the burglar, and happen during the day. These episodes are completely unlike the stereotype of media reports and pub conversation.

As we have seen, statistics of decision-making in criminal justice can often stimulate further investigation into apparent disparities, which can in turn be measured against a variety of possible yardsticks such as fairness, humanity or effectiveness. Decisions are made by people and are about people – which the form in which statistics are collected tends to conceal – hence the welcome which should be accorded to perspectives in which the *person* is the central unit of analysis, as in data on criminal careers, victimization surveys, and studies of the fear of crime. Just as we should not allow statistics to make us forget the people behind the numbers, neither should we allow ourselves to forget the primacy of objectives, principles and policies. The value of statistical information can only be assessed against the objectives it is meant to reach and the principles and policies which inform its scope and focus. At virtually every stage of the criminal process, the final stumbling block to a coherent evaluation of current practice is that objectives and principles remain unarticulated. However the very existence of routine information allows one to infer these partially, and to challenge their areas of ambiguity. Until principles are fully clarified, the task of full assessment remains impossible, and any search for consistency can achieve only the empty shell of unprincipled uniformity.

Bibliography

Arnott, A.J.E. and Duncan, J.A. (1970). *The Scottish Criminal*. Edinburgh, Edinburgh University Press.

Ashworth, A.J. (1983). *Sentencing and Penal Policy*. London, Weidenfeld and Nicolson.

Ashworth, A.J. (1984). *The English Criminal Process: A Review of Empirical Research*. Occasional Paper No. 11. Oxford, Centre for Criminological Research, University of Oxford.

Ashworth, A.J. *et al.* (1984). *Sentencing in the Crown Court*. Occasional Paper No. 10. Oxford, Centre for Criminological Research, University of Oxford.

Auglin, M.D. (1983). 'Drugs and Crime: Behavioural Aspects'. In S.H. Kadish (ed.) *Encyclopaedia of Crime and Justice*. London, Collier–Macmillan.

Baldock, J.C. (1980). 'Why the prison population has grown larger and younger'. *The Howard Journal of Penology and Crime Prevention, 19*, 142–55.

Baldwin, J. and McConville, M. (1977). *Negotiated Justice: Pressures on Defendants to Plead Guilty*. London, Martin Robertson.

Baldwin, J. and McConville, M. (1978). 'The new Home Office figures on pleas and acquittals – what sense do they make?' *Criminal Law Review*, 196–201.

Bates, J.V. and Heap, C. (1982). 'Delays in the Magistrates' Courts'. *Justice of the Peace, 146*, 334–7.

Belson, W.A. (1968). 'The extent of stealing by London boys and some of its origins'. *The Advancement of Science, 25*, 171–84.

Black Report (1979). *Report of the Children and Young Persons Review Group*. Belfast, HMSO.

Blumstein, A. and Cohen, J. (1973). 'A theory of the stability of punishment'. *Journal of Criminal Law and Criminology, 64*, 198–207.

Blumstein, A. *et al.* (1976). 'The dynamics of a homeostatic punishment process'. *Journal of Criminal Law, Criminology and Police Science, 67*, 317–34.

Borrie, G.J. and Varcoe, J.R. (1971). *Legal Aid in Criminal Proceedings: A Regional Survey*. Birmingham, Institute of Judicial Administration, University of Birmingham.

Bottomley, A.K. (1970). *Prison Before Trial*. London, Bell.

Bottomley, A.K. (1973). *Decisions in the Penal Process.* London, Martin Robertson.

Bottomley, A.K. and Coleman, C.A. (1981). *Understanding Crime Rates: Police and Public Roles in the Production of Official Statistics.* Farnborough, Gower.

Bottoms, A.E. (1977). 'Reflections on the renaissance of dangerousness'. *Howard Journal, 16,* 70–96.

Bottoms, A.E. (1981). 'The suspended sentence in England, 1967–1978'. *British Journal of Criminology, 21,* 1–26.

Bottoms, A.E. (1983). 'Neglected Features of Contemporary Penal Systems'. In D. Garland and P. Young (eds) *The Power to Punish: Contemporary Penality and Social Analysis.* London, Heinemann.

Bottoms, A.E. and McClean, J.D. (1976). *Defendants in the Criminal Process.* London, Routledge and Kegan Paul.

Box, S. (1983). *Power, Crime and Mystification.* London, Tavistock.

Box, S. and Hale, C. (1982). 'Economic crisis and the rising prisoner population in England and Wales, 1949–1979'. *Crime and Social Justice, 16,* 20–35.

Braithwaite, J. (1984). *Corporate Crime in the Pharmaceutical Industry.* London, Routledge.

Brantingham, P.J. and Brantingham, P.L. (1981). *Environmental Criminology.* Beverly Hills Calif., Sage.

Burrows, J. and Tarling, R. (1982). *Clearing Up Crime.* Home Office Research Study No. 73, London, HMSO.

Butler, S. (1983). *Acquittal Rates.* Research and Planning Unit Paper 16, London, Home Office.

Carr-Hill, R.A. and Stern, N.H. (1979). *Crime, The Police and Criminal Statistics.* London, Academic Press.

Chambers, G. and Millar, A. (1983). *Investigating Sexual Assault.* Edinburgh, HMSO.

Chambers, G. and Tombs, J. (1984). *The British Crime Survey Scotland.* Edinburgh, HMSO.

Chatterton, M.R. (1976). 'Police in Social Control'. In J.F.S. King (ed) *Control Without Custody?* Cambridge, Institute of Criminology, University of Cambridge.

Chatterton, M.R. (1983). 'Police Work and Assault Charges'. In M. Punch (ed) *Control in the Police Organisation.* Cambridge Mass., MIT Press.

C.I.P.F.A. (1978). *Police Statistics: Estimates 1978/9.* London, CIPFA Statistical Information Service.

C.I.P.F.A. (1984). *Police Statistics: Estimates 1984/5.* London, CIPFA Statistical Information Service.

Clarke, R.V.G. *et al.* (1985). 'Elderly Victims of Crime and Exposure to Risk'. *Howard Journal of Criminal Justice, 24,* 1–9.

Clarke, R.V.G. and Hough, M. (1984). *Crime and Police Effectiveness.* Home Office Research Study No. 79, London, HMSO.

Cohen, S. (1979). 'The punitive city: notes on the dispersal of social control'. '*Contemporary Crises, 3,* 339–63.

Cohen, S. (1985). *Visions of Social Control: Crime, Punishment and Classification.* Oxford, Polity Press.

Crow, I. and Cove, J. (1984). 'Ethnic minorities and the courts'. *Criminal Law Review,* 413–17.

Ditchfield, J.A. (1976). *Police Cautioning in England and Wales.* Home Office Research Study No. 37, London, HMSO.

Ditton, J. (1977). *Part-time Crime: An Ethnography of Fiddling and Pilferage.* London, Macmillan.

Dominelli, L. (1984). 'Differential justice: domestic labour, community service and female offenders'. *Probation Journal, 31,* 100–103.

Downes, D.M. (1983). *Law and Order: Theft of an Issue.* London, Fabian Society.

Duff, P. (1985). 'Crime on Offshore Installations'. *Howard Journal of Criminal Justice, 24,* 188–29.

Farrington, D.P. and Bennett, T. (1981). 'Police Cautioning of Juveniles in London'. *British Journal of Criminology, 21,* 123–35.

Farrington, D.P. and Dowds, E.A. (1985). 'Disentangling Criminal Behaviour and Police Reaction'. In D.P. Farrington and J. Gunn (eds) *Reactions to Crime: the Police, Courts and Prisons.* Chichester, Wiley.

Farrington, D.P. and Morris, A.M. (1983). 'Sex, sentencing and reconviction'. *British Journal of Criminology, 23,* 229–48.

Fisher, C.J. and Mawby, R.I. (1982). 'Juvenile delinquency and police discretion in an inner-city area'. *British Journal of Criminology, 22,* 63–75.

Fitzmaurice, C. and Pease, K. (1982). 'Prison sentences and population: a comparison of some European countries'. *Justice of the Peace, 146,* 575–9.

Frankenburg, C. and Tarling, R. (1983). *Time Taken to Deal with Juveniles Under Criminal Proceedings.* Research and Planning Unit Paper 18. London, Home Office.

Gandossy, R.P., Williams, J.R., Cohen, J., and Harwood, H.J. (1980). *Drugs and Crime: A Survey and Analysis of the Literature.* Mimeo, available from Superintendent of Documents GPO, Washington DC, 20402.

Garofalo, J. (1981). 'The fear of crime: causes and consequences'. *Journal of Criminal Law and Criminology, 72,* 839–57.

Gemmill, R. and Morgan-Giles, R.F. (1980). *Arrest, Charge and Summons: Current Practice and Resource Implications.* Royal Commission on Criminal Procedure Research Study No. 9, London, HMSO.

Gibson, E. (1960). *Time Spent Awaiting Trial.* Studies in the Causes of Delinquency and the Treatment of Offenders No. 2, London, HMSO.

Gladstone, F. (1979). 'Crime and the crystal ball'. Home Office Research Unit *Research Bulletin, 7,* 36–41.

Gormally, B. (1978). 'Pick them up or put them down: an assessment of the Black Report'. *The Howard Journal of Penology and Crime Prevention, 16,* 144–52.

Gormally, B. *et al.* (1981). *Unemployment and Young Offenders in Northern Ireland.* Belfast, Northern Ireland Association for the Care and Resettlement of Offenders.

Gottfredson, M.R. (1984). *Victims of Crime: The Dimensions of Risk*. Home Office Research Study No. 81, London, HMSO.

Gottfredson, M.R. and Hindelang, M.J. (1979). 'A study of "The Behaviour of Law" '. *American Sociological Review, 44*, 3–18.

Greenberg, D.F. (1980). 'Penal sanctions in Poland: a test of alternative models'. *Social Problems, 28*, 194–204.

Greenberg, D.F. (1983). 'Age and Crime'. In S.H. Kadish (ed) *Encyclopaedia of Crime and Justice*. London, Collier-Macmillan.

Gregory, J. (1976). *Crown Court or Magistrates' Court?* OPCS Social Survey Division, London, HMSO.

Hakim, C. (1982). 'The social consequences of high unemployment'. *Journal of Social Policy, 11*, 433–67.

Heise, D.R. (1975). *Causal Analysis*. New York, Wiley.

Henry, S. (1978). *The Hidden Economy: the Context and Control of Borderline Crime*. Oxford, Martin Robertson.

Hirschi, T. (1969). *Causes of Delinquency*. Berkeley, University of California Press.

Holdaway, S. (1984). *Inside the British Police*. Oxford, Basil Blackwell.

Home Office (1956). *Report of the Commissioners of Prisons 1955*, Cmnd 1956, London, HMSO.

Home Office (1961). *Report of the Interdepartmental Committee on the Business of the Criminal Courts*. (Streatfeild Committee) Cmnd. 1289, London, HMSO.

Home Office (1964). *The Sentence of the Court: A Handbook for Courts on the Treatment of Offenders*. 1st edn, London, HMSO.

Home Office (1966). *Report of the Departmental Committee on Legal Aid in Criminal Proceedings*. (Widgery Committee) Cmnd. 2934, London, HMSO.

Home Office (1975). *The Distribution of Criminal Business between the Crown Court and Magistrates' Courts*. (James Committee) Cmnd. 6323, London, HMSO.

Home Office (1977). *Criminal Statistics, England and Wales 1976*. Cmnd. 6909, London, HMSO.

Home Office (1978a). *The Sentence of the Court: A Handbook for Courts on the Treatment of Offenders*. 3rd. edn, London, HMSO.

Home Office (1978b). *Prison Statistics England and Wales 1977*. Cmnd. 7286, London, HMSO.

Home Office (1979a) *Criminal Statistics England and Wales 1978*. Cmnd. 7670, London, HMSO.

Home Office (1979b) *Statistics of the Criminal Justice System England and Wales 1968–78*. London, HMSO.

Home Office (1980). *Criminal Statistics England and Wales 1979*. Cmnd. 8098, London, HMSO.

Home Office (1982). *Unrecorded Offences of Burglary and Theft in a Dwelling in England and Wales: Estimates from the General Household Survey*. Home Office Statistical Bulletin 11/82. London, Home Office.

Home Office (1983). *Crime Statistics for the Metropolitan Police District Analysed by Ethnic Group*. Home Office Statistical Bulletin 22/83, London, Home Office.

Home Office (1984a). *Cautioning by the Police: A Consultative Document.* London, Home Office.

Home Office (1984b). *Criminal Statistics England and Wales 1983.* Cmnd. 9349, London, HMSO.

Home Office (1984c). *Prison Statistics England and Wales 1983.* Cmnd. 9363, London, HMSO.

Home Office (1984d). *Probation Statistics England and Wales 1983.* London, Home Office.

Home Office (1984e). *Criminal Justice: A Working Paper.* London, Home Office.

Home Office (1984f). *Report on the Work of the Prison Department 1983.* Cmnd. 9306. London, HMSO.

Home Office (1985a). *Young Offenders in Prison Department Establishments Under the Criminal Justice Act 1982: July 1983–June 1984.* Home Office Statistical Bulletin 2/85, London, Home Office.

Home Office (1985b). *Criminal Careers of Those Born in 1953, 1958 and 1963.* Home Office Statistical Bulletin 7/85, London, Home Office.

Home Office (1985c). *The Sentencing of Young Offenders Under the Criminal Justice Act 1982: July 1983–June 1984.* Home Office Statistical Bulletin 12/85, London, Home Office.

Home Office (1985d). *Report of the Parole Board 1984.* HOC 411. London, HMSO.

Hood, R.G. (1962). *Sentencing in Magistrates' Courts.* London, Stevens.

Hood, R.G. (1972). *Sentencing the Motoring Offender.* London, Heinemann.

Hood, R.G. and Sparks, R.F. (1970). *Key Issues in Criminology.* London, Weidenfeld and Nicolson.

Hope, T.J. (1984). 'The first British Crime Survey: current and future research'. Home Office Research and Planning Unit, *Research Bulletin, 18,* 12–15.

Hough, J.M. and Mayhew, P. (1983). *The British Crime Survey: First Report.* Home Office Research Study No. 76, London, HMSO.

Hough, J.M. and Mayhew, P. (1985). *Taking Account of Crime.* Home Office Research Study No. 85, London, HMSO.

Jardine, E. (1983). 'Police Cautioning in Northern Ireland'. *Lynx, 8,* October 1983.

Jardine, E. *et al.* (1983). 'Community Service Orders, Employment and the Tariff'. *Criminal Law Review,* 17–20.

Johnson, R.E. (1979). *Juvenile Delinquency and its Origins.* Cambridge, Cambridge University Press.

Kilbrandon Report (1964). *Children and Young Persons (Scotland).* Cmnd. 2306, Edinburgh, HMSO.

King, M. (1971). *Bail or Custody.* London, Cobden Trust.

Kinsey, R. (1984). *Merseyside Crime Survey: First Report, November 1984.* Liverpool, Merseyside County Council.

Krisberg, B. and Schwartz, I. (1983). 'Rethinking Juvenile Justice'. *Crime and Delinquency, 29,* 333–64.

Lambert, J.R. (1970). *Crime, Police and Race Relations.* London, Oxford University Press.

Landau, S.F. and Nathan, G. (1983). 'Selecting delinquents for cautioning in the London Metropolitan area'. *British Journal of Criminology, 23,* 128–49.

Laycock, G. and Tarling, R. (1985). 'Police force cautioning: policy and practice'. *Howard Journal of Criminal Justice, 24,* 81–92.

Lenke, L. (1980). 'Drugs and Criminality in Scandinavia'. In N. Bishop (Ed) *Crime and Crime Control in Scandinavia 1976–80.* Oslo, Scandinavian Research Council for Criminology.

Lidstone, K.W. *et al.* (1980). *Prosecutions by Private Individuals and Non-Police Agencies.* Royal Commission on Criminal Procedure Research Study No. 10. London, HMSO.

Litton, R. and Pease, K. (1984). 'Crimes and Claims: the Case of Burglary Insurance'. In R.V.G Clarke and T.J. Hope (eds) *Coping with Burglary.* Lancaster, Kluwer-Nijhoff.

Lord Chancellor's Department (1973). *Statistics on Judicial Administration.* London, HMSO.

Lord Chancellor's Department (1984). *Judicial Statistics 1983.* London, HMSO.

McCabe, S. and Purves, R. (1972). *The Jury at Work.* Oxford, Basil Blackwell.

McCabe, S. and Sutcliffe, F. (1978). *Defining Crime: A Study of Police Decisions.* Oxford, Basil Blackwell.

McCabe, S. and Treitel, P. (1984). *Juvenile Justice in the United Kingdom: Comparisons and Suggestions for Change.* London, New Approaches to Juvenile Crime.

McClintock, F.H. and Avison, N.H. (1968). *Crime in England and Wales.* London, Heinemann.

McConville, M. and Baldwin, J. (1981). *Courts, Prosecution and Conviction.* Oxford, Oxford University Press.

McConville, M. and Baldwin, J. (1982). 'The influence of race on sentencing in England'. *Criminal Law Review,* 652–58.

Mannheim, H. (1965). *Comparative Criminology.* London, Routledge and Kegan Paul.

Mars, G. (1982). *Cheats at Work: An Anthology of Workplace Crime.* London, Allen and Unwin.

Marshall, J. (1974). *How to Survive in the Nick.* London, Allison and Busby.

Mawby, R.I. (1977). 'Sexual Discrimination in the Law'. *Probation Journal, 24,* 42–53.

Mawby, R.I. (1979). *Policing the City.* Farnborough, Gower.

Maxfield, M.G. (1984). *Fear of Crime in England and Wales.* Home Office Research Study No. 78. London, HMSO.

Merton, R.K. (1957). *Social Theory and Social Structure.* New York, Free Press.

Morris, P. and Heal, K. (1981). *Crime Control and the Police.* Home Office Research Study No. 67. London, HMSO.

Mott, J. (1983). 'Police decisions for dealing with juvenile offenders'. *British Journal of Criminology, 23,* 249–62.

Moxon, D. (1983). 'Fine default: unemployment and the use of imprisonment'. Home Office Research and Planning Unit. *Research Bulletin, 16,* 38–41.

NACRO (1981). *Fine Default.* Report of a NACRO Working Party, London, NACRO.

Northern Ireland Office (1984). *A Commentary on Northern Ireland Crime Statistics 1969-1982.* Policy Planning and Research Unit (PPRU) Occasional Paper 5, Belfast, Northern Ireland Office.

Northumbria Police (1980). *Annual Report of the Chief Constable.* Ponteland, Northumbria Police.

Nuttall, C.P. *et al.* (1977). *Parole in England and Wales.* Home Office Research Study No. 38, London, HMSO.

Parker, H. *et al.* (1981). *Receiving Juvenile Justice.* Oxford, Basil Blackwell.

Pease, K. (1980). 'Community Service and Prison: Are They Alternatives?' In K. Pease and W.W. McWilliams (eds) *Community Service by Order.* Edinburgh, Scottish Academic Press.

Pease, K. (1981). *Community Service Orders: A First Decade of Promise.* London, Howard League for Penal Reform.

Pease, K. (1983). 'Did the Falklands War Reduce Crime?' *Justice of the Peace, 147,* 724-33.

Pease, K. (1985a). 'Community Service Orders'. In M.H. Tonry and N. Morris (eds) *Crime and Justice: An Annual Review of Research, 6,* Chicago, University of Chicago Press.

Pease, K. (1985b). 'What Risk of Reconviction for Juveniles?' *Justice of the Peace, 149,* 329.

Pease, K. *et al.* (1977). *Community Service Assessed in 1976.* Home Office Research Study No. 39. London, HMSO.

Pease, K. and Sampson, M. (1977). 'Doing Time and Marking Time'. *Howard Journal of Penology and Crime Prevention, 16,* 59-64.

Philips, D. (1977). *Crime and Authority in Victorian England: The Black Country, 1835-60.* London, Croom Helm.

Phillpotts, G.J.O. and Lancucki, L.B. (1979). *Previous Convictions, Sentence and Reconviction.* Home Office Research Study No. 53. London, HMSO.

Poulin, J.E. (1980). *Juveniles in Detention Centres and Jails: An Analysis of State Variations during the Mid-1970s.* Reports of the National Juvenile Justice Assessment Centres, US Government Printing Office, Washington DC.

Pratt, J. (1985). 'Delinquency as a Scarce Resource'. *Howard Journal of Criminal Justice, 24,* 93-107.

Priestley, P. *et al.* (1977). *Justice for Juveniles.* London, Routledge and Kegan Paul.

Robertson, G. (1984). 'Changes in the Use of the Criminal Provisions of the 1959 Mental Health Act'. In Williams, T. *et al.* (eds) *Options for the Mentally Abnormal Offender.* Leicester, British Psychological Society.

Rose G.N.G. (1968). 'The Artificial Delinquent Generation'. *Journal of Criminal law, Criminology and Police Science, 59,* 370-85.

Rossi, P.H. *et al.* (1974). 'The Seriousness of Crimes: Normative Structures and Individual Differences'. *American Sociological Review, 39,* 224-37.

Royal Commission on Criminal Procedure (1981). *Report.* Cmnd. 8092, London, HMSO.

Rutherford. A. (1984). *Prisons and the Process of Justice: The Reductionist Challenge.* London, Heinemann.

Sapsford, R. J. (1978). 'Further research applications of the Parole Prediction Index'. *International Journal of Criminology and Penology, 6,* 247–54.

Schwartz, I.M. *et al.* (1984). 'The "hidden" system of juvenile control'. *Crime and Delinquency, 30,* 371–85.

Scottish Home and Health Department (1984). *Criminal Statistics (Scotland) 1980–1982.* Cmnd. 9403. Edinburgh, HMSO.

Sebba, L. (1967). 'Decision-making in juvenile cases – a comment'. *Criminal Law Review,* 347–55.

Shaw, S. (1980). *Paying the Penalty: An Analysis of the Cost of Penal Sanctions.* London, NACRO.

Simon, F. and Weatheritt, M. (1974). *The Use of Bail and Custody by London Magistrates' Courts Before and After the Criminal Justice Act 1967.* Home Office Research Study No. 20. London, HMSO.

Sinclair, I. and Miller, C. (1984). *Measures of Police Effectiveness and Efficiency.* Home Office Research and Planning Unit Paper 25. London, Home Office.

Skogan, W. (1984). 'Reporting crimes to the police: the status of world research'. *Journal of Research in Crime and Delinquency, 21,* 113–37.

Skogan, W.G. and Maxfield, M.G. (1981). *Coping with Crime.* Beverly Hills California, Sage.

Smart, C. (1979). 'The new female criminal: reality or myth?' *British Journal of Criminology, 19,* 50–59.

Social Work Services Group (1984). *Children's Hearings Statistics 1982.* Statistical Bulletin No. CH 7/1984. Edinburgh, Scottish Education Department.

Softley, P. (1973). *A Survey of Fine Enforcement.* Home Office Research Study 16. London, HMSO.

Softley, P. (1976). 'A comparison of acquittal rates in magistrates' courts and the Crown Court'. *Justice of the Peace, 140,* 455–6.

Softley, P. (1978). *Fines in Magistrates' Courts.* Home Office Research Study No. 46. London, HMSO.

Softley. P. (1980). *Police Interrogation: An Observational Study in Four Police Stations.* Royal Commission on Criminal Procedure, Research Study No. 4. London, HMSO.

Somerville, J.G. (1969). 'A study of the preventive aspect of police work with juveniles'. *Criminal Law Review,* 407–14, 472–84.

Southgate, P. and Ekblom, P. (1984). *Contacts Between Police and Public.* Home Office Research Study No. 77. London, HMSO.

Sparks, R.F. (1971). 'The use of suspended sentences'. *Criminal Law Review.* 384–401.

Sparks, R.F. (1973), 'The enforcement of fines: the process from sentence to committal'. *British Journal of Criminology, 13,* 92–107.

Sparks, R.F. *et al.* (1977). *Surveying Victims: A Study of the Measurement of Criminal Victimization.* New York, Wiley.

Steadman, H.J. and Cocozza, J.J. (1974). *Careers of the Criminally Insane.* Lexington DC, Heath.

Steer, D. (1970). *Police Cautions – A Study in the Exercise of Police Discretion.* Oxford, Basil Blackwell.

Steer, D. (1980). *Uncovering Crime: The Police Role.* Royal Commission on Criminal Procedure, Research Study No. 7. London, HMSO.

Stevens, P. and Willis, C.F. (1979). *Race, Crime and Arrests.* Home Office Research Study No. 58. London, HMSO.

Tarling, R. (1979). *Sentencing Practice in Magistrates' Courts.* Home Office Research Study No. 56. London, HMSO.

Tarling, R. (1982). 'Unemployment and Crime'. Home Office Research and Planning Unit, *Research Bulletin, 14,* 28–33.

Thomas, D.A. (1979). *Principles of Sentencing.* 2nd edn London, Heinemann.

Thornberry, T.P. and Christensen, R.L. (1984). 'Unemployment and criminal involvement: an investigation of reciprocal causal structures'. *American Sociological Review, 49,* 398–411.

Thorpe, D.H. *et al.* (1980). *Out of Care: the Community Support of Juvenile Offenders.* London, Allen and Unwin.

Tutt, N. (1981). 'A decade of policy'. *British Journal of Criminology, 21,* 246–56.

Tutt, N. (1984). 'Diverting children from custody'. In D.J. Muller *et al.* (eds) *Psychology and Law.* Chichester, Wiley.

Tutt, N. and Giller, H. (1983). 'Police cautioning of juveniles: the practice of diversity'. *Criminal Law Review,* 587–94.

Tversky, A. and Kahneman D. (1982). 'Causal schemas in judgements under uncertainty'. In D. Kahneman *et al.* (eds) *Judgement under Uncertainty: Heuristics and Biases.* Cambridge, Cambridge University Press.

Vass, A.A. (1984). *Sentenced to Labour: Close Encounters with a Prison Substitute.* St. Ives, Venus Academica.

Vennard, J. (1980). *Contested Trials in Magistrates' Courts: the Case for the Prosecution.* Royal Commission on Criminal Procedure, Research Study No. 6, London, HMSO.

Vennard, J. (1981). 'Acquittal rates in magistrates' courts'. Home Office Research and Planning Unit, *Research Bulletin, 11,* 21–3.

Walker, M.A. (1981). 'Review of "Crime, the Police and Criminal Statistics" '. *British Journal of Criminology, 21,* 88–9.

Walker, M.A. (1983). 'Some problems in interpreting statistics relating to crime'. *Journal of the Royal Statistical Society, 146,* 281–93.

Walker, N. (1981a). 'A note on parole and sentence lengths'. *Criminal Law Review.* 829–30.

Walker, N. (1981b). 'Feminists' Extravaganzas'. *Criminal Law Review,* 379–86.

Walker, N. (1985). *Sentencing: Theory, Law and Practice.* London, Butterworths.

Waller, I. and Chan, J. (1974). 'Prison use: a Canadian and international comparison'. *Criminal Law Quarterly, 17,* 47–71.

Wardlaw, G. (1978). *Drug Use and Crime – An Examination of Drug Users and*

Associated Persons and their Influence on Crime Patterns in Australia. Woden, Australian Institute of Criminology.

West, D.J. (1982). *Delinquency: Its Roots, Careers and Prospects.* London, Heinemann.

Wilkins, L.T. (1984). *Consumerist Criminology.* London, Heinemann.

Wilkins L.T. *et al.* (1986). 'Income inequality and crime'. In preparation.

Zander, M. (1971). 'A study of bail/custody decisions in London magistrates' courts'. *Criminal Law Review,* 191–211.

Author Index

Subject Index